IDIOT

A MEMOIR

WIND

PETER KALDHEIM

IDIOT

A MEMOIR

WIND

CANONGATE

First published in Great Britain, the USA and Canada in 2019
by Canongate Books Ltd, 14 High Street, Edinburgh EH1 1TE

Distributed in the USA by Publishers Group West
and in Canada by Publishers Group Canada

canongate.co.uk

1

British Library Cataloguing-in-Publication Data
A catalogue record for this book is available on
request from the British Library

ISBN 978 1 78689 736 7

Typeset in Perpetua by Palimpsest Book Production Ltd,
Falkirk, Stirlingshire

Printed and bound in Great Britain by Clays Ltd,
Elcograf S.p.A.

For Gerald Howard and Susanne Williams

'Remember only that in life are many useless things, and but few which tend toward a solid end.'
— Theophrastus, *The Characters*

CHAPTER 1

*O*n *the night* I escaped from the land of giants, I set off into a blizzard I feared would soon make the roads completely impassable. Gale-force winds were blowing in from the northeast, churning the snow into a white froth that reduced visibility to near zero, but, despite the conditions, there was one thing I had no trouble seeing with perfect clarity: running for my life was the only choice I had.

It was the Monday after Super Bowl XXI – 26 January 1987 – and the sports pages of the New York tabloids were full of exultant headlines celebrating the hometown Giants' victory over the Denver Broncos, most of which, I confess, I can no longer recall. Only the back-page headline of the late-edition *Post* has remained fixed in my mind – as I knew it would the moment I spotted it. At the time, I was riding the IRT subway uptown from Chambers Street, on my way to the Port Authority bus terminal in midtown, praying I'd still be in time to catch a bus — any bus — out of town before the snowstorm forced Greyhound to suspend service. When the train reached Fourteenth Street, one of the other passengers got off, leaving behind a copy of the *Post* on the seat beside me. I promptly scavenged it, and as the train continued rattling north to Times Square I flipped through the paper until I eventually came to the back page. The three-word headline I encountered hit me with such an immediate shock of recognition I couldn't help flinching.

LAND OF GIANTS!

I suspect most New Yorkers took these three words as nothing more than justifiable hyperbole, but in my agitated state of mind that night they struck me as something else entirely. To me, they were a timely — and painful — reminder of just how small my life had become.

How small *I* had become.

Perhaps I was being paranoid, but to a man in my situation it was hard not to take it as a cosmic rebuke.

And what, exactly, was my situation? Well, for starters, I was thirty-seven years old, unemployed and flat-out broke. On top of that, I was also homeless, except for the pay locker in Penn Station where I stored my clothes and toiletries. In short, my life had become nothing to brag about, only something to survive, and for that I had no one to blame but myself and my accomplices: alcohol, cocaine and a deep-seated streak of what my old Greek philosophy professor would call *akrasia* — a weakness of will that allows one to act against one's better judgement. If Greek's not your thing, call it what Bob Dylan does: idiot wind. That's what I came to call it, and for nearly a dozen years it had been blowing my life ragged. Along the way, I'd watched it carry off just about everything that should have mattered to me. My marriage. My career. The respect of my parents and friends. Even a place to lay my head at night. All gone. Gone with the idiot wind.

And now, thanks to the stunt I'd pulled on Bobby Bats over Super Bowl weekend, I was also about to lose the city I loved.

Bobby Battaglia was not a dealer you could screw over with impunity. They didn't call him 'Bobby Bats' for nothing. I'd once seen him splinter a guy's shinbone in three places, just for talking trash in a pick-up basketball game at the city gym on Carmine Street. Back then, he was just a teenage sociopath with a Louisville slugger, who ran with a pack of like-minded Italian kids from the West Village. Now Bobby Bats was a twenty-nine-year-old sociopath who had pumped so much iron over the years he could no longer shoot a jump shot that didn't clang off the rim and ricochet to half-court. But he could still swing a bat, and what he'd do to a guy who'd just stiffed him for a thousand dollars' worth of coke was something I was determined not to find out.

Common sense should have warned me against doing business on credit with someone like Bobby Bats, but somehow common sense never seemed to factor into the equation when I had the idiot wind at my back and a 'sure-fire' scheme to make a score. I figured Super Bowl weekend with a New York team in the mix would be a golden opportunity. The bars in Tribeca – where I'd been hustling grams and half-grams for a living ever since I'd proved myself too unreliable for more legitimate employment – would no doubt be packed all weekend with Giants fans looking to score something to help snort the home team to victory. All I had to do was show up with the product and the cash would come rolling in. At least, that was the theory. And as theories go, it wasn't all that far-fetched. It was the eighties, after all. Bright lights, big city. Even the starving artists in the neighbourhood would turn out their pockets for a half-gram when they saw 'Pete the Hat' walk into the bar.

And so, with some – but not enough – trepidation, I went up to the West Village on the Friday before the big game and, following Bobby Bats' established protocols, I placed a call to his apartment from a pay phone on the corner of Carmine and Bedford Streets, just down the block from his apartment. No one got buzzed into Bobby Bats' building by simply ringing his doorbell. You had to call from the street first, where he could check you out from his second-floor bedroom window. If he told you it was okay to come up, you rang the bell once, and once only. Then he'd buzz you into the building and he'd be waiting with his bat in hand on the second-floor landing to make sure it was only you coming through the door. (Lately, he favoured aluminum bats. Said he'd got tired of the wood ones cracking.)

Once you got up to Bobby Bats' apartment, he'd check his watch. The rule was, you couldn't leave for at least a half-hour. *I'm not the fucking 7-Eleven*, he'd say. *You come up, you stay long enough to make it look like a social call, or else forget about it. Keeps the neighbours off my ass that way.* He did his best to keep his business low-profile, I'll give him that. You'd never catch him slinging Sno-Seal packets in a bar-room toilet like I did. Bobby Bats only dealt 'weight', in quarter-ounce increments, and only to a select clientele. That way he kept the traffic at his apartment to a minimum.

As I've said, I had known Bobby Bats since he was a teenager, but, even so, he would never have taken me on as a buyer just because we'd played hoops in the same gym. You had to be vouched for by someone who was already one of his regulars, and it wasn't until a friend of mine who owned a bar on Hudson Street gave Bobby the go-ahead one night after hours that we started doing deals together. At first, it was strictly cash-and-carry. Then, as he got more comfortable dealing with me, I'd occasionally convince him to front me a quarter-ounce and he'd give me two or three days to come up with what I owed him. Which should never have been a problem if I'd handled my business properly. Bobby sold some of the purest Peruvian flake in the city – coke potent enough to take a good stepping-on with baby laxative or powdered vitamin B and still leave you with blow that gave your customers the jolt they were looking for. I could buy a quarter-ounce for five hundred dollars, step on it till seven grams turned into fourteen and, at a hundred bucks per gram, double my investment, no problem, with a few grams left over to feed my own nose.

Sometimes things worked out that way and I came out ahead. Other times I 'fucked up the package', as they say in the trade, getting high on my own supply, and as the deadline for repaying Bobby Bats came closing in I had to scramble around borrowing money or taking 'pre-orders' from any of my customers gullible enough to entrust me with their cash in advance of delivery. I did whatever it took. If I had to string some people along for a while, so be it, as long as Bobby Bats got his money on time. And so far, despite some close calls, I had never failed to hold up my end of the bargain. Which is why I was fairly confident I could talk him into doubling down for Super Bowl weekend and fronting me a half-ounce instead of my usual quarter.

Of course, I knew better than to broach my proposal too

quickly. In his own way, Bobby was as much a stickler for the niceties of gracious hospitality as any Bedouin sheik. That Friday was no exception. He ushered me into his narrow railroad flat, propped his aluminum bat against the doorjamb, nodded toward his zebra-striped leather couch and told me to get comfortable. Then, looking every bit as cramped as a grizzly bear in an Airstream trailer, he squeezed his considerable bulk into the tiny galley kitchen to fix me a cup of espresso and a plate of cannoli from Ferraro's Bakery in Little Italy, where he sent his live-in girlfriend, Gina, to pick up fresh pastries every morning. (She was just nineteen, a real stunner, and her only job was running errands for Bobby. It wasn't a bad gig. It kept her in leather boots and rabbit-fur jackets. And all the coke she cared to hoover.)

When my espresso was ready, Bobby brought it out to the living room and set it down on the weight-lifting bench that doubled as his coffee table. We sipped our coffee and munched cannoli and passed the time making small talk about the local sports teams. The Knicks were still going nowhere. The Rangers had a shot. Phil Simms would need to have a damned good game to beat the Broncos. Once we'd finished our snack and the dishes were cleared, Bobby Bats reached into the drawer of the end table beside his armchair and pulled out a big vial filled with his personal stash of uncut coke. He dumped out a mound on a ceramic tray he kept handy and chopped out two thick lines for each of us. Then he passed me the tray. Visitors first, always.

I took two long snorts and instantly felt the burn rushing all the way to the back of my skull. 'Oh, Jesus!' I muttered, as my head snapped back in recoil. It was crazy good shit. Train-jumped-the-track shit. Just two lines, and I was off the rails.

And with that all my big plans for the weekend took a screeching lurch toward disaster. I just didn't see it at the time. My eyes were too full of dollar signs.

Flush with alkaloid-fuelled bravado, I made my pitch to Bobby Bats and waited expectantly for his reaction. He seemed to hesitate a moment, narrowing his gaze as he fixed me with an appraising look, but then he shrugged his muscle-bound shoulders and, just as I'd suspected he would, said, 'Okay, let's do it. Just give me a minute.'

Actually it was more like five minutes before he emerged from the bedroom at the front of the apartment. I assumed he had some kind of safe in there where he locked up his product, but that was just my guess. I'd never once seen inside. The door was always closed whenever he had visitors. Another of his house rules, and he was scrupulous about it.

When Bobby Bats finally returned to the living room, he was carrying his industrial-grade Ohaus triple-beam scale and a Tupperware container full of pre-bagged rocks of coke. 'Take your pick,' he said, passing me the Tupperware. 'They're all halves.' That's how he always worked. He'd pre-weigh all the packages before bagging them, but he'd let you pick the bag that caught your eye. Then he'd zero out the scale and weigh your package right in front of you, so there'd be no doubt you were getting good weight. It was a sign of respect – and as Italian as the neighbourhood butcher shops.

I made my selection and Bobby went through his triple-beam routine. I then borrowed his screen-mesh hand grinder and spent the next fifteen minutes cranking the handle till all the rocks in my bag were reduced to a fine powder, ready to be stepped-on with cut. I'd add the cut later, once I got back downtown to Tribeca. Bobby Bats wouldn't let you cut the stuff

7

at his place. He understood it was part of the business, but it pained him to see perfectly good coke being fucked with in his presence and he wouldn't put up with it. I could see his point. But, hey, not everyone can afford to be a purist.

It was going on five o'clock by the time I finished grinding, and as soon as I was done bagging up the coke I stashed it in my backpack with the rest of the tools of my trade. I stood up to put my coat on, then headed for the door, thanking Bobby Bats for the 'taste' and promising I'd be back to settle up with him on Monday.

'You can't fuck this up, Hat. You know that, right?' Bobby Bats cautioned me as he unlocked the deadbolts and opened his door to let me out. A word to the wise. Unfortunately, I failed to take it to heart — as the next seventy-two hours would make abundantly clear.

'No problem, Bobby,' I blithely assured him, and out the door I went.

It was already dark when I stepped out into the street. A crisp, cold winter night, the air faintly redolent of exhaust fumes from the evening rush hour. I was so wired I couldn't face riding the subway. Instead, I decided to make the trek downtown on foot, figuring the cold air would clear my head by the time I made it all the way to the Raccoon Lodge. So I turned up the collar of my overcoat and set off south on Seventh Avenue at a brisk pace. At Canal Street, I had to weave my way through the usual rush-hour log-jam of Jersey-bound cars inching in fits and starts toward the entrance to the Holland Tunnel, but once I got past that obstacle it was an easy ten-minute walk down Hudson Street the rest of the way. I made it to the Raccoon Lodge in plenty of time to catch the tail end of Happy Hour.

The Raccoon Lodge, my de facto base of operations, was

a long, narrow bar tucked into an old six-storey yellow-brick building at 59 Warren Street, a few steps east of West Broadway, down in the shadows of the ill-fated Twin Towers. There were plenty of pretentiously hip new bars downtown in those days of the Tribeca renaissance, along with a dwindling handful of old-time, unpretentious watering holes, but the Raccoon Lodge was a rare hybrid. It somehow managed to be both hip *and* unpretentious in equal measure, which is a neat trick I've never seen successfully duplicated by any other bar I've ever raised a glass in.

The Raccoon harboured one of the last coin-op pool tables left in lower Manhattan, and a gem of a jukebox eclectically stocked with hard-to-find treasures that ranged from rockabilly to roots reggae, from vintage Motown to Mississippi Delta blues. The jukebox alone was reason enough to seek the place out. But for me the bar's biggest draw was the mix of customers it attracted, a shifting cast of characters every bit as eclectic as the evening's playlist.

Where else but the Raccoon could you belly up to the bar and rub elbows with commodities traders and high-steel iron-workers, secretaries and kinetic sculptors, truck drivers and abstract painters, schoolteachers and struggling actors? Or shoot pool with Keith Richards? Or shoot eyes at Debra Winger? Or shoot the shit with Jay McInerney? You never knew who might walk through the door, or what they'd have to say for themselves when they started bending your ear, but it was rarely a boring conversation. To a motor-mouth cokehead like me, there could hardly have been a more congenial place to ply my trade.

The bar was extra busy when I walked in that night, as it always was on Fridays. Thirty or forty drinkers, mostly regulars, the majority of them waving empty glasses at the bartenders and clamouring for refills before Happy Hour expired. I worked my way through the crowd and squeezed into my usual spot at the far corner of the bar, down near the pool table. I was still feeling chilled from my hike downtown, so I ordered a double Akvavit to turn the heat up and a bottle of Rolling Rock to chase it. The first shot went down so good I ordered another. Then I stepped over to the pool table and added a quarter to the queue lined up on the rail. There were six quarters ahead of mine. I'd be waiting a while for a turn at the table. I didn't mind. I needed time to do a little business first anyway.

I didn't have long to wait on that score. One of my regular customers was standing, cue in hand, beside the table, watching his opponent line up a shot, and as I passed him by he gave me that expectant look they all get, right before they ask you, sotto voce, 'You holding?'

I flashed him a grin and nodded. 'Just give me a few minutes, Dave,' I said. 'I'll get back to you.'

This was a good sign. I hadn't even had time to shuck my pack and take off my coat and already I had my first order. Now all I had to do was duck downstairs to the basement storeroom and get busy cutting the coke and portioning it into packets. Then I could open for business.

The door to the Raccoon's basement beer-storage room was posted with a sign that said 'Employees Only'. I paid it no mind. I wasn't on the payroll at the Raccoon, but I served as the unofficial 'bar-back' on busy nights, fetching cases of beer whenever the bartenders needed to restock. My efforts were repaid in free drinks, and – more importantly – in unfettered access to the storeroom whenever I needed a little privacy to package up some coke. As long as I came upstairs toting a case of beer, no one got suspicious. I was part of the scenery, as inconspicuous as the dusty framed photos of Jackie Gleason hanging on the bar's wood-panelled walls.

The beer storeroom occupied the building's former coal cellar and extended partway under the sidewalk in front of the bar. Up top, there was a metal hatch covering the hole through which the coal used to be dumped. Now the hatch was used for keg deliveries. The beer-truck drivers would open the hatch and drop the barrels of beer straight down through the hole onto a cushioning pile of old tyres arranged on the floor beneath the opening. It was a handy system.

Fruit flies infested the storeroom much of the year, but fortunately they disappeared once the weather turned cold, so I didn't have to worry about getting black specks in the coke I was about to cut that night. But as I unloaded my pack onto the top of a stack of beer cases and laid out my supplies I discovered I had a bigger problem. My bottle of cut was practically empty.

I shook my head in disbelief. What a dipshit I was! My only recourse was to hit the street again and hustle over to the smoke shop around the corner on West Broadway, where the turbaned Pakistani who ran the shop did a booming business peddling drug paraphernalia to the neighborhood's burgeoning population of cokeheads. I knew he stocked jars of powdered vitamin B. I'd bought from him before. I prayed the shop would still be open. Otherwise, I was fucked.

I hurried upstairs and was immediately buttonholed by Dave, who was impatiently waiting to collect the gram he always ordered. 'Slight snag,' I told him. 'I've got to run out and pick up a pack of Sno-Seal papers. Hang tight, I'll be right back.' Which was a lie, of course, but 'cut' is a word best left unsaid when talking to a customer.

My heart sank when I turned the corner onto West Broadway and saw the smoke shop's security gates already locked for the night. The smoke shop must have closed at six. I'd missed my chance by minutes. What the fuck was I going to do now? I knew of another shop in the Village, but there was no guarantee that place wouldn't be closed, too, by the time I could get there. Besides, I already had a good buzz going, thanks to the Akvavit and the lingering effects of Bobby Bats' free sample. Why ruin it with a fruitless trip uptown? Better to just stay put and bite the bullet. I could sell a few grams of uncut coke to Dave and whoever else was lucky enough to take advantage of my stupidity. Once I had a little walking-around cash in my pocket I would close up shop for the night and hold on to the rest of my stash until I could replenish my supply of cut when the shops reopened on Saturday. It would put a crimp in my timeline for recouping the cash I owed Bobby Bats, there was no denying that. But with any luck I could pick up the slack over the next few days. At least that's what I told myself.

Back at the Raccoon, I returned to the beer cellar and got busy creasing Sno-Seal papers and weighing out coke on the mini-scale I kept in my pack. When I was done, I had six half-gram packets ready for sale. For my personal use, I scooped out another half-gram, loading it into one of those little glass vials every cokehead carried back then – the kind with the tiny brass coke spoon attached to the screw-top by a short length of chain. The remaining ten-plus grams I stored away in my pack, cursing myself all the while. It was galling to think how much business I'd be passing up before the night was over.

Before heading back upstairs I helped myself to a couple of bumps from my vial, which improved my mood. Then I stashed my backpack in a dim corner of the storeroom for safekeeping and grabbed a case of Bud longnecks to carry up to the bar.

'Thanks, Pete, you read my mind,' Ace said when I set the case on the corner of the bar. 'What are you drinking?'

I ordered another round of Akvavit and Rolling Rock, and while I waited for Ace to bring my drinks I caught Dave's eye and nodded toward the men's room door. He got the message and nodded back. Two minutes later, we crowded into the single-stall bathroom, locking the door behind us.

'You're going to love this shit, Dave,' I said, with painful confidence, as I passed him two half-gram packets.

'Well, let's see, shall we?' he replied, smiling through his wiry black beard. 'Join me for a bump?'

'I wouldn't say no,' I grinned back. When had I *ever* said no?

'First things first,' he said, pulling five twenties from his pants' pocket. They were bunched in a damp roll. He must have been clutching them tight in one of his clammy palms the whole time he'd been waiting for me.

I unpeeled the bills from the roll and slipped them into my wallet, while Dave opened one of his packets and produced a sip-straw from the breast pocket of his rumpled Wall Street suit. He snorted two good hits and I could see his eyes light up as he handed me the straw.

'Damn, Hat, you weren't kidding! This shit's the real deal.'

'Told you,' I smiled, and helped myself to a couple of bumps.

After stashing the straw and the packet of coke back in his breast pocket, Dave checked his nose in the stall's mirror and rubbed away any telltale traces of white. I did the same. Anybody seeing us emerge could probably guess what we'd been up to, but there was no sense being sloppy about it.

'We good?' Dave asked.

'We're good,' I answered.

'Okay then, let's go,' he said, unlatching the door. 'We've got drinking to do.'

I waited a respectable minute after Dave left the bathroom, then slipped out the door myself and joined him at the bar, where he was surreptitiously tucking one of the coke packets into his wife Andi's pocketbook. It was her turn to powder her nose. She excused herself and headed for the ladies' room while Dave ordered us all a round of beers.

'To the Giants,' Dave toasted, clinking his bottle of Bud Light against my Rolling Rock.

'To the Giants,' I repeated.

The party was under way.

By seven-thirty I had sold the four half-grams I was holding, which left me with cash in my pockets but, regrettably, nothing for the latecomers. All I could do to soften the bad news was to offer the unlucky ones a few hits from my personal stash, discreetly passing them my vial so they could visit the bathroom on their own. I figured my largesse would pay off in the long run. Looking at the grins on their faces when they returned from the john, I knew they'd be back for more tomorrow.

As the night wore on, the number of freebies I was doling out began to add up at a rate that should have been alarming. That is, of course, if I had been in any condition to heed an alarm. But I had long since morphed into Mr Magnanimous, heedless of anything but the cokehead's prime directive. Keep the party going! Whenever the vial came back empty, I'd duck down to the beer cellar and reload.

And a good time was had by all.

The rest of the night whizzed by, and next thing I knew the bartenders were shouting last call. Dave and Andi greeted this announcement with a good-natured chorus of boos. It was four in the morning, and they'd just spent ten hours straight in the Raccoon Lodge, but they were still raring to go. As was I. So when Dave proposed we move the party elsewhere, he didn't have to twist my arm.

'Houston Street?' Dave suggested, as he dropped a twenty on the bar for the tip cup.

'Works for me,' I replied, and threw a twenty down myself. 'Let me just grab my stuff from the cellar.'

'Meet you outside,' Dave said.

We didn't have to wait long for a cab. There were always plenty of taxis cruising the streets of Tribeca at closing time. Dave flagged down a yellow Checker and we all piled in.

'Corner of Houston and Mercer,' Dave instructed the driver.

'The after-hours club?' the cabbie asked. Every grave-yard-shift cabbie knew the place.

'You got it,' Dave replied.

The Houston Street after-hours was a Mafia-owned club on the northern edge of SoHo, housed in a former auto mechanic's shop – a windowless, single-storey cinderblock box, totally nondescript. There wasn't a sign anywhere on the building, just a small brass plaque on the reinforced steel door that opened onto Mercer Street. Members Only. That was it. Like Bobby Bats, the club did its best to keep a low profile. You could have walked past the place a hundred times and had no clue what went on in there. Unless, of course, you happened by the place at four in the morning. Then there was a long line of nocturnal specimens queued up on the sidewalk, all waiting their turn to stand in the glare of the spotlight mounted above the entrance and present their ID and membership cards to the hard-guy leather jacket working the door.

The doorman turned away anyone without ID and a club membership card. If you had no card but showed up with someone who did, that person could sponsor you, and you'd be sent upstairs with your sponsor to the loft office. There you'd have to pass muster with the no-nonsense lesbian who managed the place. If she deigned to add you to the membership rolls and issue you a card, your sponsor's name would be linked with yours in the ledger; in the event you caused a problem, you weren't the only one who'd be called to account.

Of course, the whole operation was completely illegal, so it made sense to be careful who you let through the door. But as difficult as it was to gain entrance to the club, to me the more difficult part by far was getting out once I was in. In that shadowy space throbbing with jukebox bass, the time–space continuum ceased to apply. You'd pop in at four for a nightcap or two, nothing more, and invariably get caught in the club's quicksand till the houselights came up at 10 a.m. and the bouncers bum-rushed you out the door into the merciless light of day.

You could have made a killing selling sunglasses on that corner.

Dave, Andi and I were card-carrying members of the club, and when the shuffling line finally delivered us to the door we were waved in quickly. 'Watch your step on the stairs,' the doorman cautioned. His standard warning. The two steps that led down to the sunken floor of the club were notorious for sending people stumbling. The management purposely kept the place as dark as the opium den in Robert Altman's *McCabe & Mrs. Miller*. Which was exactly how the night owls who haunted the club preferred it.

The shadows offered cover. Cover to indulge in indiscretions

– both sexual and pharmacological – you would never get away with elsewhere. Couched in the candle-lit gloom of one of the high-backed booths that lined the club's west wall, you could lay out lines on the varnished pine table and discreetly snort coke to your heart's content. Or, if you preferred, you could treat yourself to a hand-job from one of the coke whores who hovered around the booths like fruit flies over a beer keg. As long as you didn't cause a ruckus, the bouncers would just let you go about your business.

There was a price you paid for all this laissez-faire treatment, of course, and it was exacted every time you stepped up to the bar. Even if you ordered nothing fancier than Pabst, and maybe the occasional shot of schnapps, you could easily drop the better part of a hundred bucks in just a few hours. I knew that all too well. I'd done it many times over the years. And here I was, with a wallet full of cash I should have been saving for Bobby Bats, on my way to doing it once again.

No worries, whispered the idiot wind. *You can make it up tomorrow.*

The club was filling fast when we arrived, but there were still a few unoccupied booths and we grabbed one while we could. I dumped my stuff on one of the seats and told Dave and Andi to hold the fort while I fetched the first round from the bar. As my eyes adjusted to the light, I spotted some familiar faces on the raised dance floor at the back of the club, where the jukebox was pumping out Billy Ocean's 'Caribbean Queen' at full volume. Bartenders and waitresses, mostly, out to unwind a little after working the night shift. I could never predict who I'd run into at Houston Street, but I'd been knocking around the West Village and SoHo and Tribeca for so many years that it was a safe bet I'd run into *somebody* I'd shared a drink or a hit

17

of coke with in my travels. And, sure enough, tonight there were plenty of candidates giving me the nod as I made my way to the bar.

I was happy to see my favourite bartender working. Gwen was a blonde with a Rubenesque figure, and her quick smile and sunny disposition always made the club seem a little less sepulchral. Like me, she was a Norwegian 'squarehead' born in Bay Ridge, Brooklyn, and we'd been swapping bad *lutefisk* jokes ever since I started hanging out at Houston Street back in the mid-seventies. That night, however, the frown she turned on me when I stepped up to the bar told me she was in no mood for jokes.

'Well, well, look who finally decided to show his face,' she said, sounding miffed.

For a split second, I stood there wondering why. Then it dawned on me.

Oh, shit, I still owe her two hundred bucks!

The last time I'd seen Gwen I'd been scrambling to cover a debt to Bobby Bats, and I'd hit her up for cash, with the promise I'd get the money back to her within a week. That was more than a month ago.

No wonder she was pissed.

'I know, I know, I'm a fucking asshole,' I said, feeling mortified. 'I'm sorry, Gwen, what can I say?'

'How about, "Thanks for the loan, Gwen. Here's your money"?'

'Okay,' I said, grinning sheepishly as I pulled out my wallet. 'Thanks for the loan, Gwen. Here's your money.'

'That's more like it.' Gwen finally smiled. 'What can I get you?'

Glad that she wasn't one to hold a grudge, I ordered three beers and three shots of peppermint schnapps, and when I settled the bill I guiltily tipped Gwen an extra twenty before heading back to the booth.

'Thanks, Hat,' Dave said, as I set the cork tray down on the table. 'Next round's on me.'

It better be, I told myself. One trip to the bar and my wallet was close to empty. I'd definitely have to make some kind of move in the club before the night was over, there was no getting around it. First, though, a drink.

'To the Giants!' we toasted, and I quickly downed my shot of schnapps.

'Freelance dealing' was one of the few activities not tolerated at the Houston Street club. The Italians had their own people moving drugs in the place and anyone they caught poaching on their turf would quickly get the boot (or worse). I knew I'd be taking a risk if I tried moving product in there, but I was so strapped for cash at that point I was willing to take my chances. And so, when Andi dragged Dave off for a spin on the dance floor, I hunkered down in the booth, keeping a wary eye out for the roving bouncers, and fiddled around in my pack on the seat beside me until I had three Sno-Seal packets filled with what I hoped was no more than a gram each. Fooling with a scale would have gotten me caught in a heartbeat. All I could do, under the circumstances, was to eyeball the amounts and pray I wasn't being overly generous.

When Dave and Andi returned to the booth, I excused myself and started making the rounds. Miraculously, within a half-hour I managed to discreetly unload the three grams to some of the people I'd spotted on my trip to the bar and the bouncers were none the wiser. And suddenly the pressure was off. Once again, I had money to burn. And before the long night was over I would burn through plenty.

Predictably, the party kept right on cranking along until the house lights flared at 10 a.m. and sent us scurrying out into the streets of SoHo like so many startled cockroaches. The three of us were starving by then, so we caught a taxi back down to Tribeca and had the cabbie drop us at a Greek diner on Hudson Street, where our motor-mouths made short work of three huge breakfast platters. Six thousand greasy calories later, we finally parted company. Dave and Andi flagged a cab and headed downtown to their harbour-view apartment in one of the new high-rise buildings that flanked the World Financial Center complex. I set off south down Hudson to pay a visit to the smoke shop. It was just past eleven and he'd be open for business and happy to sell me a bottle of exorbitantly over-priced vitamin-B powder.

Outside the smoke shop, I stashed the bottle of cut in my backpack and headed up the block to Chambers Street and the Bond Hotel, an SRO flophouse where the hallways reeked of roach spray and bad hygiene, and the bathroom faucets spat out rust-red water for the first few minutes after you opened the tap. Like the down-and-outers who made up its customer base, the Bond Hotel had seen better days. But it hadn't always been a flophouse. Back in the mid-nineteenth century, when the hotel was built, it was called the Cosmopolitan and it catered to a posh clientele. Then in the late 1930s the building had gone up in flames, a victim of arson. The place was eventually refurbished and renamed the Bond Hotel, but it never regained its former glory and by the 1980s it was as dreary a place to stay as any hellhole on the Bowery.

The Bond, however, still had three things to recommend it. First, it was close to the Raccoon Lodge. Second, its rates were as cheap as you could find anywhere in Manhattan. And third – but not least – its rooms had solid doors and sturdy locks, which is something you come to value when you need a place to process illegal drugs. All of which made it my flophouse of choice whenever I could spare the cost of a room.

I would hardly have called myself a regular at the hotel, but I had stayed there enough that the desk clerk recognised me as a familiar face, which helped me convince him to rent me a twenty-dollar room several hours earlier than the customary check-in. I was grateful for that. I'd already been up for more than twenty-four hours. The sooner I could hit the rack, the better.

You would think that after snorting coke for sixteen hours nonstop, sleep would be hard to come by. Not true. Despite all the marching powder in my system, as soon as I stripped down to my skivvies and flopped on the sagging bed I was out for the count. And I stayed out for the next five hours, until my bladder finally rang the Apache alarm clock and forced me out of bed.

Groaning in protest, I threw on some clothes and hurried down the hall to the toilet. In hotels like the Bond, the rooms come equipped with nothing more than a hand sink and a blurry mirror. The bathroom is always 'down the hall'. Which makes for some urgent traffic in the corridors, as you can well imagine. (And probably more in-room sink-pissing than anyone in management would care to acknowledge.)

Back in my room, the view through the grimy window showed the sun sinking low over the Hudson as dusk overtook the streets of Tribeca. Happy Hour must already have been under way. It was time to get busy prepping product for the night ahead.

I switched on the ceiling globe so I'd have light to work by, then steeled myself as I opened my pack to see how much coke had survived the night. I knew one thing for certain: it wasn't going to be as much as I hoped. Nevertheless, even with my lowered expectations I was shocked when I weighed what remained and discovered I had barely five grams left of the fourteen I'd picked up from Bobby Bats only twenty-four hours earlier.

And what did I have to show for my efforts? Twelve measly dollars. That's all that was left in my wallet after I'd forked over twenty for the room. Even for me this was an all-time fuck-up. *What now?* I asked myself, again and again, as I sat on the edge of the bed and tried to wrap my head around the full dimensions of this disaster.

True, I had just enough coke left to cover my debt to Bobby Bats, if I stepped on it with five grams of cut and mustered the restraint to peddle all ten grams without dipping into the stash for my own enjoyment. An unlikely scenario, granted, but still within the realm of possibility.

Sure, go for it, you can still make it work, the optimist in me insisted.

But the realist in me would have none of it. *Who the fuck are you kidding? It'll never happen.*

The realist proved himself right by pulling out the coke spoon and helping himself to two hefty scoops from my dwindling stash.

As the rush cut through my hangover, my mind began to focus, and suddenly, with a clarity verging on clairvoyance, I could see that my life was about to take a radical turn into uncharted territory. Come Monday, I would have to abandon New York for parts unknown. It was that simple. A scary prospect, but to tell the truth I accepted it with relief more than resignation.

How many years had I been longing to escape the rut my life in New York had become?

More than I cared to count.

And how many years had I failed to summon the will to make the changes that would have freed me?

Ditto.

Now that the idiot wind had forced my hand, I finally had my way out. A sorry way out, to be sure, but I welcomed it nonetheless. The key would be raising enough cash over the next two days to bankroll my getaway. Barring a repeat of last night's performance, I was confident I could make that happen. And so, in blissful ignorance of how events would actually unfold over the course of the next two nights, I broke out my supplies and got busy cutting and packaging what remained of the coke, no easy chore with hands as shaky as mine after the previous night's excesses. Ten packets were all I could complete before frustration got the better of me and I called it quits. But that would be enough for starters.

When I was done cutting and portioning out the coke, I still had five grams left to work with after the first ten packets sold out – a reserve stash I immediately proceeded to diminish by treating myself to a couple of celebratory snorts for a job well done.

I was buzzing nicely by the time I finished packing away my supplies, and after freshening up with a whore's bath at the tiny hand sink, I got dressed, checked the angle of my Bogart fedora in the blurry mirror and, satisfied I was ready to face the night, headed out in search of customers.

It was pushing seven when I walked into the Raccoon, and the crowd was sparse. Gary and Ace, the Raccoon's two principal owners, were working behind the bar that evening, as they usually did on weekends. I said my hellos and ordered a tall rum and Coke. Then I stepped over to the jukebox, dropped in a quarter and punched the buttons for a 1972 rarity by Leon Russell called 'I'm Slipping into Christmas'. It was a record Ace inserted into the rotation when the holiday season rolled around, a deeply bluesy loser's lament I always thought would make the perfect background music for a Christmas-time wrist-slitting beneath the mistletoe. I loved it the first time I heard it – loser's laments had a certain undeniable resonance for me in those days. There was no telling when I'd next get the chance to hear it again, so I seized the opportunity to play it one last time.

In light of how the rest of the night went, that Leon Russell dirge would prove to be a prescient selection. By the time I stumbled out of the Houston Street after-hours club the following morning – for the second time in as many days – I was a bigger loser than ever, with plenty to lament. Once again, I had spent the night doling out free hits like they were party favours – only this time I had spread my largesse over a wider territory by wandering from bar to bar on the Tribeca circuit. Puffy's. Whitey's Tavern. The North River Bar. The Ear Inn. In every bar, I made more friends than profits.

It wasn't that I didn't unload any product along the way. Six of the ten packets I'd prepped at the Bond actually turned into cash in my wallet. But the three hundred bucks I collected had somehow been reduced by half by the time I left the after-hours club – which would have depressed me more if I hadn't already reached the stage where I couldn't give a fuck. I was so sick of the grind and so ready to put it all behind me that I didn't care whether I left town with money in my pocket or not.

Still, my prospects weren't totally bleak. There was every

chance I could move a few more grams during the big game on Sunday night. Or so I told myself as I crawled back into bed at the Bond Hotel to catch a few hours' sleep before the festivities kicked off at a pre-game party one of my customers was throwing at his loft on Church Street. Good thing I had laid out another twenty at the hotel desk on my way in that morning, otherwise I would have had to check out by noon, and I definitely needed more sleep than that if I was going to make it through the Super Bowl.

The loft party at Ari and Mandy's place was in full swing by the time I finally made my appearance. Ari owned one of the bigger job-lot electronics stores on Church Street. His wife Mandy kept the store's books and dabbled in photography. The loft's whitewashed brick walls were hung with dozens of her black-and-white abstracts, most of them close-focus shots of vintage architectural features from the neighbourhood's buildings.

Dozens of locals were milling around the cavernous space, clutching cups of Bloody Marys and shouting over the music blasting from Ari's Bang & Olufsen sound system. Blind Faith, playing 'Can't Find My Way Home'.

Ari's collection of vinyl LPs from the sixties and seventies was a marvel to behold. He must have had twenty linear feet of albums packed into the long, low storage unit that lined the living room's north wall, all standing upright, cheek-by-jowl, impeccably in alphabetical order. Ari and I were the same age and had similar tastes in music, so whenever I attended one of his parties I'd pepper him with requests. I can't remember ever requesting a song that he couldn't find somewhere in his library.

'Hey, Pete, glad you could make it,' Ari greeted me, as I made my way toward the Bloody Mary punch bowl.

'Hey, Ari,' I said, shaking his hand. 'Thanks for the invite. Looks like I'm a bit underdressed, though.'

Everywhere I looked, Giants jerseys and caps were much in evidence. All I had on was my wide-brimmed grey felt fedora and the same tweed sports coat and black turtleneck I'd been wearing all weekend.

Ari grinned. 'As long as you aren't wearing Broncos orange, you've got nothing to worry about.'

Christ, don't I wish that were true, I thought to myself. I had worries galore, but this wasn't the place to air them.

'Good turnout,' I said, as I took a sip of Bloody Mary, which was heavy on the vodka and laced with an eye-watering dosage of Tabasco. In other words, perfect.

'Any tune requests?' Ari asked.

'Got any Nazz?' I replied, hoping to stump him for once.

'Shit, yeah,' Ari said. 'I love Todd Rundgren.'

Foiled again, but I was glad. Todd Rundgren had seen me through a lot of all-night acid trips in my college days.

Minutes later, the loft filled with Rundgren's voice, vintage 1968, singing 'Open My Eyes'.

'Way to go, Ari,' I shouted in his ear. 'Let me tip the DJ,' I said, pulling out my vial of coke. Ari and his wife were regular customers of mine at the Raccoon.

'You're too kind,' Ari smiled.

So we adjourned to the kidney-shaped glass coffee table that fronted his big sectional couch, where a half-dozen other partygoers were already gathered, chopping lines and wielding straws, revving up their team spirit. I tapped out four generous lines from my vial, and Ari and I joined in on the fun.

The fun kept right on coming for the next two hours, until the party started breaking up around six. Everyone was heading out to catch the game at whatever big-screen bar they fancied. A good many in the crowd at Ari's were planning to watch it at the Galway, an Irish-run joint on Varick Street that was famous for its Super Bowl half-time buffet. I figured it was as good a place as any, so I tagged along with Ari and Mandy on the short walk uptown from their loft to the bar.

We arrived a good two hours before kick-off, but the place was filling up fast with people who had made their reservations weeks earlier. It was always a reservations-only affair. Ari and Mandy were on the list, of course. I hadn't booked a spot in advance, but the off-duty bartender who'd been pressed into service as the doorman was one of my frequent customers.

'Hey, Jimmy,' I said.

'Hey, Hat, come on in,' he replied, waving me through without so much as a glance at his clipboard. Lowly as my adopted profession might be, you couldn't deny it came with perks.

After two hours of guzzling Ari's Bloody Marys on an empty stomach I was feeling no pain when I squeezed into a corner spot at the bar with a decent line of sight to the giant screen in the back. The spot I picked was in a shadowy little alcove with a single two-top table tucked up hard against the bar's tinted front window – an out-of-the way place to surreptitiously snort the occasional hit.

Of course, the 'occasional' hits got less occasional by the hour, and by the time the strains of the national anthem started echoing through the room I was Mr Magnanimous once more, buying rounds of drinks for everyone and treating an ever-growing circle of friends to free hits from my stash.

Go, Giants!

Or, as Mr Magnanimous would say, *Go crazy!*

And that's exactly what I did as the first half played out.

The only hint of sanity in my whole performance was when I took the time to unload a few of the packets I'd prepped at the Bond before visiting Ari and Mandy. Otherwise I would have been tapped out after the first few rounds.

Half-time came, with the Giants in the lead, and the happy crowd began queuing up at the big buffet table. I should have joined the line, but the blow had suppressed my appetite, so I stayed put at the bar. Which was fortunate, because otherwise I might have missed Elena's entrance.

I saw her step through the front door, and she caught my eye immediately. She just stood there, looking a bit perplexed as she scanned the packed room, trying to spot an opening.

She looked familiar, but it took me a moment to place her. She was a waitress at the Greek diner on Hudson Street where Dave and Andi and I had eaten breakfast on Saturday morning. I was so used to seeing her in a frumpy waitress uniform it was a surprise to see her dolled up in tight-fitting designer jeans, high black leather boots and a faux-leopard jacket. It was a fashion statement with an unmistakably outer-borough accent, but it showcased her curves with more flair than the smock dress and apron I was used to seeing her wear.

As soon as I recognised her, I waved her over to my corner and gave up my stool at the crowded bar. She seemed grateful for the welcome, but the look on her face told me she was having the same trouble placing me that I'd had with her.

'I'm Pete,' I said, extending my hand. 'I eat at your diner all the time. I'm the guy who always orders the meatloaf special.'

That seemed to jog her memory.

'Elena,' she said, smiling as she shook my hand with a strong grip. 'I *thought* you looked familiar. Thanks for the seat. I just got off shift. I've been on my feet for the last eight hours.'

'Can I buy you a drink?' I offered.

'Sure,' she said. 'I'd like a double shot of ouzo and a wine cooler.'

Whoa, this girl wastes no time getting up to speed! I thought to myself.

In the spirit of *eudemonia,* I ordered a double shot of ouzo, too, and lifted my glass to hers in honour of the occasion.

'To the New York Giants,' I toasted.

'To whatever,' she smiled, clinking glasses before she downed her double shot without a flinch. 'To tell you the truth, I'm not really into American football. I just came for the party. I've got the next two days off, and I'm not leaving here tonight until I'm so drunk I pass out on the cab ride back to Brooklyn.'

To a man in my condition, this seemed an entirely reasonable goal, and I decided then and there that I would help her reach it.

'Well, then, we'd better have another round. You've got some catching up to do.'

When the half-time hoopla ended and the second half kicked off, we were already working on our third round of drinks, and Elena was getting more affectionate by the minute. By the fourth quarter, when New York had the game well in hand, Elena was putting up less resistance than the Denver Broncos' defence, and – lucky me – it looked like Phil Simms and the Giants wouldn't be the only ones with something to celebrate that night.

It would be flattering to think that my charm and wit were what won Elena over, but odds are my success had more to do with the baggie of coke I kept passing to her beneath the apron of the bar. Apparently Elena had as big an appetite for marching powder as she did for ouzo.

The Giants' 39–20 triumph sent the crowd in the Galway into a frenzy of back-slapping and high-fives. Elena and I skipped all that. We were too busy making out in the shadows of the alcove. It was the sort of public display that would normally have provoked cries of 'Get a room!' but in the euphoria and the general pandemonium nobody paid us any mind. Not that it mattered. By that point in the evening we were well past caring about public opinion.

At 3 a.m. the party was winding down, and Elena and I decided to head home to her place. Outside, on Varick Street, it was snowing lightly as we flagged down a cab and set off for Brooklyn.

'Should I take the bridge?' the cabbie asked.

'No, take the Battery Tunnel,' Elena told him. 'It's quicker.'

Up until that point, Elena hadn't mentioned exactly where she lived in Brooklyn, but when I heard her recite her address to the cabbie, I realised we were heading to – of all places – Bay Ridge, my native ground. I hadn't set foot in that part of Brooklyn in many years. And now, on what would be my last night in New York, I was returning to my roots, slipping back into the old neighbourhood under cover of darkness for a one-night stand.

At the time, it struck me as an odd coincidence. But months later, and many miles away, after I'd had time to mull over the symmetry of that farewell visit, I would come to think of it as fate.

As we cruised along the shore of the Narrows, I could barely make out the running lights of the ghostly freighters out on the water beneath the Verrazzano Bridge. The snow was several inches deep when we climbed out of the cab in front of Elena's place, a two-storey brownstone on a quiet side street off Fifth Avenue. It was one of those old-style row houses you enter by mounting a ridiculously high set of front steps, and what with the snow underfoot, and Elena's compromised equilibrium, it was quite an adventure coaxing her up to her first-floor apartment.

As soon as we were safely inside, Elena triple-locked her front door and dragged me straight to her bedroom. After our make-out session at the Galway, any attempt at foreplay would have been redundant, so we skipped the preliminaries and, without further ado, we stripped off our clothes and got busy. And we stayed busy for quite some time.

When our bodies finally untangled, the only thing I craved was a good night's sleep. Elena, however, wasn't quite done. Before turning off the bedroom lamp, she reached for the empty baggie on the nightstand – the baggie that had once been full of Bobby Bats' coke – and turned it inside out. Then, like a cat lapping milk, she gave the white-dusted plastic a thorough licking with her pert little tongue. 'Dessert,' she called it, and in a way that's exactly what it was.

The final act before you leave the table.

I just hoped I'd be well out the door before the bill came.

With that unsettling thought in mind, I rolled over, passed out and didn't awaken until hours later, when the sound of Elena's panicked voice roused me into groggy consciousness.

'Oh, shit! Oh, shit! Oh, shit!' she moaned, throwing back the covers and hopping out of bed. 'Wake up, Pete. Hurry, you've got to go!'

'What's the problem?'

'It's already one-thirty!' she exclaimed. As if that explained anything.

'What's the rush? You told me you had the day off.'

'I do,' she said. 'But I forgot about Demetri!'

'Demetri?' I repeated. 'Who the fuck's Demetri? Your boyfriend?'

'No, Demetri's my older brother,' she explained. 'He's coming over at two to fix my washing machine, and you can't be here when he shows up.'

'Why not?' I asked. 'It's your place, isn't it? You're a big girl. What's the big deal?'

She shook her head. 'You don't get it. Demetri still thinks I'm a virgin.'

She was right. I didn't get it. The girl had to be twenty-three or twenty-four if she was a day. Who stays a virgin that long in this day and age? I'd have accused her of pulling my leg if she hadn't seemed so genuinely upset. She was frantically scurrying around the bedroom, plucking my clothes from the carpet and tossing them onto the foot of the bed.

'Quick!' she said. 'Get dressed! He could be here any minute.'

'Okay, calm down,' I said, as I threw back the covers and climbed out of bed. 'Let me use the bathroom first. I've got time to take a piss, at least, don't I?'

'I guess,' she said. 'But hurry, please!'

Four minutes later I was buttoning my overcoat as Elena herded me to the door and whisked me out with a peck on the cheek and a parting apology.

'Sorry, Pete. I'll make it up to you next time, I promise.'

'I'm going to hold you to that,' I said, and left her with a smile.

I knew there would never be a next time, but what else was I going to say to her? *Have a nice life, you'll never see me again?* I liked her. I couldn't do that. Sometimes the truth is just too cold.

And sometimes so is the world, as I discovered the moment I stepped outside Elena's door. While we'd been hunkered down in the darkness of Elena's black-out-shaded bedroom, the storm had grown into a full-blown blizzard. The snow on the streets was knee-deep, and at the rate the clouds were dumping more there'd be another foot on the ground by nightfall. After the warmth of Elena's bed, it was a real shock to my system, but there was nothing I could do about it except turn up my collar and start slogging through the whiteout towards the BMT subway station on 86th Street, eight long blocks away. Even if some miracle had sent a cab my way, I couldn't have afforded to catch it. Last night's cab ride out to Bay Ridge had cost me the last of my cash. I had nothing left in my pockets but loose change and a couple of subway tokens.

The wind was against me the entire way, whipping snow into my face so hard it stung like hornets. For a good part of the trek, I was forced to walk backwards to make any progress at all. By the time I reached the shelter of the subway station, my ears and cheeks were practically frostbitten.

How the hell am I going to get out of town in weather like this? The question was gnawing at me as I boarded the RR local for the forty-minute ride back to Manhattan.

When you don't have a dollar to your name, hitchhiking is usually your only option, but that was off the table. The only affordable alternative was Greyhound, if I could somehow scrape together the price of a bus ticket. Which wasn't going to be easy. I couldn't really borrow the money for a ticket. Anyone I knew well enough to hit up for a loan had already learned from experience that lending money to me was a losing proposition. That left me with only one solution. One I would rather not have resorted to, but I couldn't see any other way to raise the cash I needed in a hurry.

I was going to have to scam one of my customers.

If I put in an appearance at the Raccoon Lodge, the odds were good that someone would approach me for coke, and when they did I'd tell them I was on my way to 're-up'. I'd take their buy-money up front and promise to be back within the hour. And that would be the last they'd see of me. Somewhere down the line I'd just have to send a money order back to the Raccoon to square the debt and ease my conscience. At least, that's what I told myself to make the idea more palatable.

I got off at Chambers Street and reluctantly started trudging south toward the Raccoon Lodge. The snow was still falling without let-up, but the howling wind I'd faced in Brooklyn had blown itself out, leaving behind a residual calm that felt somehow more threatening. Overhead, the sky was a solid mass of grey clouds getting darker by the minute, and the winter light, pale and weak, was fading fast.

It was only a little past three in the afternoon, yet the electronics stores along Church Street were already locked up tight, shut down early by the storm. The scene was the same when I turned the corner onto Warren Street. Every shop gated and dark. But down at the far end of the block, the lights of the Raccoon Lodge beckoned like a beacon in the twilight gloom. I just hoped the bar wouldn't be empty when I got there. You can't run a con without a mark.

Nearing the end of the block, I could see the neon glow from the beer signs in the bar's window tinting the snow as it swirled past the plate glass. Snowflakes in borrowed colours – Budweiser red, Pabst blue, Rolling Rock green – danced in the air like party confetti. It was a festive sight, but it didn't cheer me. The party was over, and I knew it. One for the road and I'd be on my way.

When I stepped inside and started stomping my snow-crusted Reeboks on the doormat, I drew the attention of every person in the bar. All three of them. In the corner by the pay phone two meter maids in ear-flap hats sat huddled over mugs of hot chocolate, no doubt sheltering from the storm while they waited for their shift to end. The only familiar face belonged to Susan, the weekday bartender. Susan and I had been close friends for years. She looked up from the pile of supermarket tabloids she was leafing through and sized me up with a jaundiced eye.

'Oh, Christ, look what the cat dragged in,' she remarked, when I joined her at the far end of the bar. 'You okay? You look like shit.'

That was what I liked best about Susan. The girl pulled no punches.

'Duly noted,' I said. 'Thanks.'

'What can I get you?' she asked. 'Coffee? Visine? A blood transfusion?'

'Very funny,' I muttered. 'A cup of coffee will be just fine.'

'Cup of coffee, coming right up,' she grinned. 'How do you want it?'

'Straight up black,' I said. 'No cream, no sugar, no editorial comments.'

'Ooh, poor baby!' she cooed, mocking me. 'Feeling a little thin-skinned today, are we?'

'You might say that,' I replied. 'So cut me some slack, okay?'

'If you insist,' she said, pouring me a mug of coffee. 'Not that you deserve it.'

Susan's tone of voice when she delivered that last comment left me with the suspicion that I might have offended her at some point during my weekend-long binge. Offhand, I couldn't recall anything specific, but that didn't mean I had nothing to regret. For all I knew, it might have been my binge itself that offended her. Susan was the kind of friend who will tell you the truth even when you don't want to hear it – and she'd been hounding me to clean up my act for ages. It pained me to think I had hurt her feelings. Of all the things I would miss when I left New York, Susan's hard-nosed friendship was high on the list. Still, probing for gory details wasn't how I wanted to spend our parting moments.

Of course, Susan had no clue that I was about to skip town, and I meant to keep it that way. Somewhere down the road I'd have to pick up a phone and ease her mind. In the meantime, secrecy seemed to be the easiest – if not the bravest – exit strategy. But the look of concern in Susan's eyes when I'd walked into the bar made it that much harder to keep her in the dark, and I squirmed inside at the thought of sitting there much longer under the pressure of her worried gaze.

'Oh, by the way,' Susan said, 'some guy named Bobby's been calling here for you. I told him to call back at Happy Hour.'

Some guy named Bobby's been calling.

'Okay, thanks,' I said, though the news was hardly something to be thankful for. 'Not much of a crowd today,' I said, quickly changing the subject. 'Any of the regulars been in yet?'

'One too many,' Susan replied, cryptically. It didn't take me long to figure out what she meant. A moment later I heard the telltale creak of the men's room door, and I pivoted on my stool just in time to see Kentucky Fried Danny stumble out of the john and carom off the pool table as he made his unsteady way back to the bar.

'Jesus, he looks extra crispy,' I observed. 'How long's he been here?'

Susan rolled her eyes and gave me the damage report. 'They shut down his job site at ten this morning and I've had the pleasure ever since.'

As Danny approached, Susan retreated to the middle of the bar and made a show of restocking the speed wells – leaving me to deal with the mess she'd made.

It was no small mess.

'There he is, Pete the Hat, my main man!' Danny proclaimed when he got close enough to focus on me. He was still dressed in his ironworker's clothes – a grimy set of Carhart coveralls smeared with iron rust, which had the unsettling appearance of dried blood. His greasy blond hair was still matted in a circular pattern by the webbing of the hard hat he'd shed hours ago. Danny was an overgrown kid from the hills of Kentucky, an apprentice ironworker who'd been shipped north by his union to work on one of the new skyscrapers down at the World Financial Center. He'd been in New York for almost a year, and in that time he'd become a fixture at the Raccoon Lodge – and, thanks to his union wages, one of my better customers.

As Danny approached, I could see that his eyelids were droopy, but the rest of his baby face was frozen in a rictus-like grin. The grin was a dead giveaway. Young Danny was already deeply fried. But the sight of me seemed to pull him partway out of his stupor and he stood a little straighter as he walked up and clamped a beefy hand on my shoulder.

'Brother, am I glad to see *you*!' he blubbered in my ear. 'Let me buy you a drink. What'll you have?'

The last thing I needed at that point was alcohol, but when

Danny was on a tear it was a waste of time trying to argue with him. So I let him order me a peppermint schnapps. Not much of a drink, but I figured my breath could use the help. For himself, he ordered a double Jack and Coke.

Susan brought us our drinks and the change from the twenty Danny had given her.

'That's for you, darlin',' Danny said, pushing back a five.

Susan nodded her thanks and gave the mahogany bar two quick raps with her knuckles before retreating toward her tip jar. The moment she was out of range Danny got right down to business.

'You holding?' he asked. As usual, he cupped a furtive hand over his mouth when he popped the question. I'm sure in his backwoods way he thought that was proper form for conducting clandestine business in public, but all it ever did was draw attention to our transactions. Such a bush-league move annoyed me, yet I was never able to break him of the habit. This time, however, I let it slide. Considering the scam I was about to pull on him, it seemed the least I could do.

'Not at the moment,' I told him. 'But I'm on my way to re-up right now. How much you looking for?'

Before answering, Danny slipped his wallet out of his coveralls and checked to see how much cash he had left.

'I could go for a half, I guess,' he said, folding two twenties and a ten together and passing them to me beneath the bar.

'No problem,' I said, pocketing his cash. 'Give me half an hour.'

I took a final swig of coffee and got up off the barstool. Susan saw me buttoning my overcoat and shouldering my pack and she shot me a look of disapproval. She knew what was up. Or *thought* she did.

'Leaving us so soon?' she asked sarcastically, as I headed for the door.

'Duty calls, but I'll be right back,' I lied, and then hurried out into the storm.

In those days, when lying was my stock in trade, Susan had always been the one person I had never tried to deceive. The thought that I'd saved my farewell lie for her made the chill in the air feel that much colder. But the tears that filled my eyes as I retraced my steps to the subway for the trip uptown to the Port Authority proved I still had a conscience, so maybe there was hope for me yet.

As long as the Greyhound buses were still running.

CHAPTER 2

*W*hen *I surfaced* from the subway, Times Square was ghostly white and hushed to a whisper. The only sounds were the clinking of tyre chains on a crosstown bus and the distant scraping of a plough blade echoing from somewhere up in the Theater District. Forty-Second Street was deserted, and as I headed for the Port Authority the loneliness that suddenly overwhelmed me was as harsh as the wind off the Hudson. I was totally on my own now, and that was painful to admit. Yet what did I expect? Once the last bridge is burnt, every addict becomes an island, no matter what John Donne says.

The question is, why would anyone choose that path? I'd been ducking that question for fifteen years, afraid to face the answers I might find, and this was the result. In my heart, I knew there was no point running for my life if all I was running toward was more of the same. Somewhere down the road I'd have to find the courage to take the hard look that was necessary. But

I'd been dodging the truth for so long I wondered if I still had it in me to face it. And that scared me more than Bobby Bats.

My trousers were caked with snow up to my thighs by the time I reached the Port Authority and I was shedding clumps with every stride as I rushed through the concourse, praying I hadn't missed the last bus out. When I checked the Greyhound Arrivals and Departures board, the storm's impact was evident. Every bus heading north or west of the city had already been cancelled. But the board did offer one ray of hope from the sunny south – a bus to Miami was scheduled to depart at 6 p.m. and it hadn't yet been added to the cancellations list. I was in luck! Would the fifty dollars I'd scammed from Danny be enough to buy a ticket to Miami? I doubted it. In any case, I'd have to hold back some cash for food.

'How far south will the Miami bus take me for thirty bucks?' I asked the churchy-looking black woman behind the counter.

She sniffed and gave me the fisheye before consulting her rate book. 'Best I can do for you is Richmond, Virginia. A one-way ticket will cost you thirty-six dollars.'

I almost replied 'Praise Jesus!' but thought better of it. Heartfelt or not, it would have earned me another sniff, no question. Instead, I pushed two twenties across the counter. Eighty per cent of my net worth, gone. But I surrendered it with little regret. If it got me clear of the storm, it would be money well spent.

'Bus leaves at six, from Gate 8, Mezzanine Level,' the clerk said, as she passed me my ticket and change. 'Don't miss it, son. Might be the last bus leavin' out of here tonight.'

'Gate 8, thanks,' I said, and hurried off to check the concourse clock. It was 5.40. I had made it with twenty minutes to spare. As the tension drained from my body, I realised I was starving. The concourse food shops were still open, but I couldn't afford to pay their jacked-up prices, so I made a mad dash across the street to the Korean grocery store on Ninth Avenue.

The Korean grandma behind the counter looked up when I entered, and as I rushed up and down the aisles frantically grabbing items off the shelves she watched me suspiciously, her face a stern mask of concern or disapproval – I couldn't tell which. But I didn't want her getting spooked and dialling 911, so I called out over my shoulder, 'Sorry, I'm in a real hurry.'

When I dumped my supplies on the counter and pulled out my last ten-dollar bill, the grandma's stern expression softened and she rang up my order on a well-worn abacus. There wasn't much to ring up. A loaf of Wonder Bread. A jar of Welch's grape jelly. A twin-pack of Bic disposable razors. A travel-sized tube of Colgate toothpaste. And a pouch of Bugler brand roll-your-own tobacco. No one could say I wasn't travelling light.

'Nine dolla,' the grandma announced, when the beads stopped clicking. To my surprise, as she handed over my change, she flashed me a gap-toothed smile and said in a flat, uninflected Korean accent that left me puzzled, 'You go far.'

I had no clue whether I'd just been delivered a prophecy or asked a simple question.

'Go far?' I repeated, unsure what else to say.

'You go far, I put extra bag. Bad weather,' she said, nodding toward the store window.

'Oh, right,' I smiled, getting the picture. 'Thanks, an extra bag would be great.'

The Miami bus rolled up to Gate 8 on the dot of six and was greeted by murmurs of relief from everyone in line. The doors popped open with a pneumatic hiss and the lanky, grey-haired driver stepped off and started collecting tickets. As I handed him mine, I asked, 'How bad are the roads out there?'

'Seen worse,' he replied with a Down East accent that eased my mind. In Maine, you don't survive long enough to get grey hair unless you've mastered the art of driving in snow.

The bench seat in the rear of the bus was unoccupied, and I immediately claimed it. It's the one seat on a Greyhound that lets you get horizontal, even if only in the foetal position, and I figured I'd better get what sleep I could on the ride to Richmond because there was no telling where or when I'd next get the chance to bed down in a warm place. After shucking my coat and my snow-filled Reeboks, I broke out the Wonder Bread and grape jelly, and belatedly realised I'd forgotten to ask the Korean grandma for some plastic utensils. I was forced to improvise, and I felt completely ridiculous as I sat there spreading jelly on bread with the only utensil I had available – the hollow plastic handle of a Bic disposable razor. But the jelly sandwiches cured my hunger pangs, and as the bus headed into the Lincoln Tunnel I felt the sugar start to perk me up. I welcomed the rush. It had been twelve hours since I'd snorted my last line of coke and abstinence was gnawing at my synapses with sharp little teeth.

The tunnel's sodium lights cast a jaundiced glow on the white-tiled walls as I gazed out the window, intent on catching a parting glimpse of the blue-tiled strip at midpoint, which marks the border line between New York and New Jersey. When it eventually flashed by, it left me with mixed feelings. In a sense, it was the starting line for the marathon race I now had to run to reclaim my life, and of course that was something to be glad about. But on the flip side it was also very much a finish line: a here-and-gone reminder that my life in New York was now behind me. And that was a sad thing to acknowledge – as shattered dreams always are.

<center>~~~</center>

Fifteen years earlier, fresh out of Dartmouth with an honours degree in English, I had moved back to New York from New Hampshire and landed my first job in the publishing business: a copy editor's position in the college textbook division at Harcourt Brace Jovanovich. *This is it!* I thought. My childhood dreams of a literary career in the Big City were becoming a reality. I was twenty-two at the time, and everything seemed to be going to plan. Two months after hiring on at HBJ, I capped a five-year courtship by marrying my high-school sweetheart, Marie – despite my father's repeated attempts to talk me out of it. He said I'd be foolish to rush into marriage with the first (and only) girl I'd ever dated. I ignored his warnings. I was young and in love and sure I would prove him wrong.

Marie and I moved into a tiny one-bedroom apartment in Bay Ridge. Our budget was too tight for anything grander. But we didn't mind. We were two kids from blue-collar families and no strangers to stretching a dollar. Besides, like all newly-weds, we had faith that love would conquer all – and that better days were coming. And for a few charmed years our optimism seemed justified. Marie was promoted to head buyer for women's sportswear at Gimbel's department store in Manhattan, and shortly thereafter I was promoted to chief copy editor at HBJ. When our raises came through, we moved to a bigger apartment in neighbouring Dyker Heights, where I converted the spare bedroom into a writer's den. It was a welcome change; in our old apartment the only place I could set up my typewriter was on the Formica dinette table in the roach-infested kitchen.

And while at first that had seemed a suitably bohemian setting for writing a debut novel, it had quickly lost its romantic appeal. Now I had a proper desk in a roach-free space, and I vowed to start putting in more time at the typewriter.

Unfortunately, that vow was easier to make than to keep, as Marie and I began spending more and more of our evenings caught up in the whirl of Manhattan's nightlife. Between Marie's connections in the fashion business and mine in the publishing world, we were constantly being invited to parties that kept us in the city late, and by the time we'd wobbled off the RR train in Bay Ridge and grabbed a cab home I was rarely in any shape to hit the typewriter. In my sober hours I'd look through the paltry pile of manuscript pages I'd produced since I'd left college, and my heart would sink. I had set myself a goal after graduation, to publish my first novel by my twenty-fifth birthday. That deadline was already in the rear-view mirror. I began to doubt I'd ever reach my goal. However, instead of redoubling my efforts, I started feeling sorry for myself. And that's when my troubles began to multiply.

Before then, I'd never had to wrestle with self-doubt. I'd sailed through school with honours at every level, accomplishing everything I'd put my mind to. So when I set my sights on a writing career after college I naively assumed I'd succeed, as I always had. Now, the limits of my abilities were becoming painfully apparent. And since my early success had left me woefully unprepared to deal with disappointment, my first reaction was to sulk and play the 'if only' game. *If only I didn't have to slave at HBJ for rent money, I'd have finished the book by now. If only I hadn't married Marie so soon, I'd have had more solitude for writing.* Which only made things worse because I knew I was making excuses, not progress. Before long, Happy Hour at the

Lion's Head was the only time of day I felt good about myself, and as the months dragged on I began drinking more heavily than I had in my fraternity days at college.

As my Irish nana used to say, 'a burden shared is a burden halved'. In hindsight, I have no doubt I should have confided in Marie. After all, how many thousands of hours had we spent sharing everything on our minds since the night we'd first met at a Sadie Hawkins dance in the Sachem High School gym? But instead of opening up to the one person who could best have understood what I was going through, I kept my troubles to myself. I had too much stubborn pride, I guess; I could never bring myself to confess to Marie that her Ivy League wonder boy now felt like a loser.

Marie could hardly ignore the changes in my behaviour, however, and began to complain about all the 'overtime' I claimed to be working at the office – my fallback excuse for the hours I spent drinking every evening in the West Village, fooling myself that hanging out with real writers was the next best thing to being one myself. A pathetic delusion only alcohol could sustain. By the time I showed my guilty face at home, it would be after nine o'clock and Marie would already have eaten dinner and retired to bed without me. But her patience was wearing thin. One grim night I arrived home to find all the house lights blazing – and Marie crying hysterically on the living-room couch. She had reached her limit.

'My God, Marie, what's the matter?' I asked, as if I didn't already know.

'I can't take this any more, Pete,' she sobbed. 'If you can't make time for me, what's the point of staying together?'

It was wrenching to look at her weeping face and see not the polished sophisticate she'd grown into during her years in the rag trade but the vulnerable teenager she'd been when we first started dating. I'd made her miserable, and misery had stripped her bare. I felt so ashamed it was hard to meet her eyes as I stammered my apologies and swore that I still loved her. To my relief, Marie followed her heart and believed me. I even believed it myself. Yet, for all my good intentions, it wasn't long before I betrayed her trust again, even more egregiously, by climbing into bed with another woman while Marie was overseas scouting the latest French fashions at the Paris Prêt-à-Porter show.

Drunks save their lamest alibis for themselves, and though I knew this latest betrayal was only another selfish attempt to distract myself from what ailed me I told myself it was just a one-night stand – my shot at a taste of the free love I'd stead-fastly refrained from during my hippie days in college, out of loyalty to Marie. But my infatuation with Bobbi B – a husky-voiced siren ten years my senior – was stronger than I'd expected. Our first hook-up soon led to another, and eventually blossomed into a year-long affair that only ended when Bobbi – like Marie – discovered how hollow my promises could be.

Bobbi was an ad exec who occasionally had to fly out to LA to oversee production of TV commercials and sometimes she'd give me the key to her apartment on Barrow Street and ask me to collect her mail while she was away. On her final trip before our break-up she asked an additional favour. 'I left some cash on the kitchen table. Will you go down to the Con Ed office and pay my electric bill when it shows up in the mail?'

'Sure,' I promised, and then forgot all about it – until Bobbi returned two weeks later to find her power shut off and her refrigerator full of rotting food. After that, she washed her hands of me. 'You're a great fuck, Pete, but a lousy friend,' were her parting words. Which stung, because I couldn't deny it – any more than I could deny I was a drunk or a lousy husband.

Soon afterward, Marie reached the same conclusion and informed me she was filing for an annulment. It crushed me to hear her say it at last. But I knew it was the ending I'd seen coming for a long time. There was no point pretending I could fix what I'd broken.

My father was right, after all. I wasn't the exception that proved the rule. I was just another naive fool who'd rushed into marriage prematurely – and hurt a good woman who deserved better. There was nothing to do now but bow out gracefully, and with tears streaming down my face I picked up the phone and called one of my HBJ co-workers to ask if I could rent the spare bedroom in his apartment on the Upper West Side. The following morning – a cold, grey Saturday at the start of America's Bicentennial year – Marie helped me stow my belongings in a rental van. We hugged goodbye in tearful silence. There were no words that could have made our parting any easier. And so, with a feeble toot of the horn and a farewell wave, I set off for Manhattan to see what I could salvage from the wreckage.

Remarkably, the problems that plagued my personal life hadn't yet affected my performance at work. Hungover or not, I showed up at my desk every morning and gave HBJ my best effort. But shortly after my split with Marie I left HBJ to take a job as acquisitions editor for the textbook division of D. Van Nostrand Company in their offices near Madison Square Garden. The new position was a rung higher on the corporate ladder and the bump in salary it brought me would pay a lot of bar tabs, so I thought it was a change for the better. Instead, it proved to be my undoing.

Acquisitions editors spend a lot of their time meeting with professors who claim to have the next big idea for a bestselling textbook. In that regard, the job comes with built-in excuses for absenting yourself from the office. If I said I was going to spend the afternoon on the Columbia University campus, or pop over to Brooklyn to interview someone at Pratt Institute, my superiors had no objection. In fact, they took it as a sign of diligence. They had no clue that most of my so-called scouting trips were just a convenient cover for my increasingly frequent bouts of midday drinking – at least not at first. But six months into my tenure, as it became obvious that my time away from the office wasn't producing any signed contracts, I could sense my bosses growing skeptical about my ability to get the job done.

I knew I was headed for a reckoning. I had stepped up my drinking to reckless levels after Marie sent me packing. But in the end it wasn't my failure to sign new authors that sealed my fate. Instead, it was my failure to meet a pressing editorial deadline for one of the textbook projects I'd inherited from my predecessor – a freshman-level primer on textile design. For months, I'd been bluffing about my progress editing the manuscript, when in fact I'd hardly made a dent in the first chapter. The deadline for transmitting the text to the printer for galley production was rapidly approaching, and the textbook's author was calling me nearly every day from her office at Ithaca College to ask why I hadn't sent her an edited manuscript. When she finally threatened to take the matter up with the managing editor, the only way I could stall her was by promising to fly up to Ithaca that weekend with the edited manuscript so we could work through all the changes together.

There was little chance I could edit the entire four-hundred-page manuscript in the two days I had left before our meeting, but I was desperate enough to try. That evening I went down to the Village to connect with the dealer Bobbi B had always bought her speed from, hoping a supply of bootleg Black Beauties would boost my productivity. However, even wired on amphetamines I couldn't outrun the ticking clock, and when I flew upstate on Saturday morning I had less than a quarter of the manuscript ready for inspection. I arrived in Ithaca strung out from a two-day speed jag and half-drunk from the three Bloody Marys I'd downed on the plane – in no shape to make a good first impression, even after I'd popped a few breath mints and ducked into the restroom to splash my face with water. Still, there was no turning back now, so I hailed a cab and grimly set off for the professor's apartment.

Despite her hectoring tone in our recent phone conversations, the professor greeted me warmly when I turned up at her door. She was a big-boned blonde in her late thirties, with a pageboy haircut and the open, guileless smile of a Midwestern farm girl.

'Nice to finally meet you, Peter. Come on in,' she said, and ushered me to the dining-room table, which she'd cleared off to use as our workspace.

While I dug the manuscript out of my briefcase, she poured coffee, then we settled down to go through my suggested changes. By the time we took a break for lunch, we had nearly run through all the pages I'd had a chance to edit and my stomach was so tied up in knots I could barely choke down the ham and cheese sandwich she fixed me.

The moment I'd been dreading was upon me at last, and with no hope of avoiding it any longer I pushed my plate aside, cleared my throat and confessed the true state of affairs. The poor woman was stunned.

'You haven't even *touched* the last three hundred pages?' she gasped. 'We'll never make the printer's deadline now! How could you let this happen?'

I owed her the truth, and she got it. The whole sorry tale of my break-up with Marie and ensuing slide into alcoholic irresponsibility. I had tears in my eyes by the time I finished, and her eyes were brimming too, but her sympathy for my personal problems didn't deter her from telling me she'd be calling my boss on Monday to insist that he reassign her book to an editor she could trust. It was the only sensible thing to do, and I didn't try to dissuade her. But I begged her not to act until I'd had a chance to break the news to my boss first. I was grateful when she grudgingly agreed to delay her call until ten o'clock on Monday morning.

Back in Manhattan, I typed my letter of resignation as soon as I'd unpacked, then spent the remainder of the weekend at the White Horse Tavern, getting falling-down drunk like Dylan Thomas. *Fuck it!* I told myself. *Why go gently?* If you drink hard enough, you reach a point where you quit worrying about your screw-ups and just accept the fact that whatever happens next will be something you richly deserve. 'Martyred to drink', as the Irish would have it. I'd jumped on that cross like I was born to it. And perhaps I was. Shake my family tree and you'd have Irish martyrs dropping all around you – as I often reminded myself whenever I was tired of shouldering all the blame. At heart, I always knew that was a cop-out. But when you're stumbling off a barstool, you'll grab any crutch that's handy – shillelaghs not excluded.

First thing Monday morning, looking every bit as miserable as I felt, I walked into the managing editor's office, repeated my tale of woe and tendered my immediate resignation. Mr Pak's reaction to the news wasn't the angry dressing-down I'd been expecting. Instead, with enviable equanimity, he nodded his head in regret and said sadly, 'You should have come to me sooner.' Mr Pak seemed even sorrier for my loss of face than I was. Which shamed me worse than any tirade could have – as if my self-esteem weren't dragging in the dirt already. Mr Pak hadn't cursed me out, but I cursed myself plenty back out in the street, and that morning I swore I was going to make some changes. Then I popped into the first Blarney Stone I passed and raised a glass to the future.

To make ends meet after the debacle at Van Nostrand, I began soliciting freelance copy-editing and proofreading jobs from my contacts in the business, and for a while it looked like I might have a third act. I should have known better. If I'd had the self-discipline you need to be a successful freelancer, I wouldn't have been freelancing in the first place. Inevitably I began missing deadlines and getting blackballed from future assignments, and within eighteen months the ruin of my publishing career was complete. Not surprisingly, those same months marked the steady growth of my newly acquired taste for cocaine. From then on, I had the idiot wind at my back, sweeping me toward a future that would bring no end of fresh regrets.

Enough! I vowed, as the bus emerged from the tunnel and fought for traction on the Weehawken hill. The damage was done. Brooding over it was pointless. It was time to start looking ahead. Fortunately, my harried existence as a coke addict hadn't completely sapped my capacity for optimism, and as the bus pushed south through New Jersey I soothed my mind with the consoling fiction that the uncertain road ahead would provide me with the Kerouacian adventures I'd been longing to experience ever since I first read *On the Road* as a high-school sophomore. *Who knows?* I thought. *There might even be a book in it.*

In my daydreams of hitting the road like Jack Kerouac, I'd always pictured myself as the Sal Paradise character, Kerouac's fictional stand-in. Now here I was, hitting the road in the guise of Sal's drug-addled sidekick, Dean Moriarty. This was a worrying role-reversal. One I'd have to overcome – and soon – to avoid the fate of Dean's real-life model, Neal Cassady, who died aged forty-one with a bellyful of booze and pills, the hapless victim of his own excesses. I didn't want an end like that. I doubt poor Neal wanted it either. But we'll never know. He died alone by the side of a railroad track on a freezing night in Mexico, a holy fool who kept his own counsel to the end.

Of course, in the back of my mind I realised that my pretensions of following in Kerouac's footsteps were a self-aggrandising fantasy that allowed me to distance myself emotionally from the dismal situation in which I now found myself, but when you're down and out you'll clutch at the flimsiest of straws to convince yourself you're not totally worthless. If clinging to my Kerouac fantasies was the only way to keep my spirits up out on the road, so be it. At least I'd be in good company.

My hands and face were a sticky mess by the time I finished the jelly sandwiches, so I grabbed my pack and squeezed into the toilet cubicle to wash up and shave. When my blurry image in the sheet metal mirror looked marginally less disreputable, I finished cleaning up my act by removing all the drug paraphernalia from my pack and burying it deep beneath a pile of wadded paper towels at the bottom of the waste bin. Now, if a highway cop nabbed me for hitchhiking and started nosing around in my pack, the worst I'd be facing were vagrancy charges. *Foresight*, I grinned. When was the last time I'd exercised any of that?

The bus was barely doing thirty on the snow-clogged New Jersey Turnpike. Which was fine with me. The longer it took to reach Richmond, the longer I'd have to sleep. We were just passing Rahway when I bundled my coat for a pillow and turned in for the night. *The next time I open my eyes*, I told myself, *all the snow will be behind me.*

The trip through the Garden State must have triggered it – Kate, bless her soul, was a Jersey girl from Bergen. A chestnut-haired, Scots-Irish beauty with a hint of Cherokee in her cheekbones and a smile that could gladden my heart from a block away. I met her one night in the Lion's Head, about a year after my break-up with Marie. By then, I was back to dating and in no hurry to abandon the life of a bed-hopping bachelor in post-pill Manhattan – but from the moment Kate and her raucous girl-friend Flossie came laughing into the bar that night, tipsy and on the prowl, my bachelor days were numbered.

Eight months later, we were standing before a justice of the peace in the Sinatra-haunted town of Hoboken, repeating vows both of us had broken before. This time, though, we'd get it right. We were sure of it. Our failed first marriages had made us wiser, and the bitter lessons we'd learned could only make our second bite of the apple that much sweeter. And for the next few years, it *was* sweet. While Kate finished up her coursework for a BA in English at the New School – a goal she'd been deferring since her first marriage broke up – I buckled down at the typewriter and began publishing articles in *High Times* and the *SoHo News*, as well as a chapbook of short stories issued by Cooper Union Press. We bought a Dodge van that I fitted out for camping and cele-brated our second anniversary with a road trip to San Francisco, laughing our way from state to state, with Van Morrison's just-released *Wavelength* album blasting from the cassette player on constant replay. At the top of our lungs, we sang along with Van the Man, our voices sometimes out of key, but our hearts in perfect harmony – and as the miles rolled by it seemed nothing could spoil our happiness. But all the while the spoiler was lurking in the wings, and when the idiot wind finally retook the stage during our fourth year together I began backsliding into the same routines that had doomed my marriage to Marie.

Kate was an occasional coke user herself, so she'd never pressed me to kick my habit. I wish she had. Then at least I wouldn't have had a running start when things started going downhill. Still, it was no one's fault but my own when I reverted to form and began hanging out till the wee hours with my coke-head buddies in Tribeca. Come sunrise, I'd slink home to Hoboken on the PATH train with a mouthful of alibis so lame they insulted Kate's intelligence. Which only infuriated her more. From the start, she'd made it clear she wouldn't tolerate deceit. She'd lived a lie while she was cheating on her first husband, and afterwards she'd promised herself she'd never live that way again.

On the eve of our fifth anniversary, Kate kept that promise and told me to pack my stuff and move out. She called it a 'trial separation', which left me with a scrap of hope to cling to when I headed across the river to an unfinished loft on Washington Street, around the corner from the Ear Inn. The air mattress we'd put to such happy use on our cross-country trip was now my only piece of furniture, and in the weeks ahead I salted it nightly with my tears as I lay in the dark wondering why the fuck I couldn't quit making the same damned mistakes. The answer, of course, was as plain as the runny nose on my face, but until I was ready to accept it nothing would change.

Though I had no doubt which of us was on trial, in the end our separation was a trial for both of us, because, despite all the heartache and acrimony, we hadn't stopped loving each other. Every few months, Kate would invite me back to Hoboken for the weekend, and the old spark would flare like it always had. But she was looking for more than that. What Kate really wanted was some sign that I'd started to turn my life around – the proverbial light at the end of the tunnel. Sadly, I kept disappointing her. The only turn my life had taken since we'd separated was a turn for the worse. By that point, I couldn't hold a job more than a week before getting pink-slipped for poor attendance, and slinging coke in bar-room toilets had become my primary source of income. Yet Kate remained hopeful. How, I don't know, but she did. The heart is an organ of manifold mystery.

Two years into our separation, the ongoing gentrification of Hoboken priced Kate out of her apartment on Garden Street and she moved to a more affordable place in Jersey City. It meant a longer ride on the PATH train for me, but I never passed up the chance to spend a weekend with her whenever she extended one of her periodic invitations – the last of which came on a wintry weekend at the start of 1984. When I arrived at her apartment at suppertime that Saturday evening, Kate was bustling around the kitchen in a flour-dusted apron, fixing us a meal of buttermilk fried chicken and homemade biscuits, one of her Southern specialities (she'd been raised in Alabama, before her father moved the family north to New Jersey during her freshman year in high school). After dinner, stuffed and happy, we retired to the bedroom and spent the rest of the night just lolling around, smoking weed and watching *Saturday Night Live* until we both drifted off to sleep.

The following morning we slept in late, until Kate finally decided it was time for coffee. She got up to make a pot. I threw on some clothes and hit the streets to fetch breakfast rolls and a Sunday *Times*. I got back fifteen minutes later, sprinkled with snow from the flurries that were falling, and we sat down to a leisurely breakfast before taking the paper back to bed with us. For the next few hours we lay side-by-side, sharing the paper, until about two in the afternoon, when Kate announced she was feeling sleepy. 'I think I'll take a little nap,' she said. 'But wake me up in an hour or so. I don't want to sleep all day.' I promised her I would – but it was a promise I never got to keep.

Within minutes, Kate was snoring softly. I continued working my way through the Book Review. And she kept dozing peacefully for the next half-hour. So peacefully, in fact, she was lulling me to sleep, too. But suddenly the bed began to shake, and when I turned toward Kate I was horrified to see her thrashing convulsively beneath the covers. Immediately, I grabbed her shoulder and shook it, calling out her name, hoping it was only a bad dream. But she didn't wake up. Her body just kept bucking with spasms.

In a panic I grabbed the phone and called for an ambulance. The paramedics arrived only four minutes later. By that time, I had scooped Kate up from the bed and laid her on the floor to perform CPR. The paramedics brushed me aside and took over, to no visible effect. Kate's face had already gone blue, and as I stood uselessly to the side watching them ready her for transport, I knew in my heart I had lost her forever. A brain aneurysm. That's what the post-mortem report said. For thirty-three years, Kate had graced the world with her smile. Now she was gone too soon – and our trial separation was over at last.

Two years had passed since that awful afternoon in Jersey City, but Kate's death continued to haunt my dreams, and it was just such a nightmare that had me in its grip as the bus arrived in Richmond. I was fast asleep when the bus rolled into the station, and suddenly I could feel my body begin to shake. In my dream, I panicked. I was sure I'd just been stricken by an aneurysm and was convulsing like Kate. It felt so terrifyingly real, it *had* to be true. Until I opened my eyes and saw the Greyhound driver, who was shaking my shoulder and barking some message I was slow to process.

'What time is it?' I mumbled.

'Time to wake up,' the driver replied. 'This is Richmond, son. End of the line for you.'

End of the line for you – I didn't like the sound of that. But he'd gotten me to Richmond in one piece, so I said thanks as I stuffed my feet into my sneakers and got off the bus to face whatever Richmond had in store for me. Which turned out to be shock, followed instantly by disappointment when I saw that the parking lot was hemmed in on three sides by mountains of snow! Mountains being raised ever higher by a pair of Bobcat front-loaders that were zipping around in the predawn darkness, scraping and scooping for all they were worth. It was a thoroughly dispiriting tableau. So much for my dreams of putting the snow behind me.

Inside, there weren't more than a dozen people in the waiting area. A dozy mix of vagrants and stranded travellers, bathed in fluorescent light. Those who were awake looked weary and stunned into submission, like nighthawks in an Edward Hopper diner. That same look deadened my own face when I spotted the clock above the shuttered ticket window. Three-thirty. A bleak hour, for sure. I decided I'd better sit tight at the station till daylight. Outside, the temperature was well below freezing, and the roads were empty – it was no night for hitchhiking.

With hours left to kill, I headed to the men's room and treated myself to a sink bath, taking advantage of the facilities while I had the chance. Come dawn, I'd be entering hostile territory: the realm of 'Restrooms for Customers Only'. I had five bucks left to my name, so I wouldn't be a customer much longer. For the moment, though, I was still a man of means and willing to spring for a 'Bottomless Cup of Coffee' in the concourse coffee shop. My body was jonesing for coke. A jolt of caffeine would take the edge off.

The coffee shop advertised '24-Hour Service', yet there wasn't a server in sight. No customers either. Which seemed weird, until I approached the counter and peeked into the kitchen through the pick-up window. A skinny young waitress was standing at the stove, with her back to me, stirring the contents of a stock pot with a long wooden spoon. I coughed to attract her attention, and she flinched like a startled squirrel before she spun around to peer through the window.

'No rush,' I called out, sorry I'd spooked her.

She mustered a sheepish grin and called back, 'Just a sec, I'll be right with you.' She stepped out to the counter and hurried over with a menu. 'Sorry, I had to stir the chilli,' she said. 'We're shorthanded tonight. Our graveyard cook never showed. He couldn't make it in through the storm. The swing shift cook stayed over to cover, but he's passed out on some flour sacks in the pantry. Claims he's resting up for the break-fast rush, but that's a crock. With the roads the way they are, there won't be any rush this morning. We've been dead all night. Till you walked in, anyway. What can I get you, mister?'

Listening to her babble, I thought she must be starved for company. But my junkie's radar kicked in when I noticed how she kept pulling a crumpled paper napkin from her apron pocket to dab her runny nose. I realised she was tweaking her ass off. Her dilated pupils – and her spiky crown of black hair – gave her the waifish look of a Japanese Manga heroine. A heroine whose name badge said 'Charlene'.

'You from New York?' she asked, pouring the cup of coffee I'd ordered.

'Used to be,' I said. 'How'd you guess?'

'Soon as you said *caw-fee* I kind of figured. You an actor or something?'

'An actor?' I smiled. 'What makes you think that?'

'Your hat, I guess. Don't see too many hats like yours in this town, except on TV. I could see you playing a G-man in *The Untouchables*. My dad used to love that show.'

'I'm a writer, actually,' I replied. A tenuous claim, I'll admit. I hadn't published anything new in years. Still, I figured 'writer' was a better profession to claim than 'homeless junkie'.

'A writer? That's cool,' Charlene said. 'What do you write?'

'This and that,' I said. 'Short stories, magazine pieces for *High Times*.'

'*High Times*, wow!' she gushed. 'You must be famous.'

'Only in my own mind,' I laughed.

'What are you working on now?'

'Just gathering material,' I said, feeding her the same line I'd been feeding myself for longer than I cared to admit. 'But I'm thinking of doing a book about hitchhiking across the country, like Jack Kerouac's *On the Road*. Ever read it?'

'Nope, never heard of it,' Charlene admitted. 'What's it about?'

'Two road buddies back in the beatnik days, bumming around the country, high on speed.'

'Speed, huh?' Charlene said, her interest piqued. 'What, like crystal meth?'

'Pretty much,' I said. 'But they were popping Benzedrine pills. They called them bennies back then.'

'So, what, are you a speed freak too?' A fair question, after I'd just told her I wrote for *High Times*.

'Not any more,' I smiled. Twenty-four hours clean and I was already bragging. But it felt good to say it anyway – until my guilty conscience reminded me that I had nothing to brag about. Not after leaving poor Susan and Danny in the lurch.

'Wish I could say the same,' Charlene said, swiping at her nose with the paper napkin. 'I've been trying to kick, but it's not that easy.' And with that the empty coffee shop became a confessional, and in a tone of voice as bitter as the coffee she kept pouring into my 'bottomless' cup, Charlene launched into the story of her troubles.

She said she hated being hooked on meth. But she hated her parents even more for using her addiction against her. They'd denounced her as an unfit mother and convinced a judge to grant them custody of her infant daughter, Kylie. The child's father had no say in the matter – he'd hanged himself in a jail cell while awaiting trial after his arrest for meth-dealing. Charlene blamed his death on her parents, too. The sheriff in the rural Blue Ridge town where she'd grown up was her mother's cousin. Family strings had been pulled, and Daryl, the college-drop-out boyfriend, had been taken out of circulation. But not before he'd gotten Charlene pregnant in her senior year of high school.

'Daryl's blood is on their hands, the fuckers,' Charlene swore. 'He never even got to see his baby girl. His sister and I buried him a month before Kylie was born. Then my parents stole Kylie away and packed me off to Bible College in the Ozarks. A tight-assed Baptist school where they told me God would "rehabilitate" me, if I'd just open my wicked heart and let Him in. What a fucking joke. I wouldn't have lasted a night in that place if I hadn't scored a bag on the bus ride to Missouri. I stuck it out for a week, till my stash ran out, and then I bolted.'

'Then what?' I prompted, earning another refill.

'I hitchhiked to a bus station and spent my book allowance on a ticket to Richmond.'

'Why Richmond?'

'Daryl's sister lives here. I didn't know who else to turn to. I've been crashing in the guest room at her co-op ever since. Taking night classes in commercial art, and then dragging my ass over here to waitress on the graveyard shift. I get so tired some days, crystal's all that keeps me going.'

'So, you had no problem making a connection here? Does Daryl's sister use?'

'God, no,' Charlene said. 'Amanda's a nurse. She'd never mess with crank. I score from my art school friends. Half those people are hard-core tweakers. Keeps their creative juices flowing, they say. Maybe so, I tell them, but you're all still junkies, same as me.'

'How are the art classes going?' I asked, steering for calmer waters.

The sheepish smile returned. 'Not bad, really. Twenty more credits and I'll earn my certificate. Then I'm going to find a job in advertising. One that'll pay me enough to hire a lawyer and start fighting to get Kylie back.'

'Think you can win?' I asked.

'If I can pass a piss test, yeah,' she said, but with little conviction. 'Getting clean's the hard part. I kick for a few days, and then I relapse. Every time. Amanda offered to get me into an inpatient rehab programme, but I keep putting it off. I want to finish my degree first. At least that's what I tell Amanda. Truth is, I'm scared I couldn't handle it.'

'When the time comes, trust me, you'll find a way,' I said, and even as the words left my mouth I thought, *Bullshit!* Who was I to be acting wise and avuncular? So far, all I'd done to change my life was to put a few hundred miles between me and Bobby Bats. I could fool Charlene, but I couldn't fool myself. I was just as afraid of what the future might hold as she was. The hard work was all still ahead of me and, like Charlene, I wasn't sure I could handle it.

Tears welled up in her Manga eyes, and Charlene dabbed them back with her napkin. 'For Kylie's sake, I hope you're right.'

I hoped I was right, too. For both of us.

Two Richmond cops walked in just then and settled on stools at the far end of the counter. Charlene gave her eyes another quick dab and hurried off to take their order while I headed for the restroom. Call it junkie paranoia, but when I finished in the bathroom I was reluctant to return to the coffee shop. Not with the cops still at the counter. So far, my gangster fedora hadn't attracted any unwanted attention, but why press my luck?

I was biding my time in the waiting room when it suddenly dawned on me that I hadn't given my wallet a thorough going-through before I left New York. When I was on a tear, I'd sometimes squirrel away cash in the wallet's hidden crevices and then forget all about it. I didn't have much hope I'd get lucky, but I had nothing better to do, so I pulled out my wallet and rifled every cranny. Alas, my search produced no squirrelled twenties, but it wasn't a wasted effort, because I discovered a business card I'd forgotten I was carrying – one that might prove more valuable than any cash I might have found.

My friend Tanner had slipped it to me at Christmas time, when he'd stopped into the Raccoon for a few drinks before heading to the airport to catch a flight back to his new home in San Francisco. In his heyday in the early eighties, Tanner had made a pile in the drug trade, using his cover as an importer of Himalayan handicrafts to smuggle high-grade Nepalese and Afghani hash into the States. Unlike most drug dealers, Tanner was smart enough to quit while he was ahead, and when he closed shop in 1985 he took his profits to San Francisco and began investing in real estate. Now he was buying old commercial warehouses and converting them to luxury condos. When I'd seen him in December, I'd half-jokingly suggested I might head west and hit him up for a job one of these days. It was only drunken blather on my part, but Tanner took me seriously.

'Can you hang drywall?' he asked.

'As a matter of fact . . .' I said, and told him about the weeks I'd spent hanging drywall for a buddy of mine who'd been contracted to build a new sound room on the top floor of Jimi Hendrix's old Greenwich Village recording studio, Electric Lady. Every wall on that job had to be triple-hung – three layers of wallboard sandwiched together to ensure the room would be soundproof. So, yes, I had hung a bit of drywall.

'Well, then, I've got work for you if you turn up,' Tanner said, and handed me his business card.

It was two-forty-five in the morning in San Francisco, but Tanner had always been a night owl, so I wasn't worried my call would rouse him out of bed. Tanner picked up on the second ring and sounded wide awake as he dealt with the operator, who asked him, in her Southern drawl, whether he'd accept a collect call from someone she dubiously called 'a Pete the Hat'.

'Sure,' Tanner said. 'Put him on.'

'Tanner! Good to hear your voice, brother. Hope I didn't wake you.'

'Hell, no,' he said. 'What's shaking, Hat?'

'Funny thing,' I said. 'I just found your number in a bus station.'

'Yeah, yeah, I know. "For a good time, call Tanner." What can I say? My fans are legion. What bus station? Where are you?'

'Richmond fucking Virginia. Enjoying the balmy Southern weather. But I'm heading west, and I was wondering if you could still use a drywall man.'

'Absolutely,' Tanner said.

My spirits surged. Thank God, he was someone I'd never screwed over. I only wished I could say the same about Bobby Bats. I was already far enough from Manhattan to quit worrying about him tracking me down, but that didn't make me feel any better about how I'd left him hanging. No way to shuck it – that was baggage I'd have to carry with me, however far I travelled.

'How soon are you coming?' he asked.

'I'm thumbing it, so figure three days, maybe four?'

'Okay, great,' Tanner said. 'Call me when you get to town and I'll give you directions to the job site. You can crash in one of the empty condo spaces till we find you a place of your own.'

'Awesome,' I said. And it was. A job *and* a place to crash! What more could I hope for? 'Thanks, Tanner, I owe you big time.'

'No sweat,' Tanner said, like he hadn't just saved my bacon. 'Anyway, after the solid you did me in Nepal, I'd say I'm the one who owes *you*. Try not to catch any rides with axe-murderers. I'll see you when you get here.'

I was glad Tanner had brought up the favour I'd done for him. It made me feel less guilty about sponging off his generosity. A few years back, when Tanner was still in the import business, I'd arranged for him to meet a Dartmouth classmate of mine who was related to the Nepalese Royal Family. On his next 'buying' trip to the Himalayas, Tanner stopped off in Kathmandu to look my classmate up, and while they were making small talk Tanner happened to mention that he was an avid fly fisherman. That was all my classmate needed to hear.

Next thing Tanner knew, they were bumping along in a Land-Rover, heading up into the hills outside the city to try their luck in a private lake reserved for members of the Royal Family. On his very first cast, Tanner hooked the biggest trout of his life — a sixteen-pound German brown that put up a tremendous fight. And that was just the start of the fun. Tanner caught so many big fish that day, when he got back to the States he couldn't stop raving about the 'monster browns of Nepal'.

I was grinning ear-to-ear when I returned to the coffee shop. And there were no cops in sight to spoil my mood. 'There you are,' Charlene said. 'I thought I'd lost you.'

'I had to make a phone call.'

'Way you're grinning, must have been a good call.'

'An *excellent* call,' I beamed. 'I just landed a job in San Francisco.'

'Well, good on you,' Charlene smiled. 'Congratulations.'

'Thanks. I guess you'd better cash me out. It's time I got moving.'

'Sorry for bending your ear all night. I don't usually yammer on to strangers like that, but you're a good listener. Good luck out on the road. Collect a lot of stories for your book.'

'Good luck to you, too,' I said. 'I hope you get Kylie back real soon. I'll keep a good thought.'

The sun was up when I stepped out of the bus station, and in the clear light of day I suddenly realised I had no idea how to get back to I-95. Then I remembered I'd seen a local street map posted in the station. I hurried back inside to consult it, and that's when I noticed that the campus of Virginia Commonwealth University wasn't far away. VCU! Why hadn't I thought of that sooner? Kate had attended VCU for her first three years of college, and we'd visited Richmond several times while we were married to see friends she'd made as an under-graduate. One of her friends, a painter named Brett Stuart, had taken a teaching position in the Arts Department after gradu-ation. If I could find him, I was sure he'd float me a small loan to tide me over till I made it to the coast. His number was listed in the phone book. Big relief. I jotted it down and set off on the three-mile hike to the VCU campus through the cheek-stinging cold. At that early hour, the streets were nearly empty, and by the time I reached the Quad I'll bet I passed more statues of Confederate war heroes than I did pedestrians. And every one of those snow-mantled statues was only slightly stiffer than me as I stood stamping my frozen feet outside the locked doors of the Arts building, reading a handwritten sign that said all classes had been cancelled till further notice. *At least Brett's got the day off*, I thought. *Might as well give him a call right now.*

Seeking a warm place with a pay phone, I followed the scent of frying bacon to a funky bar and grill on the edge of campus, where the ceiling instantly caught my eye. *Of all the gin joints in all the towns in the world*, I smiled, as I stood there gawking at the amazing collection of hats that were tacked to the acoustic tiles. Everything from coonskin caps to Laurel and Hardy bowlers, and quite a few felt fedoras just like the one on my head. Naturally, I took it as a good omen. Magical thinking, yet how could I resist? I'd been a hat fan ever since Aunt Mary, my spinster godmother, gave me a French beret for my tenth birthday. But when I dialled Brett's number, all I got was a recorded message that his number was no longer in service. *What now?* I frowned. Then I remembered someone I could call to check on Brett's whereabouts – his mentor, Morris Yarowsky.

Morris was an accomplished abstract painter and long-time member of the faculty in VCU's Art Department – and a fellow Dartmouth alum. If anyone could help me locate Brett, it would be Morris. But when I called him, Morris said Brett had resigned his teaching job the previous semester and moved to Ohio.

Well, that's that, I thought, and was on the verge of hanging up when I decided to throw a Hail Mary. 'Listen, Morris, here's the thing,' I said, and explained my situation. Half an hour later, I was on the road again, hiking to the interstate with two crisp twenties in my wallet.

Morris had shown up at the restaurant within ten minutes of my call. After offering his condolences for Kate's death, he surprised me by handing over double what I'd asked to borrow. His generosity humbled me, but in my heart I knew it was really Kate I had to thank – and it saddened me to think I'd traded on her memory to raise a bit of pocket change. One more debt I could never repay her. I could only pray she'd understand.

I'd had my fill of trudging through snow by the time I got back to the interstate, and I couldn't wait to put Richmond behind me, but the town refused to cut me loose. For the next three hours, as I lost all feeling in my toes, car after car passed me by, and I began to suspect my *Untouchables* hat – as Charlene had called it – was jinxing me. By then I was desperate enough to believe a change of hat might change my luck, so I reluctantly backtracked into town to search for a clothing store. I found my way to a run-down neighbourhood that was obviously well outside the watershed of Ronald Reagan's 'trickle-down economics'. Whole blocks of storefronts stood empty, their windows soaped-over and hung with 'For Rent' signs. It didn't look promising.

I pressed on anyway, and eventually spotted a little shop that sold discontinued stock from a local woollen mill. The outlet occupied a storefront that had once been a dry cleaner's, and the faded letters on the facade above the doorway spelled out the slogan: Alterations While U Wait.

Here we go, I grinned. A timely alteration was exactly what I needed – preferably, a knit watch cap like the one my dad wore in the old snapshots from his navy days. But when I stepped inside and asked the counter clerk if she had any watch caps in stock she scratched her cornrows in confusion and admitted she didn't know what I meant. I described what I was looking for and finally her eyes lit up. 'Oh, I get you,' she said. 'You want a *toe-boggin*.'

Now it was my turn to scratch my head. 'A *toe-boggin*?'

'Yeah, you know, a hat you wear when you go sledding.'

I almost laughed when I finally figured out she was saying *toboggan*, but I kept my composure as she pointed me toward a fifty-gallon cardboard barrel full of mittens and scarves and knitted hats, all dyed in such hideous colours it was easy to see why they'd ended up in a remainder bin. I picked out the least garish cap I could find and, for the princely sum of one dollar, I walked out of the shop the proud new owner of a bile-yellow *toe-boggin*. Okay, proud is probably stretching it – the thing was uglier than poisoned-rat puke. That didn't stop me from ditching my fedora in the nearest trash can, just as I'd done with my drug paraphernalia on the bus. Little by little, I was shedding my New York persona. And I was glad to see it go.

It was mid-afternoon when I made it back to the ramp. I prayed I'd catch a ride before nightfall, otherwise I'd be forced to blow Morris's money on another Greyhound ticket. I would hate to do it, but, now that I had a job waiting in San Francisco, wasting another night in Richmond was out of the question. I needed my new toboggan hat to work its magic fast. And damned if it didn't come through for me just minutes later, when I heard the jingling crunch of snow-chained tyres easing to a stop behind me. Before I'd even had a chance to stick out my thumb. An old blue Suburban. Seemingly conjured out of thin air!

'Where you headed, son?' the driver asked. He was a big-bellied, middle-aged man with close-cropped hair and a jowly face bracketed by bushy mutton-chop sideburns.

'San Francisco,' I said, and the driver's brows wedged up like frost heaves.

'That's quite a trip,' he said.

'It should be, if I can ever get moving. I've been stuck in Richmond since three-thirty this morning.'

'Well, I can take you as far as Petersburg. It's only sixty miles down the road, but it'll get you out of Richmond. Up to you. Would you rather hop out and wait for a longer ride?'

That wasn't happening. No way in hell. He could have been one of Tanner's axe murderers, with a goddamn bloody axe sitting right there on the seat beside him, and I would still have taken my chances. 'No, Petersburg sounds good to me,' I said. To someone named Pete, how could it not?

'Name's Randall,' the driver said. 'What's yours? Might's well not be strangers.'

'Pete,' I said.

'Pete, huh? Well, then, maybe Petersburg will bring you luck,' he smiled.

'Let's hope so,' I said. 'Is Petersburg where you live, Randall?'

'Yessir, all my life. I teach wood shop at the high school, but they cancelled classes today, so I came up to Richmond to visit my sister. Poor gal just had a hip replaced. I was on my way home from the hospital when I spotted you.'

'Thank God you did,' I said. 'I was starting to think I'd get frostbite before anyone stopped.'

'I do quite a bit of travelling myself,' Randall said. 'In the summertime, mind you, when there's no school to tie me down. Never been to the West Coast, but I've been all over the South, doing Civil War reenactments. Been my hobby nearly fifteen years now, and it never gets old.'

It was hard to picture a man of Randall's girth surviving on field rations of hardtack and hominy, much less charging across a battlefield, but it turned out Randall never had to charge very far because he was a specialist. As most reenactors are, he informed me. Randall's specialty was getting gut-shot and dying on the field of glory – preferably as early in the skirmish as possible. Whereupon he'd do his part for the Rebel cause in a supine position for the remainder of the battle.

As we rode south, Randall entertained me with accounts of his many deaths. At Manassas ('First *and* Second'). At Shiloh. At Chickamauga. At Vicksburg. The man was a veteran campaigner. Some of the battlegrounds he mentioned I'd never even heard of, but Randall knew the terrain of every one by heart, even those yet to be graced by his bloodied corpse. Like a mountain climber who sets his sights on summiting the highest peaks on every continent, Randall was a man driven by a vision – a vision as ambitious as it was macabre. He dreamed of dying gut-shot on every sacred battlefield in the Confederate States. Odd as his quest seemed to me, I had to admire his persistence. Maybe that's why the road sent him my way. To drop a hint. I'd certainly need plenty of persistence to make this fresh start work.

'My sister thinks I'm crazy,' he grinned, as we turned off the highway at Petersburg. 'She says I'll never pull it off. But you know what I tell her?'

'What?'

'If I can't die at all of them, I can always die trying.'

'I'll be rooting for you, Randall,' I laughed. 'I wish you many deaths before you die.'

Smiling, I took up my post beneath a streetlight on the southbound on-ramp – where I stood clouded in my own frozen breath for the next two hours, feeling as abandoned as a dumpster baby, while the temperature sank into the teens and not a single car passed my way. *Lucky namesake town, my ass!* Persistence was getting me nowhere, except closer to hypothermia. I was shivering so hard my muscles were cramping, and I knew I had to make a move. Ten minutes more and I'd have dropped from the cold like poor Neal Cassady.

The only shelter in sight was a quarter-mile up the road, where a blue neon 'Vacancy' sign was pulsing outside a small motel court. I started shuffling toward it, and as my numb feet crunched through the crusty snow I gave thanks for Morris's generosity.

The money he'd lent me was about to save my life.

CHAPTER 3

Room 29 *at* the Pine Tree Inn was no luxury suite, but it had its own electric heater and that was luxury enough for me. 'What a day!' I groaned, as I cranked the thermostat and slumped into a chair in front of the blower. Who knew it would take sixteen hours to make sixty miles of headway? At this rate, I'd be lucky to reach San Francisco by Paddy's Day. I doubted it would come to that, but who could say?

If today's ordeal had taught me anything, it was that the road is full of surprises. I mean, what were the odds I'd spend my first hours in Richmond lending a sympathetic ear to a fellow junkie? Yet there Charlene was, waiting to kick off my trip with a sad story so much like mine it was hard not to think I'd been fated to hear it. And what about Tanner? Who'd have predicted I'd find his business card just when I needed it most? Or that Morris, a man I barely knew and hadn't seen in years, would reappear in my life and humble me with his generosity? Maybe fatigue was messing with my head, but it all seemed somehow preordained. As though the road were saying, if you want to change your life, here's how you start – with empathy, with loyalty, with charity.

Real or imagined, it was good advice, and I knew if I didn't take it to heart now there was little hope I'd get another chance. I couldn't let that happen. I was sick of treating others shabbily and blaming booze and drugs for my bad behaviour. More than anything else, what I wanted from my fresh start was to wake up every morning without regretting what I'd done the day before. Was that too much to ask? I hoped to God it wasn't, because otherwise I'd be just as miserable in San Francisco as I'd been in New York – and that was a future too depressing to contemplate.

As soon as I thawed out, the heat in the room began to make me drowsy, and I could barely keep my eyes open as I polished off the last of my bread and jelly. But, tired as I was, I couldn't turn in for the night just yet. Not until I'd scrubbed my clothes in the bathtub and hung them to dry by the heater. With all my spare clothes now on their way to becoming abandoned property in a Penn Station pay locker, the clothes on my back were all I had, and I didn't want to hit the road in the morning smelling like a goat. What kind of fresh start would that be?

Now, this is more like it, I thought, grinning to myself as I slipped between the sheets butt naked – blissfully unaware that I'd have one more surprise to deal with before the night was through.

When I woke to use the bathroom several hours later, I immediately sensed that something wasn't right. Except for a glimmer of moonlight peeking through a gap in the curtains, the room was as dark as a root cellar. What had happened to the lights I had left on? And why was the room so fucking cold?

I was already shivering beneath the covers, but as soon as the words *power outage* registered in my groggy brain I felt a fresh chill hit me. Jumping out of bed, I pulled back the curtains to confirm my fears. Sure enough, the motel's sign was dark – and so was every streetlight in the neighbourhood. *This can't be happening!* I cursed. I felt like that jinxed character in the Li'l Abner comics, Joe Btfsplk, the poor bastard with a perpetual cloud of misfortune hanging over his head. I had no idea when the power might be restored. All I knew was that I was freezing my bare ass off in a room with a now-useless electric heater. But what could I do about it, except hunker down and try to survive? So I threw on my overcoat, tugged my knit cap down over my face and burrowed in beneath the covers, hoping I'd stop shivering long enough to catch a few more hours of sleep.

Despite the cold, I eventually did nod off and I didn't open my eyes again until after dawn, when I was abruptly awakened by a flat Midwestern voice reciting the latest prices for soybean futures. *What the fuck?* Then I remembered I'd left the TV on when I'd gone to bed, and I realised the power must be back. Hallelujah! I'd finally caught a break! But my good mood quickly soured when I hopped out of bed to check my laundry and discovered that all my clothes were still sopping wet. There went my plans for an early getaway. *What now?*

Collect lots of stories for your book. Weren't those Charlene's parting words? Well, my first day on the run had certainly provided its quota, and while I waited for my clothes to dry I filled several sheets of motel stationery with notes for my road journal. It had been ages since I'd felt the excitement of throwing myself into a new project and in the end I was glad the power outage had delayed my departure. I'd been dreaming of making my mark as a writer ever since I'd got my first taste of literary acclaim in Miss Heit's third-grade class, for a rhyming story I'd written that mimicked the Dr Seuss classic *And to Think That I Saw It on Mulberry Street*. Unbeknownst to me, Miss Heit had entered my story in a state-wide creative writing contest, and it placed in the top five in the grade-school category. Several months later, to my surprise, the principal called me to the stage during the year-end school assembly and presented me with a gilt-edged certificate of merit from the New York State Teachers' Association. From then on, whenever anyone asked what I wanted to be when I grew up, my answer never varied. (Oddly enough, ten years later I wound up mimicking Dr Seuss again, by enrolling at Dartmouth College – Theodore Geisel's alma mater. Wheels within wheels . . .)

It was nearly eleven when I finally hit the highway, hoping to catch a quick ride and make up for lost time, but all I caught for the next hour were suspicious glances from a steady parade of looky-loos who sized me up in passing and then left me standing in the cold. 'Kerouac forgot to mention this part,' I muttered to myself. Then again, maybe he hadn't gotten stranded quite as often. America had been less paranoid when Kerouac was on the road in the late forties. Thanks to psychos like Charlie Manson and Ted Bundy, people thought twice about picking up a stranger anymore. Understandable caution, I supposed, but it was sad to see how much harder hitchhiking had gotten, even since the sixties, when I used to thumb home from college to visit Marie nearly every month. Hell, in my hippie days I looked scruffier than I did now, and I could still thumb from Hanover to Brooklyn in less time than it would have taken me on a Greyhound bus. Apparently, those days were long gone.

Hitchhiking to the West Coast was going to take more patience than pluck, I could see that now. Still, what could I do about it, except put on my best 'I'm-not-a-serial-killer' face and wait for my luck to change?

Then I suddenly realised there *was* something I could do. So far I'd been hitchhiking legally by sticking to the entrance ramp, rather than risk getting hassled by highway cops for thumbing on the interstate. But playing it safe was getting me nowhere, so I jogged down the ramp to the highway shoulder. Within minutes a shiny Renault sedan pulled over to pick me up. *Should have made this move an hour ago, dummy,* I chided myself as I ran to the car. But I was all smiles when I climbed in and shook hands with the deeply tanned crewcut kid behind the wheel.

'Thanks for stopping,' I said. 'I was starting to think I was invisible.'

The kid asked where I was headed, and when I told him San Francisco he said, 'Well, I can take you far as Selma, if that'll help.'

'Selma, Alabama?' I asked him. It was the only Selma I could think of.

He laughed, 'That's what my shipmates always think, too. But I'm from Selma, North Car'lina. About a hundred forty miles down the road. Keep you out of the cold for a few hours, anyway.'

A hundred and forty miles! String together a few more rides like that and I'd be in Florida in no time.

'You in the navy?' I asked. He was dressed in street clothes, but he looked a little too shipshape for a merchant seaman.

'Yes, sir. Goin' on three years now.'

'Where you stationed? Norfolk?' I asked, thinking of my

father. My dad had spent most of his two-year enlistment in the navy giving crewcuts in the base barber shop at Norfolk, Virginia, before leaving the service in 1948 to play his part in the postwar baby boom.

He and my mother were no shirkers: I was born a year later, and by 1955 I had three younger brothers – all of us doomed to go through our school years shorn like sheep by my dad's heavy hand on the clippers. Which might have been okay if we'd been home-schooled at an Aryan Brotherhood compound, but in the public schools on Long Island it just made us bait for skinhead jokes. Is it any wonder I'd developed a thing for hats?

'No fuck?' he scoffed. 'What a hole. No, I've been stationed at Andros Island for the last year and a half. Sweetest base in the Atlantic.'

'Andros Island? Must be a sunny place. That's quite a tan you've got going on.'

'Not many places sunnier than the Bahamas,' he grinned.

'That explains it,' I said. 'I didn't know we had a base in the Bahamas. What do you do down there?'

'I'm a sonar tech at AUTEC,' he said. 'That's navy shorthand for Atlantic Undersea Testing and Evaluation Center. AUTEC's where submarine captains get certified on underwater weapons systems. We do beta-testing of next-gen sonar equipment there, too. Some of the gear we're testing now would blow your mind. A fish takes a shit two miles below the surface, we can not only detect it, we can tell you what the sucker had for breakfast.'

I laughed. 'You're pulling my leg, right?'

'Okay, I'm exaggerating a little,' he admitted. 'But the day is coming, believe me.'

'I'll take your word for it,' I said. And I did. Though it was hard to imagine a scenario in which our national security would hinge on accurate analysis of fish shit. But I must admit, by the time we reached Selma I knew more about sonar systems than I'd ever learned watching late-night reruns of *Run Silent, Run Deep*.

'Enjoy the rest of your leave,' I said, hopping out at the exit.

'Two more days and I'm out of here,' he grinned. 'I can't wait to get back where it's warm.'

That makes two of us, I thought, hoping my next ride would finally take me south of the snow line.

If I could *catch* a next ride, that is. Three frustrating hours later I was still stuck in the Selma doldrums, with darkness coming on and the temperature dropping fast. Now I was getting nervous. I had barely enough money to buy supper when I hiked across the service road to warm up at a KFC, so there'd be no bailing out to a motel room tonight. If I didn't catch a ride out soon, I was going to be in trouble.

Fortunately, as soon as I got back to the highway, a furniture delivery truck pulled over for me. 'You're a lifesaver, man,' I said, climbing into the cab beside a sandy-haired young guy with a mullet haircut and a Van Halen T-shirt under his quilted thermal vest. Nineteen, maybe twenty, I guessed.

'Don't know about that,' he said, 'but I can take you as far as Fayetteville.'

'How far is that?' I asked, hoping for a big number.

'Fifty miles south,' he said. 'Where you headed?'

'San Francisco, eventually,' I told him. 'But right now I'd settle for anywhere that isn't freezing. If I can make Florida by daybreak, I'll be a happy camper.'

'Well, there's a truck stop in Fayetteville where I can drop you. Lot of long-haul drivers fuel up there. Might catch you a good ride south if you ask around in the parking lot.'

'I like the sound of that,' I said, as he gunned the big Mercedes diesel and got rolling. 'You hauling furniture to Fayetteville?'

'Nope, I'm dead-heading back to the warehouse. Dropped my last load up in Virginia a couple hours ago. In fucking Petersburg,' he sneered.

'Funny,' I said. 'I just spent the night there. Not your favourite town, I take it?'

'I got into a fender-bender there last month. Some dried-up old bitch ran a red light and clipped my back end. She gets a hot flash, and I'm the one facing jail time. Just my luck.'

'Jail time for what?' I asked. 'If she blew the red light, how's that your fault?'

'Problem is, I'm on probation in North Carolina. Leaving the state without permission is a violation. I never bothered telling my PO I was making deliveries out of state. Soon as the Petersburg cops ran my licence, I knew I was screwed.'

'That sucks,' I said.

'Big time,' he agreed. 'I've got a probation hearing scheduled tomorrow morning. If they decide to violate me, I'll be locked up by lunchtime.'

'Jesus,' I said. 'Guess you won't be getting much sleep tonight.'

'Tonight? Shit, I haven't had a good night's sleep in weeks. Whatever happens tomorrow, I'll be glad to just get it over with.'

I felt sorry for the kid. I knew what he was facing. Eight months after Kate's death I got popped for selling blow to a confidential informant – a seductively dressed coke whore the narco squad sent into the Raccoon one night to fish for drugs with a pocketful of marked 'buy' money. I was the sucker who took the bait. It cost me six months on Rikers Island, during which I learned all I'd ever needed to know about the hardships of life behind bars, so the kid's story was falling on sympathetic ears and I couldn't help rooting for him. Despite all his worries, he'd been goodhearted enough to give a stranger a lift and that counted for something in my book. As we approached Fayetteville, he even went the extra yard by putting out a call on his CB radio, asking any truckers in the area to holler back if they could take on a southbound passenger. Nothing panned out, but I was grateful he'd even tried.

The truck stop where the Van Halen kid dropped me turned out to be a bust. There were a few big rigs parked out back, but the counterman in the diner told me their drivers had already bedded down for the night — which left me in a black mood as I started the five-mile hike back to the interstate. But my morale improved considerably when I noticed that none of the ramshackle houses along the access road had snow in their yards. *South of the snow line at last!* Two miles down the road, the houses gave way to pine forest bordered by chain-link fencing, with signs every hundred yards that said: Fort Bragg – Government Property – No Trespassing. It was spooky country to be hiking through in the dark, so I was relieved when I finally heard a car approaching. But when I spun around and stuck my thumb out, I immediately wished I hadn't.

The dark-coloured Crown Vic had *unmarked cop car* written all over it. Seeing it roll up on me real slow, like a cop would, I started to sweat and braced myself for my first encounter with a Southern sheriff. Fortunately, instead of a cop, it was just an elderly Baptist preacher who'd decided to play the Good Samaritan on his way home from prayer service. Big exhale.

'Where you from, son?' he asked me when I climbed in.

'New York,' I said.

'New York, eh? Well, you're in the so-called Bible Belt now,' he smiled – a bit impishly for a preacher, it seemed to me.

'Yeah, but I thought it was supposed to be warmer down here in God's country.'

'You'll feel warmer when I drop you off in Lumberton. It's only thirty-five miles south, but for some reason it's always three or four degrees warmer than Fayetteville. Don't ask me why.'

I didn't really care why, so long as he was right. When he pulled onto the interstate, I glanced across the highway and noticed a pack of unmarked cop cars staked out on the shoulder of the northbound lanes.

'Quite the speed trap the cops have got set up over there,' I remarked.

'That's not a speed trap,' the preacher said. 'It's a drag line for dope smugglers. They catch plenty coming through here on their way up from Florida. Too bad they can't catch them all. It's a shame to see so many young people these days throwing their lives away just to get high.'

It was hard to argue with that. Not when I was sitting there beside him as Exhibit A.

'Mind you, I understand the temptation,' the preacher added. 'I tried smoking jimson weed when I was young. We called it "loco weed" back then. Makes you see crazy things. I guess some folks think that's fun, but it scared me silly. You ever fool around with drugs, son?'

'Some, when I was younger, but not any more,' I hedged. If I had confessed to all the drugs I'd experimented with in college, he'd have been appalled. The psychedelic sixties – was there ever a more enticing trap for a gullible teenager with boundless curiosity and minimal impulse control? Back then, I fancied myself the second coming of Allen Ginsberg, and I was all too willing to test my idol's theory that 'the poet becomes a seer through a long, immense, and reasoned derangement of all the senses'. LSD, mescaline, magic mushrooms, hashish – I tried them all, and never once suffered a 'bad trip'. But rather than unlocking Aldous Huxley's much-ballyhooed 'doors of perception', my experiments with psychedelics only proved I had a brain that enjoyed being chemically deranged. Which should have been a revelation that 'scared me silly' – like the preacher and his jimson weed – but instead it only made me smugly confident there was no drug I couldn't handle.

Getting high in my free time hadn't kept me from holding down three part-time jobs on campus and a place on the Dean's List, so what harm had drugs done me? None, as far as I could tell – at least, not at the time. But the false notion that I was somehow bulletproof would come back to bite me later, when I finally got around to trying cocaine and belatedly discovered that there were, indeed, drugs I couldn't handle. What happened after that would have given the preacher enough material for a dozen cautionary sermons. Luckily for him, I'd sworn off confessing to men of the cloth years ago – I'd had all I could take of that during my cassock-wearing days as a Redemptorist seminarian. I hadn't set foot in a confessional since dropping out of St Mary's Seminary midway through high school. So far, that was still the only habit I'd ever successfully kicked, and I felt no urge to start backsliding now.

On the subject of backsliding, it suddenly occurred to me how little I'd been affected by going cold turkey for the past few days. I didn't know if that was because I'd been half-frozen much of the time, or because the moment-to-moment distractions out on the road kept me too preoccupied to dwell on my withdrawal symptoms, but whatever the reasons I was grateful – I was getting off easier than any junkie had a right to expect.

The truck stop where the preacher dropped me in Lumberton was a lot busier than the one in Fayetteville, and I felt better about my chances as I hustled over to the fuel island to try my luck with the driver of a flatbed semi stacked high with irrigation pipe. But he shook his head and turned me down. 'Sorry, friend, can't help you. Wish I could, but this is a company truck. They don't let us take on riders. Most fleet trucks have the same rules. It's an insurance deal, they say. I was you, I'd just head back to the highway.'

For want of a better idea, I took the trucker's advice and hiked across the street to the highway entrance, and it wasn't long before two cars rounded a bend in the road and approached in a sweep of headlights. Squinting against the glare, I stuck my thumb out and watched the first car flash by. No luck. But the trailing car suddenly slowed down and pulled to a stop in front me. *Score!* I grinned – until my eyes adjusted to the glare and I realised I was grinning at a patrol car. This time for real. *Shit, shit, shit!*

'APPROACH THE VEHICLE SLOWLY AND KEEP YOUR HANDS WHERE I CAN SEE THEM,' the cop's bull-horn blared.

Oh boy, I thought. *Here we go.*

I shuffled forward with my palms upturned, like I was feeling for rain.

'Okay, stop right there,' the cop said when I came up to his window. 'Now, let me see some ID.' I reached for my wallet, and that's when things went from bad to worse – my back pocket was empty!

While the cop looked on skeptically, I frantically patted

myself down and failed to find my wallet anywhere. 'I can't believe this!' I groaned. 'I had my wallet when I bought supper up in Selma a few hours ago, officer, I swear!'

Paranoid scenarios began racing through my brain. What if he hauls me in on vagrancy charges? And runs my prints? And finds out he's got a convicted drug dealer on his hands? Not just a drug dealer, a *New York* drug dealer. What kind of Southern hospitality could I expect in the Lumberton lock-up once my rap sheet popped up on the screen? I had a bad feeling I was about to find out.

Happily, it didn't come to that. To my immense relief, the cop just jotted down my name and the Social Security number I recited to him, and then gave me an ultimatum. 'If you're not gone when I swing by here again at midnight, you'll be spending the rest of the night in the Lumberton jail. Do we understand each other?'

I assured him I understood perfectly, and as he pulled away I stood there shaky-kneed, thanking my stars I'd gotten off so easily. What I still couldn't fathom, though, was how my wallet had gone missing. Had the damned thing slipped out of my pocket in the furniture truck or the preacher's car? That didn't seem likely. Then it dawned on me. I must have dropped it in the bathroom stall when I hit the can after supper at the Selma KFC!

It was the only plausible explanation – and a karmically appropriate one, at that. Six hundred miles down the road, my payback for ripping off Kentucky Fried Danny had finally been delivered. All I could do was shake my head in grudging admiration. There was no denying it served me right. Still, I dreaded all the hassles I'd be facing in the days ahead, trying to make it clear across the country with no ID.

Meanwhile, I had a more pressing problem. The cop had put me on the clock and I had barely an hour left to make myself scarce before he turned up again. As if that weren't pressure enough, the wind suddenly started blowing hard from the southeast, bringing great banks of rainclouds scudding in off the Atlantic. Within minutes I was pelted by rain that was coming down so hard it left me no choice but to run for shelter.

Loitering under the canopy outside the truck stop's restaurant, I was glumly watching the downpour when the manager stepped outside and approached me. I braced myself for the bum's rush, but the young guy just held his paper hat down against the wind and invited me inside for a free cup of coffee. Southern hospitality or simple Christian charity, it made no difference to me. It was a kindness I hadn't expected, and it touched me more than I would have imagined.

'Been watching you out by the road for a while now. Thought maybe you could use a warm-up,' he said, ushering me inside to the counter.

'Yeah, it got a lot chillier once the rain hit,' I agreed.

The restaurant clock showed eleven-fifteen, and as I sat at the counter answering the manager's questions about my travels, the cop's midnight deadline continued to haunt me. How the hell was I going to get out of Lumberton in time?

'Well, I better get back to taking inventory. Sit here as long as you like. If you want more coffee, Ellie will take care of you,' the manager said, nodding at the waitress who'd just stepped behind the counter. As soon as the manager was gone, Ellie approached me with another invitation – Lumberton was turning out to be full of surprises.

'The young fella in the corner booth wants me to ask if you'd like to join him,' she said with a smile.

I swivelled on my stool to see who she meant and saw a preppy-looking kid with shaggy blond hair giving me a beckoning wave.

'Don't worry, I know him,' Ellie said, when I turned back to the counter looking skeptical. 'His name's Sean. He might talk your ear off, but he's harmless.'

'What the hell, why not?' I said. The rain was still bucketing down. I wasn't going anywhere soon. *Who knows?* I thought. *Maybe I can talk the kid into dropping me somewhere outside the Lumberton city limits.*

And so began my bizarre encounter with Sean – heir to a Lumberton real estate empire, fresh from a month-long stay in a mental ward and currently off his meds. Of course, I knew none of that when I first sat down across from him. True, he had the haggard, over-caffeinated look of a college freshman cramming for finals, but otherwise there seemed nothing peculiar about him. That is, until he opened his mouth.

'Thanks for joining me,' he said, offering his hand. 'I was watching you at the counter and I thought, "There's an interesting-looking feller. I'll bet he's got some stories to tell." My name's Sean, what's yours?'

'Pete,' I told him.

'I like your toe-boggin, Pete,' he said. 'Good hat for hitch-hiking, I'll bet.'

'Keeps my ears warm, yeah,' I replied.

'You a Christian, Pete?' he asked, apropos of what I couldn't tell, but I hoped I wasn't in for a Bible session with a true believer.

'Lapsed Catholic, but yeah, I guess you could call me a Christian.'

'I knew it! I'm a ninja warrior for Christ. I can always spot another Christian. One of my ninja skills,' he beamed, his eyes afire with a light I was beginning to suspect had nothing to do with religious fervour or caffeine consumption.

'Impressive,' I nodded. How else could I respond to such an off-the-wall claim? I couldn't imagine what he'd come out with next, but he surprised me again by veering back into more predictable territory.

'Where you hitching to, Pete?' he asked, lighting up a smoke with a heavy gold Zippo before pushing the pack across the table to me.

'Out to the West Coast, San Francisco,' I said, helping myself to one of his Parliaments.

'Whoa, that's a long way to go. How long you think it'll take you?'

I laughed. 'At the rate I'm going, might take forever. I left New York two days ago and I'm still only halfway to Florida.'

'Wouldn't it be easier to just take a Greyhound out there? I'll bet the bus could get you to San Francisco in a couple of days.'

'Probably could,' I agreed, 'if I had the money for a ticket. But I'm flat broke. Lost my wallet back in Selma. Didn't even know it was gone till I got here to Lumberton.'

'Damn, you're havin' some hard luck, aren't you? How 'bout I just buy you a bus ticket to San Francisco, one Christian to another?'

Yes, Lumberton was full of surprises.

'No, that's a generous offer, Sean, and I appreciate it, really, but a ticket to San Francisco's bound to cost close to a hundred bucks. I can't let you lay out that much money.'

'Don't worry about the money. My daddy left me plenty when he passed. Just hang out with me tonight and I'll take some cash out of my trust fund when the bank opens in the mornin'. The Greyhound station's right down the block from my bank. Get you a ticket and you'll be in San Francisco by the weekend. What do you say?'

It was a tempting proposition, I had to admit. But I was still incredulous. 'You'd do that for a total stranger? You sure?' I asked.

'You're not a stranger,' he smiled. 'You're a brother in Christ. So it's settled. I'm putting you on a bus first thing in the morning. Hey, while I think of it, there's something I've got to show you. Let me run out to my car a second.'

And with that he sprang up from the booth and rushed out the door. Ellie noticed his exit and came over with a fresh pot of coffee and a conspiratorial smile. 'You doing okay over here?' she asked. 'Sean makin' your ears bleed yet?'

'He's a talker all right,' I replied. 'Not sure we're both tuned to the same wavelength, but I'm doing my best to keep up.'

She laughed. 'I'm not sure anybody's tuned to that boy's wavelength. He took it hard when his daddy passed a few years back. Been a bit off ever since. But I'm sure he appreciates your company.'

Moments later, Sean came rushing back into the restaurant with one hand tucked out of sight inside the front of his black satin windbreaker. It gave him a wackily Napoleonic air as he crossed the room and slumped back into the booth.

'You believe in the Virgin Mary, right? Check this out,' he beamed, pulling his hand out of his jacket to reveal a sad little dirt-smudged plaster figurine that looked more like an unearthed dog bone than a statue of the Blessed Mother. 'I was digging worms by the river last year and there she was, tangled in a bunch of roots, just waiting for me to come along and set her free. Looks really ancient, right? Might be Roman or something. What do you think?' he asked, passing me his prize.

To me, it just looked like one of those cheap religious knick-knacks sold in the Botanica shops up in Spanish Harlem, but I kept that impression to myself and gave the piece the reverent examination Sean seemed to be urging. Sure enough, when I upended the statue and rubbed away a bit of dirt from the marking stamped on the base, the words *Hecho en Mexico* came to light. This, too, I kept to myself. He seemed so pleased with his find I couldn't bring myself to burst his bubble.

'I'm no expert, but it looks pretty old to me, Sean,' I said. *Old as the Industrial Revolution, anyway.* Humouring him would become my full-time job in the hours ahead, but I couldn't complain. I figured I had to earn my bus ticket somehow. Around midnight, Sean declared he was tired of sitting around, so he hustled me out to his jet-black Camaro and we set off on a nightlong prowl through the sleepy streets of Lumberton. Sean kept up a running riff on the passing scenery, and the low rumble of his muscle-car engine provided the bass line.

When we passed a stately courthouse on Main Street, Sean said it had just been used as a backdrop in a new movie called *Blue Velvet* that David Lynch had shot there a few months earlier. 'Seemed like a pretty weird movie. I think that Lynch guy's a little strange in the head,' he said.

Talk about the pot calling the kettle black, I thought to myself, but the kid was probably right. I'd seen Lynch's first film *Eraserhead* back in the early eighties and the mutant baby scenes had left me wondering what madhouse Lynch had gone AWOL from when he shot them.

Nearly everywhere we went in Lumberton, Sean pointed out some building his father's company owned. It was an impressive portfolio, and it certainly made me feel less guilty about accepting his charity. Eventually, he headed out into the surrounding countryside and we killed a few hours crunching along gravel roads through tobacco fields and pine forest, watching the night critters scatter. Whenever an opossum or raccoon ran through the headlight beams, Sean would chuckle and say, 'Everything runs from the Ghostrider.'

'What's this Ghostrider business about?' I finally asked, against my better judgement.

'That's what the Lumbee Indians around here call me. They're descended from the Croatans, the original Lost Tribe of Roanoke. I'm always out driving these roads after dark, and when they see the black Camaro with the white face in the window they say, "The Ghostrider's on the prowl again."'

The moon was getting low in the sky, and Sean's nonstop monologue was lulling me to sleep, but I woke right up when I heard him suddenly exclaim, 'Oh, crap, we're almost out of gas.' I hadn't seen a gas pump since we'd left the truck stop and I feared we were in for a long hike back from the boonies. But Sean said not to worry, he knew just where to go. A few miles down the road he pulled into the driveway of a run-down tarpaper shack, scattering the yard chickens as he pulled up beside a flat-tyred old Dodge pick-up. 'My Uncle Arlen's place,' he announced. 'He'll let me grub some gas.'

Uncle Arlen appeared at the door moments later and stepped out in his bathrobe to see what was up. Sean asked if he could get some gas, and the uncle told him to go grab a five-gallon can from the shed. As soon as Sean stepped away, Uncle Arlen approached me and asked how he was doing. He said Sean's mother was worried about him because he'd been off his meds for days and hadn't been sleeping. 'He's manic-depressive, the doctors say. He just got home last week after a month's stay in hospital to get his meds regulated, and now he won't take them. Do me a favour, son. See if you can get him to go see his mother. She really needs to talk to him. If I say anything, he'll just bark at me for meddling.'

By this point in the long night none of Uncle Arlen's revelations came as a surprise. I had pretty much reached the same diagnosis hours ago. Though I doubted it would do any good, I promised the uncle I'd put a word in Sean's ear.

We were two miles down the road when I got up the nerve to broach the subject, but Sean beat me to the punch.

'I'm hungry,' he said. 'Let's go see what Mama's got for breakfast.' We pulled up to the kerb in front of a split-level ranch house on a quiet street at the edge of town. 'I don't know if Mama will be up yet,' Sean said. 'I better take you round back and let you wait in my treehouse.'

The treehouse was a sprawling affair perched in the branches of a massive oak tree, and you could see his father's professional hand in its sturdy construction.

'Inspect the troops for a few minutes. I'll be right back,' Sean said, and left me in the treehouse to browse the shelves that held his collection of vintage lead toy soldiers.

After Sean's manic babbling, the soldiers' mute company was a tonic. But my peaceful interlude didn't last long. Within minutes, I heard Sean and his mama going at it inside the house, shouting loud enough to wake the neighbourhood. They kept it up a good five minutes before subsiding into silence. Wondering what the hell was going on, I waited in the treehouse another twenty minutes before Sean finally reappeared, now freshly washed and resplendent in a brass-buttoned blue blazer and a commodore's yachting cap. *What, are we off to a regatta now?* I wondered. Curiouser and curiouser.

'Sorry it took so long,' he apologised. 'Mama gets ornery sometimes. She wouldn't let me out of the house till I took my medicine and got washed up. Good thing I left you out here,' he grinned. 'I grabbed some raisins and salt peanuts you can eat in the car. Come on, I've got to make a stop before we go get your bus ticket.'

Sean drove us to the downtown dojo where he took martial arts lessons, and I realised why he'd claimed to be a 'ninja warrior for Christ'. He insisted I come inside to meet his master, a man named Vic Moore. The master's apartment was on the second floor, and while Sean went upstairs to fetch him I browsed the framed clippings on the dojo walls and learned that Vic Moore was the first black man to win a US national karate championship. His celebrity photo gallery included shots of Moore with Bruce Lee, Chuck Norris and Huey Newton. *This guy's the real deal*, I thought to myself, wondering why a man of his talents had set up shop in a backwater like Lumberton.

Sean came downstairs smiling and said Master Vic would join us in a moment. While we waited, he snatched a samurai sword from the weapons wall and started swinging the damned thing around with such manic energy it made me nervous. Obviously, his meds hadn't kicked in yet. I wondered what Master Vic would make of the scene when he came down to find a madman in yachting gear wildly slashing the dojo's air with a samurai sword. But as soon the big man appeared on the stairs – dressed in a conservative suit and tie – Sean calmed down immediately and meekly hung the sword back on the wall without a word from the master.

'Sensei,' he bowed, 'I'd like to introduce my friend Pete. He's on his way to San Francisco, but I wanted him to meet you before he leaves town.' And there I was, shaking hands with the only American ever quick enough to block one of Bruce Lee's speed punches. Chalk up another surprise for Lumberton.

The Greyhound ticket office was a few blocks from the dojo, and when we walked over there to check the schedule there was a westbound bus slated to leave Lumberton at two in the afternoon. Staying awake till then was going to be a struggle, but I figured I'd have plenty of opportunity to catch up on my sleep once I got on the bus. All we had to do now was hit Sean's bank and I'd be good to go. However, Lumberton had one last surprise in store for me, and the hangdog look on Sean's face when he emerged from the bank told me it wasn't going to be a good one.

It turned out Sean's mother had frozen his trust account while he'd been in the mental ward and the bank wouldn't let him touch his money until his psychiatrist declared him competent to handle his own finances again. If I'd been a tenth-degree black belt like Master Vic, I think I'd have the pulverised the first cinderblock I could find. What a letdown! Sean, of course, proposed a harebrained scheme to remedy the situation – he wanted me to go with him to his doctor's office, pose as a psychiatrist from New York and declare that I'd given Sean a clean bill of mental health!

'You're a smart guy, you could pull it off. Come on, let's try it,' Sean pressed.

'That's just plain crazy.' There, I'd said it. I felt bad for the kid, but after ten hours of biting my tongue, a dose of candour seemed in order. 'You're a generous guy, and I appreciate you trying to help me out, but I think it's time you just take me to the interstate and let me be on my way.'

Even though Sean hadn't come through with a bus ticket, my night with the Ghostrider must have brought me some luck.

As soon as he dropped me off I caught the first of three short rides that took me across the border into South Carolina. Then I hit the jackpot at a highway rest stop near Dillon, where a guy named Carl – a ponytailed hippie from Vermont – offered me a lift all the way to Florida.

Carl's rust-eaten Volvo looked ready for the scrap yard, but somehow the old beater held together as he balled the jack like Dean Moriarty and we rattled south through Georgia. By sundown, we were rolling up on the outskirts of Jacksonville, and when Carl turned west onto Interstate 10, I felt like I was finally making real progress. Twenty-five hundred miles straight down the road and I'd be watching the sun set over the Pacific.

It was dark when Carl dropped me off in the Panhandle town of Baldwin, but the night air was mild and for the first time in three days being on the road didn't feel like a trial by ice. By now, thanks to the Ghostrider, I'd gone thirty-six hours without sleep, and all I wanted was a good night's rest. Ducking into a palm grove beside the highway, I bedded down on the soft layer of dried fronds beneath the trees. *What more could you ask for?* I thought. At last things were looking up – though I'm sure my dad would have begged to differ.

When I was ten, I built a teepee in our backyard in East Northport, and all these years later it still rankled me that my father had refused to let me camp out overnight in it, no matter how much I pleaded. The way he saw it, if it was his duty to keep a roof over my head, then it was my duty to sleep under it. At the time, I thought he was just being a spoilsport. But as I lay roughing it beneath the stars that night in Baldwin I realised his final words on the matter had been prophetic. *If you want to sleep outside*, he'd told me, *go be a bum.*

CHAPTER 4

As I lay hunkered down in the dark of the palm grove, I heard rustling all around me. Mice or voles, I assumed, foraging in the dried fronds. I told myself they were no threat, but they creeped me out anyway – and called to mind another memory of my father that I hadn't thought about in years. I was three or four at the time, I'd guess, and we were living in a railroad apartment above a mice-ridden grocery store on Fifth Avenue in Bay Ridge. No doubt the mice were the source of the scary night-time noises that sometimes made me scream for my parents to come chase away the monsters under my bed, but after a few weeks of being wakened by my cries for help, my father decided it was time to break me of the habit. The way he did it taught me once and for all that there are scarier things to worry about in this world than monsters under your bed.

On that memorable night, I'd already cried monster twice, and my father had warned me that if I woke him and my mother once more I'd be sorry. But as soon as the lights were out again my fear got the better of me, and when I started howling for help the third time my father stormed into my bedroom, snatched me out of bed and hauled me into the kitchen.

'What are we doing, Daddy?' I asked, as he sat me down in the middle of the kitchen table.

'We're making a sandwich,' he said, and set a carving board and a loaf of bread beside me. Then he opened a drawer and pulled out the long carving knife and meat fork that he used for slicing the bloody roast beef my mom always cooked for Sunday dinner.

'What kind of sandwich?' I asked, already forgetting the monster as I watched my father hone the knife with a butcher's steel. Stroke, stroke, stroke.

'A *Peter* sandwich,' he replied. Which is not a phrase you want to hear from a six-foot-four Norwegian giant standing over you with a carving knife, trust me.

Still, I wasn't really convinced my father meant it. He had to be playing make-believe, right? But when he opened the fridge and pulled out a bottle of Heinz catsup, I thought, *He's really going to eat me!* My father's stint in the navy had left him in the habit of dousing everything he ate with catsup, which used to drive my mother crazy. She took it as an insult to her cooking. My father paid her no mind. He was set in his ways, and we never sat down to a meal without a bottle of Heinz on the table, so when he set the catsup bottle beside me I started wailing.

'Please, Daddy, no!' I pleaded. 'I'll be good, I promise!'

'Too late now,' he said. 'I warned you you'd be sorry. You should have listened.'

That's when I totally lost it. I howled so loud I woke my

poor mother. She was heavily pregnant with her third child, but she came shuffling to my rescue in seconds. 'What are you doing with that knife, Gus?' she barked at my father, as she scooped me off the table and hugged me to her breast.

My father grinned, a little sheepish now. He could see from my mother's glare that he'd gone too far. 'Teaching the kid a lesson he won't forget,' he said.

Well, he was right about that. From then on, I never cried out in the night – whenever I was tempted, I'd just bite my tongue and picture that carving knife.

Despite what this bizarre example of extreme parenting might suggest, my father wasn't really a heartless ogre. He was simply a clueless first-time father who'd been raised as an only child and had nothing but his own narrow experience to fall back on. My dad's father – a stern Norwegian Lutheran immigrant – had never coddled his son and my father saw no reason to treat his kids any differently. Luckily for me and my brothers, our mother, Teresa, was raised in a large and unruly Irish family, so she was more willing to let her boys be boys. Still, my mom had no qualms about threatening us with a few whacks from my father's belt if we disobeyed her while he was away at work, and many a night we sat down to supper with fresh welts on our bottoms, wishing we hadn't given her lip.

I'm sure my father didn't relish playing the enforcer after a hard day at his factory job, but he was a man who believed discipline mattered and he never gave us a last-minute reprieve. Nor did we expect one. Not from a man who spent his work-days precision-grinding components for navy helicopters. What leeway could you expect from someone who routinely worked to tolerances of a hundredth of an inch? Even when my dad mowed our lawn on weekends he'd cut it front-to-back, side-to-side, and then on the diagonal, leaving not a blade of grass untrimmed. That's just who my dad was. Meticulous by nature.

Too bad my father never found a way to pass on his self-discipline and single-mindedness to his sons. His 'spare the rod, spoil the child' tactics kept us obedient while we were children – and certainly toughened us up – but in the long run they produced no lasting benefit. As adults, my brothers and I would all struggle with impulse control and substance-abuse issues. Might we have avoided those problems if the structure in our early lives hadn't been built around fear of corporal punishment – a structure doomed to collapse as soon as we were free of my parents' control? That was a question I'd never be able to answer, but that didn't stop me from wondering about it in those self-reflective moments just before sleep, when the unquiet ghosts of childhood come back to haunt us, like a bogeyman under the bed.

Dawn was already breaking over the Panhandle when I awoke with the creepy sensation that I was being overrun by crawling bugs. I thought it was just a bad dream, until I opened my eyes and realised it was all too real. Tiny red ants were swarming all over me – skittering up my nose, inside my ears, under my clothes, everywhere. 'Holy fuck!' I shouted, jumping to my feet and breaking into a twitchy St Vitus dance as I ripped off every stitch of clothing and flailed away at the ants still left on my skin.

Anyone spying me from a passing car must have thought they'd glimpsed a madman. A naked madman frantically turning his clothes inside-out and beating them against a palm tree. It took me ten minutes to rid myself of the little buggers, and I was shivering with cold by the time I got dressed and ran out of the palm grove, feeling like Charlton Heston in *The Naked Jungle* fleeing the marabunta. Tanner was going to laugh his ass off when he heard this one.

I was still twitching and pinching at phantom ants beneath my clothes as I hiked up the road to a nearby truck stop, where I spent my last fifty cents on coffee and then wasted a half-hour in the parking lot trying to drum up a ride west. No soap, as Sal Paradise would say. Every driver gave me the same excuse I'd gotten from the trucker back in Lumberton — picking up hitchhikers was against company rules — so it was back to the highway for me. But first I scrounged up a length of baling twine from the dumpster behind the restaurant and tied up my heavy overcoat like a bedroll so I could hang it from my back-pack. The morning was getting balmier by the minute — after four days on the road, I was in shirtsleeves country at last.

When I hiked back to the interstate ramp, I saw I had compe-tition. An old codger with a scraggly white beard hanging to his belly was already stationed at the bottom of the ramp, with a cardboard sign in his hands and a battered thrift shop suitcase at his feet. *It's Billy Gibbons' grandpa!* I chuckled to myself. The old boy looked like he'd just been kicked off the ZZ Top tour bus.

'Fine mornin', ain't it?' he called out when I was still twenty yards up the ramp. 'C'mon down, I won't bite,' he said, and flashed me a toothless smile to prove it. I'd been hesitant to crowd his spot — my father had taught us that you never jump into another man's fishing hole — but the codger was apparently eager for company, and I was happy to oblige. I had a hunch he'd be a man with a brain worth picking. Someone who could steer me straight on where to score a free meal and a bed down the road. But before I could start pumping him for information, he surprised me by asking if I had anything to eat.

'Sorry, brother, can't help you,' I said, thinking he was asking for a hand-out. 'I'm tapped. Haven't had a thing to eat since yesterday.' Not since Carl the Vermonter had bought me lunch during a rest stop in Savannah.

'Well then, just a second,' he said, stooping to his suitcase. Next thing I knew he pulled out a fat bag of popcorn and a packet of peanuts and handed them to me. 'Here you go,' he smiled. 'Should hold you over till you get to the next Rescue Mission.'

'Wow,' I said, blown away by his unexpected kindness. 'You sure you can spare it?'

'Brotherhood of the road, son. You give when you can, and take when you can't. Name's Zeke. What's yours, young fella?'

'Pete,' I said. 'You just made my day, Zeke. I was starting to think Florida had it in for me.' I told him about my run-in with the red ants, and Zeke shook his head. 'Lucky for you they wasn't fire ants or you'd have been a goner.'

'Christ, you're right!' I said. I'd never even thought about fire ants. I'd got off a lot easier than I could have.

Zeke's cardboard sign read: MOBILE, ALA. He was on his way to visit a niece there. I asked him how far to Mobile and he said three hundred and sixty miles. Clear across the Panhandle to the Alabama border. 'With any luck, I should make it by suppertime. No Mission food for me tonight,' he grinned. 'My niece stuffs me like a prize hog whenever I turn up at her door.'

'Speaking of Mission food,' I said, and asked Zeke if he had any tips to offer on places to eat and sleep for free along my route to California. As I'd suspected, he had plenty, and from what he told me I wouldn't have to worry about starving. But my lack of ID was going to be a problem. Zeke said most shelters that offered free beds for the night required photo ID.

'Can't stay at the Sally without picture ID, I know that much,' he said.

'The Sally?' I asked, not catching the reference.

'Yeah, you know, the Salvation Army. That's what everyone calls it. They're a finicky bunch. Everything's by the book at the Sally.'

Just then, a dusty old Ford stake-bed truck pulled up beside us, and Zeke scuttled over and opened the passenger door to see if there was room for two. He shook his head to let me know there wasn't. I couldn't even hop on the back of the truck because the cargo bed was completely packed with rows of potted Norfolk Island pine trees. So I wished Zeke luck, and the truck pulled away, leaving me stranded in its pine-scented backdraught.

Zeke's packet of peanuts gave my rumbling stomach something to work on as I waited in the Florida sunshine for the next Samaritan to come along. While I munched I thought about Zeke's nickname for the Salvation Army: 'the Sally'. It reminded me of another nickname I used to hear around the house when I was growing up. From time to time, I'd hear my mom and dad talking cryptically about going to see 'Uncle Benny'. I'd never met any uncles named Benny, and when I asked who he was, my parents laughed. 'He's not really your uncle,' they said. 'Just a friend we go see once in a while.' But they never took us kids along when they'd paid him a visit, so he remained a mystery.

It wasn't until I was in sixth grade that I finally figured it out. I was out running errands with my father one Saturday morning when he pulled over to the kerb outside a branch office of the Beneficial Finance Company and left me waiting in the car while he ducked inside. Suddenly, it clicked. *Uncle Benny!* It had to be. I'd always known our household ran on a tight budget (I never tasted real butter till I went to Dartmouth; it was margarine or nothing in our house), but until that day I'd never known we needed quickie payday loans to make ends meet. It gave me a knot in my stomach when I realised we were poorer than I'd ever imagined.

I felt so sad for my father that day. How could we not have enough money? He'd been working two jobs at a time, day and night, for as long as I could remember. Did a skilled machinist really earn so little? It didn't seem fair. But I said nothing about Uncle Benny when my dad got back to the car. I was too embarrassed for him.

At least I'm chipping in, I thought. For the past few years, I'd been buying my own clothes with the money I earned delivering *Newsday* after school every day. Now that I was almost a teenager, I'd been hoping to quit my paper route – pedalling around with a bike basket full of heavy newspapers and getting chased by the neighbourhood dogs had begun to seem too childish and uncool. But after I discovered the truth about Uncle Benny I held on to my paper route right through junior high school and I didn't give it up until the week before I left for St Mary's Seminary, where the financial burden of feeding and housing me would fall upon the Redemptorist Order instead of my overworked dad.

In fact, my decision to enter the seminary was influenced as much by my desire to lighten the load on my parents as it was by my tenuous belief that God was calling me to the religious life. No matter what their circumstances, however, my parents never sought help from anyone but Uncle Benny. Like their immigrant parents, they were determined to make their own way in the world, too proud to even consider any sort of charity or public assistance. The only time I ever saw my father accept a handout was during a prolonged strike by the Machinists Union that kept him out of work for over a month. Even then, when we needed help the most, he was mortified to accept the carton of donated canned goods the union rep dropped off on our doorstep every week during the strike. Thank God he couldn't see his oldest son now, reduced to depending on the kindness of strangers.

◄━━━►

It took me all morning to make it forty miles down the road from Baldwin to Lake City, and along the way I got propositioned by a sad old queen out cruising for some strange before breakfast. He plopped a doughy hand on my knee and offered to take me on a scenic tour of the backroads, but when I rebuffed his advances he got pouty and dropped me off prematurely at a farm exit on a deserted stretch of road outside the town of Macclenny. There was nothing in sight but reedy marshland trilling with red-wing blackbird calls. Fearing I'd be stuck there for hours before some peanut farmer came by and took pity on me, I set off down the highway to find a busier exit. I'd probably hiked two miles before I spotted a highway patrol cop cruise by in the opposite direction. I saw him clocking me as he passed. *Uh oh, here we go again.* Sure enough, he slowed down and then hung a U-turn across the grassy median before pulling in front of me with the cruiser's blue lights flashing.

'It's illegal to hitchhike on an interstate highway in Florida, did you know that?' he asked.

I pleaded ignorance. I'd never travelled through Florida before. Then he asked to see ID, and of course all I had was a sob story. To my relief, he bought it, and only issued me a warning ticket. I folded up the flimsy copy and stuffed it in my trouser pocket, little suspecting how glad I'd be to have it in the days ahead.

'This warning will be logged in the system, understand?' the cop said. 'If you get stopped again in Florida, you won't get off as easy. Now get in the car and I'll drop you up the road at Glen St Mary. Remember, stay on the ramp and you'll stay out of trouble.'

Glen St Mary was another doldrum town, but when I finally got picked up a few hours later by a bandana-headed guitarist heading to Los Angeles I thought I'd caught the ride of my life. We'd gone a mile down the road when he made it clear he was looking for a rider willing to split the cost of gas on the trip west. 'I'm definitely not your man,' I told him, and before I knew it he was dumping me off at the Lake City exit.

At least there's a gas station here, I consoled myself. Zeke's peanuts and popcorn had left me parched and I was dying for a cold drink of water, so I scavenged a plastic Mountain Dew bottle from the fuel island trash can and filled my new canteen in the restroom. Back at the ramp, the sky grew suddenly dark and a rain squall blew in, forcing me to take shelter beneath the highway overpass. While I waited for the rain to clear, I amused myself by studying the graffiti scrawled on the curved concrete wall, communing with the ghosts of those who'd sheltered there before me. One message that put a smile on my face said: 'See America like Charles Kuralt didn't (couldn't) – hitchhike!' Even the road has its purists, it seemed. But there was another scrawl that gave me goosebumps, and its message was much grimmer: '4/4/76–4/4/86. Ten years on the road. God help me, I must be crazy.'

Yes, I thought, *the road has its tortured souls too.*

I decided these nuggets were worth saving, so I dug into

my backpack and pulled out the Wonder Bread bag I'd been using to store the road notes I'd started at the Pine Tree Inn. *Take good notes, and the story will tell itself,* my Uncle John used to say. Father John McGuire was my mother's older brother and the only published writer in our family. I always envied him his job at the Redemptorists' quarterly magazine, *The Alphonsian*, which took its name from the Order's founder, St Alphonsus de Liguori, a much-read author in his time. The pieces my uncle wrote for the magazine were mainly inspirational stories of faith and perseverance that he gathered from parishioners during his visits to Redemptorist churches around the country and in Puerto Rico, and his clear, unstuffy prose style always impressed me. The cadences of his natural speaking voice were so faithfully captured in his writing that reading his pieces was like sitting across from him at the dinner table, listening to him tell his story in person.

I wanted to write like Uncle John. More accurately, I wanted to *be* Uncle John. What a life that would be, I'd thought as a young boy. Travelling around the country, collecting stories to retell. So it was hardly a surprise to my family when I began to express an interest in going to St Mary's Seminary to follow in Uncle John's footsteps. My uncle was happy to help, and he pulled strings to make sure I was offered a full scholarship so that my parents wouldn't have to worry about scraping together the cost of tuition. I was halfway through eighth grade when I received the news that I'd been accepted to St Mary's, and after that the rest of the school year seemed to drag on interminably. I could hardly wait for summer so I could start packing my clothes and school supplies into the steamer trunk my parents bought me for the trip to the seminary's bucolic campus near Lake Erie, in the tiny town of Northeast, Pennsylvania.

I was fourteen when I entered St Mary's in 1963. I had never spent a night away from my family, so I went through a lot of Kleenex in my first few weeks on campus. But once I got over my homesickness, I settled nicely into the regimented routine of seminary life. Except for the long periods of mandatory silence each day, it wasn't much different to living under the thumb of my strict father. Learning Latin was easier than I'd imagined, and it was fun to discover how many English words had their roots in the language of Caesar and Catullus – words I began putting to work in the poems I was writing for Father Sharrock's freshman English class. The hard part, of course, was finding something worth saying, and my early efforts were all examples of what Ezra Pound called 'hunting for sentiments to fit your vocabulary'. What more could you expect from a callow fourteen-year-old?

Then came 22 November, and the news that President Kennedy, our first Catholic president, had been assassinated. A dark day for America, and especially devastating to the nation's Irish Catholics, like my mother, who I knew must be taking it hard. I wished I could have been home to share her grief, but I couldn't even call to comfort her – at St Mary's, students had no access to telephones. Still, I had to share her sorrow somehow, and in the days of mourning that followed I wrote a poem about the pain of being separated from those you love in a time of common grief. It was the first thing I'd ever written with any emotional commitment. Father Sharrock liked the poem so much he passed it on to Father Duffy, the faculty advisor for the annual literary review of student writing, and to my surprise that spring I became the first freshman to ever have a piece selected for the anthology. I could hardly believe it when I got the good news. After years of dreaming, I was finally going to see my words in print – just like Uncle John!

When the rainstorm at Lake City blew over, I caught a hundred-mile ride with a college kid in a souped-up red Toronado and when he dropped me off at Tallahassee late in the day I took a shot and asked if he could spare a little coffee money. I was hoping for a few quarters, but the kid shocked me by handing over a five-dollar bill. All he asked in return was that I say a prayer for him to do well on his final exams. I promised I would, and as soon as he pulled away I hot-footed it to the Golden Arches for supper.

The sun was dropping fast when I returned to the highway, anxious to get moving again before dark. Tallahassee was less than halfway across the Panhandle, and I still had nearly two hundred miles to go before I reached Pensacola. The first ride I caught didn't help much. The businessman who picked me up was only going down the road a few exits, to the western outskirts of Tallahassee. I took the ride anyway. I thought maybe I'd have more luck at the edge of town, away from the local traffic. Climbing into his Eldorado Caddy, I felt a blast of cold air hit me in the face and I realised the guy had his air conditioner cranked – a pleasant reminder that I was now in the Deep South and wouldn't have to worry about freezing out on the road overnight. Or so I thought.

My next ride was longer, and anything but cool. In fact, if I had known how much I'd be sweating by the time it was over I never would have gotten in the car. The lights of Tallahassee were winking on for the night when a beat-up Ford Fairlane trailing sparks from a dragging tailpipe came scraping down the ramp and pulled over on the shoulder beside me. The back door swung open and a Southern voice called out, 'Room for one more. Come on, if you're coming!' *What am I getting myself into?* I wondered, but I was tired of waiting on the ramp, so I grabbed my stuff and jumped into the back seat beside a blond teenager with a scared-rabbit look in his eyes.

'That there's Kalvin,' said the driver, twisting around in his seat to introduce me to the scrawny teenager. 'Picked him up a few miles back. I'm Virgil and this here peckerhead's my brother, Sammy,' he said, nodding at the other middle-aged redneck in the front seat. 'What's your name, hoss?' When I told him, he said, 'Well, Pete, we can take you far as the Alford turn-off. Then we're headin' north to Alabama. Sammy, pass that bottle. Let ol' Pete get a nip for the road.'

Brother Sammy swung around and shoved a pint of Wild Turkey at me, but I smiled and waved him off. 'Shoot yourself,' he grinned. 'More for me and Virgil.' Not that the two of them needed it, I thought to myself. The inside of the Fairlane smelled like the business end of a moonshine still. Kalvin's jittery look was starting to make sense. And it wasn't long before I was wearing that same look myself.

Virgil stomped on the gas, and the Fairlane fishtailed off the shoulder in a clatter of gravel. We shot out onto the highway, with the crazy redneck steering one-handed and the tailpipe spraying sparks like a grinding wheel. 'Make yourself useful, Sammy,' Virgil barked, once we were up to speed. 'Find us some Reba on the radio. Ain't a party without Reba. And don't be hogging that Turkey, you peckerhead. Give it here,' he said, letting go of the wheel with his steering hand to snatch the bottle from his brother's grasp.

With growing alarm, I wondered what kind of show-off game the fool was playing, as Virgil took a long pull from the bottle and let the Fairlane drift rudderless across two lanes of traffic. Why the hell wasn't he steering with his other hand? That's when fear sharpened my focus and I belatedly noticed the pinned-up left sleeve of Virgil's khaki fatigue jacket. I couldn't believe it – we were crossing the Panhandle in the dark with a one-armed drunk at the wheel. Could this ride get any crazier?

I glanced to my left to see how Kalvin was taking it. The poor kid looked ready to jump out of the car on the fly. I nudged him with my elbow and whispered, 'Hang tough, Kalvin. We'll get through this.'

'In how many pieces, you think?' Kalvin whispered back. Gallows humour. I liked it. The kid had more pluck than I thought. Which was a good thing, because the eighty-mile ride to Alford was a hair-raising test of nerve for both of us. Amazingly, we made it through alive. Don't ask me how. Only the angels can answer that one. All I know is, the kid and I were wrung out by the time we scrambled out of the Fairlane at the Alford exit and we both agreed to bed down for the night rather than push on in the dark.

While we were scouting around for a campsite in a clover field beside the road, a cold drizzle began falling and the only shelter available was the overpass bridge, so we climbed the steep embankment and lay down head-to-head on the wide concrete ledge beneath the roadway support beams. I nodded out for an hour or so before waking to take a piss, and when I opened my eyes I saw Kalvin sitting up wide awake beside me, hugging himself and shivering with cold. The night air had gotten much cooler after the rain and the kid's flannel lumberjack shirt wasn't cutting it.

'Why didn't you wake me up and tell me you were freezing?' I scolded him. He said he'd been scared to bother me. 'Don't be a dummy,' I said, stripping off my overcoat. 'Here, put this over you,' I told him, and when I got back we lay down beside each other beneath my coat. Eventually his teeth stopped chattering and he drifted off. But we'd only managed a couple hours' sleep before the probing beam of a cop's spotlight hit me full in the face and woke me up.

'YOU THERE, UNDER THE BRIDGE, COME DOWN WITH YOUR HANDS UP!' the bullhorn voice commanded.

Kalvin woke up muttering and asked what was going on. 'The cops want a word with us,' I whispered. 'We better get down there.'

Squinting into the bright light, we started down the steep slope, but neither of us could keep our footing on the embankment's rain-slick paving stones and ended up sliding halfway down the slope on our asses. Which might have been comical if our pratfalls hadn't landed us at the feet of an Army MP and a county sheriff who were out hunting an escaped military prisoner.

'Either of these two your man?' the local cop asked the MP, but the army cop shook his head. 'What are you guys doing under the bridge?' the sheriff asked. We told him we were holing up till daylight before thumbing west to Louisiana. He must have found our tandem tumbling act amusing, because instead of hassling us any further he and the MP just climbed back in their cruisers and drove off to resume their manhunt.

'We got lucky,' Kalvin exhaled.

'Tell that to my tailbone,' I moaned, brushing dirt off the seat of my pants. But both of us were laughing as we picked our way cautiously back up the slope and settled in to sleep off the last few hours before first light. At dawn, we climbed back up to the interstate and in the light of day it was plain to see that the redneck juicers had dropped us off in the middle of nowhere. We set off hiking along the highway toward a town called Chipley, ten miles down the line. We kept wagging our thumbs whenever a car came along, but nobody would stop and we wound up walking the entire ten-mile stretch. It took us more than two hours, our feet burning by the time we limped into Chipley.

'Nothing like a ten-mile hike to get the blood pumping, right, Kalvin?' I quipped as we neared the finish line.

'Least I'm not freezing any more,' he grinned, wiping sweat from his eyes. The morning had warmed up nicely while we were pounding pavement. At the Chipley exit there was a dinky tin-roofed general store with a single Sinclair pump out front. 'Race you there,' Kalvin challenged. 'Loser buys breakfast.'

'Find another sucker, kid,' I laughed. 'I'm beat.'

'Just kidding,' he smiled. 'I'm beat, too. And I'm not even an old man like you.'

We decided to pool our money before we went into the store. Kalvin had a little cash he'd panhandled on the trip north from Miami, and I still had a few dollars left from the Toronado kid's handout. Between us, we came up with six bucks, and we blew it all on a dozen powdered doughnuts, a half-gallon of milk and a couple of pouches of rolling tobacco. Then we took our sack of groceries down the road to a piney woodlot and hunkered beneath the trees. After we'd eaten, we tugged off our shoes and socks off to give our blistered feet an airing, and lolled around smoking and 'taking our ease', like Tom and Huck on their raft, until we finally felt rested enough to head back to the highway.

As we passed the general store again, Kalvin said, 'Hold up a minute,' and ran over to the dumpster in the parking lot. He fished out a cardboard box, tore off one of its sides and ran back to join me. 'Thought we might do better hitching with a sign,' he explained.

'Worth a shot,' I said. 'But all I've got to write with is a ballpoint. We'd need a Magic Marker to make a decent sign.'

'You mean one of these?' Kalvin asked, smiling slyly as he reached into his back pocket and pulled out a brand-new marker, still in its blister-pack.

'Where'd that come from?' I asked, though I had a feeling I already knew the answer.

'Five-finger discount. I snatched it while the cashier was ringing you up,' he confessed.

'Jesus, Kalvin, you're quite the little klepto, aren't you?'

'Guess so,' he shrugged, unabashed. 'But my handwriting sucks, so you'd better make the sign. Besides, I'm not sure I can spell Pensacola.'

A few minutes later our new sign paid off when an elderly British couple out taking the air in their Jaguar convertible stopped to give us a lift. The two diminutive Brits were wearing identical Union Jack sports car caps, looking jaunty as all get out. Cast them in porcelain, bore a few holes in their heads and they'd have made a charmingly goofy set of salt and pepper shakers.

'May we offer you a ride to Bonifay?' the wife said brightly, in her BBC accent. 'It's only the next town, I'm afraid, but you're welcome to join us.'

She didn't have to ask us twice. Not with our feet still smarting from the long hike to Chipley. So we rode in style to Bonifay, ten breezy miles down the road, and put our sign to work again, but the sign seemed to have lost its mojo. Two frustrating hours later we were still stuck in Bonifay.

Finally Kalvin said, 'Give me that sign, Pete. Let me try something.'

What's the kid up to now? I wondered, as he pulled the Magic

Marker from his pocket and embellished the sign with two thick Christian crosses, bold enough to be spotted from a long way off.

'What are we going for here, Kalvin?' I asked. 'Divine intervention?'

'A trick this dude in Miami taught me,' Kalvin explained. 'He said when you're in Baptist country always put a cross on your sign. I should've thought of it hours ago. You watch, we'll catch a ride in no time now.'

Damned if the kid wasn't right. We caught four rides in a row after that and by late afternoon we were rolling into Pensacola, where I flipped our cardboard sign over and block-printed 'MOBILE' on the blank side, adding a couple of Baptist-bait crosses for good measure. In short order, we were on our way to Alabama in a Chevy Malibu with a thirty-something hipster at the wheel. Kalvin jumped in the back seat. I rode shotgun with Richie, a cool dude who welcomed us aboard with two icy-cold Bud tallboys he pulled from a Styrofoam cooler on the seat beside him.

'Thanks,' I said, popping the flip tab. 'Glad we didn't miss Happy Hour.'

Richie said I sounded like I was from New York, and when I confirmed his hunch he said, 'Me, too. Bensonhurst, Brooklyn. Mobile's my wife's hometown. I moved down here ten years ago and opened a Brooklyn-style pizzeria. Taught the locals what a real pie tastes like. Now they stand in line half an hour just to get in the door.'

'I can believe it,' I said. 'But do you ever miss New York?'

'Yeah, sometimes. I miss the jazz clubs, mostly. You like jazz, Pete?'

I admitted I did and told him I'd been haunting the Village

jazz clubs for years. The Blue Note. The Village Vanguard. Sweet Basil. The Cookery.

'Yes, yes, check, yes, been to them all,' Richie said excitedly. 'You're going to love this then,' he said, popping a tape into the deck – and suddenly two duelling saxophones were blowing the roof off the Malibu.

'Rahsaan Roland Kirk! Playing *both* saxophones!' Richie shouted. 'Recognise it?'

'Hell, yeah,' I shouted back. 'This is "Bright Star". A classic. I saw him do this at the Vanguard back in '73. When he started playing two saxophones at the same time, my jaw dropped. I'll never forget it!'

As it happened, the night I caught Kirk's performance was also the night I first tried cocaine. Hearing Rahsaan's sax brought it all back like it was yesterday. The first set was winding down when my pal Liam, the bartender, gave me the nod to follow him into the club's back storeroom. I thought he was inviting me to share a joint, as we often did when he was working, but he surprised me by pulling out a vial of white powder instead.

'Is that coke?' I asked. When I admitted I'd never tried any, Liam looked at me like I had a hole in my head.

'You're shitting me, right? Where you been, Hat?'

'Missing out, I guess,' I grinned. *What the hell, why not?*

I trusted Liam. We'd been born only hours apart on the same February day in 1949 – a weird coincidence we didn't discover until months after we first met at the Lion's Head. Our shared birthday made me consider him my cosmic twin. However, unlike my tragically unhip childhood in the Long Island suburbs, Liam's youth had been spent on the cobblestone streets of Greenwich Village. When it came to being cool, he was always a city block ahead of me – so, naturally, I didn't think twice when he passed me the vial. *If it's good enough for Liam, it's good enough for me,* I thought. Which was exactly the kind of follow-the-leader thinking my father used to mock whenever I tried to excuse some bonehead move I'd pulled by claiming all my friends had done the same. 'If your friends jumped off the Empire State Building, would you jump too?' The answer, apparently, was yes – though I naively considered it a leap of faith, not a plunge into self-destruction. Events would prove otherwise, of course, but at the time I was hopelessly in thrall to the 'anything goes' mystique of Greenwich Village. And had been for years – ever since I'd made my first pilgrimage to the Lion's Head in 1970, while I was home on summer break before my senior year at college.

Back then I'd been hoping to meet my idol-of-the-moment, the writer Fred Exley, whose debut novel *A Fan's Notes* had blown me away with its harrowing but hysterical portrait of an alcoholic writer facing up to the fact that he'd been fated to watch from the sidelines while others – like his college classmate (and star football player) Frank Gifford – cashed in on the American Dream. *A Fan's Notes* had been billed as a 'fictional memoir', but there was no mistaking its basis in boozy reality. I'd been awestruck by Exley's gift for turning the disasters of his life into stories that were simultaneously sad and side-splittingly funny. Reading his novel was like making the Stations of the Cross high on nitrous oxide, and when I finished it I knew I'd found the newest member of my pantheon of hard-drinking writers – a worthy companion to Ernest Hemingway, Malcolm Lowry, Charles Bukowski and, of course, Jack Kerouac.

I had no idea back then why these dipsomaniacs appealed to me so much, but in retrospect I'd say it was their lack of self-control that I found alluring. All of them were writers I'd discovered only after puberty had given me good reason to doubt my own capacity for self-control, so I suppose at some unconscious level I recognised them as fellow slaves to habit, whose books offered proof that you could struggle with your demons and still turn out masterful work. But by romanticising their excesses, I suckered myself into believing I could do the same myself, and no doubt that delusion was as much to blame as my drunken condition when I accepted Liam's invitation and took the nosedive that would alter my life in ways Harold Bloom surely never envisioned when he coined the phrase 'the anxiety of influence'.

Rahsaan was still blowing strong as we crossed the causeway bridge over Mobile Bay at rush hour and were treated to a Gulf Coast sunset as gaudy as one of Kirk's tie-dyed dashikis. Minutes later, Brooklyn Richie dropped us off at a busy cloverleaf inter-section and, as I was bailing out, he did us one more solid by pressing a bag of Cheetos into my hands. Now we had supper.

'Richie, you're the best,' I told him, and gave the Malibu's roof a grateful thump as he pulled away.

'Well, Kalvin, what do you think?' I asked. 'Should we find someplace to camp?' We'd been on the road twelve hours already and it was quickly getting dark.

'Sounds good to me,' Kalvin said. 'That beer made me sleepy. Guess I'm not much of a drinker.'

'Count your blessings, kid,' I grinned. 'Let's call it a night.'

CHAPTER 5

Hitchhiking across Mississippi was harder than parsing a William Faulkner sentence, despite Kalvin's best efforts with his Magic Marker. He added so many extra crosses to our cardboard sign it began to resemble a child's sketch of a battlefield cemetery, yet we still had little luck attracting Samaritans brave enough to take on two hitchhikers at once. No doubt we'd have made better time by splitting up, but I'd told Kalvin I'd stick with him till we reached his home state of Louisiana, and I didn't want to go back on my word. The poor kid had already faced enough disappointment in his short life.

Kalvin had lost his mother to cancer a few weeks before I met him, and after his mom's funeral he'd dropped out of high school and hitchhiked to Florida, hoping to reconnect with his father, who'd abandoned his wife and only child when Kalvin was still in grade school. When he got to Miami and discovered his father no longer lived at his old address, Kalvin was forced to fend for himself. With no money and no place to stay, he wound up sleeping in city parks and shoplifting candy bars to feed himself while he continued his search. Then, after four days of nosing around, he finally met a junkie who knew his father and suggested Kalvin check the local homeless shelter.

Kalvin said he hardly recognised the old man when he found him. His heroin habit had taken a toll and he looked nothing like the photos in the family album any more. Still, his dad seemed glad to see him – at first, anyway. But then he asked Kalvin for money to buy drugs, and when Kalvin admitted he was broke his father cursed him and told him he was the same worthless kid he'd always been. I'd have cracked the heartless bastard in the mouth, but Kalvin just fled the shelter before his old man had a chance to call him a crybaby too.

Now Kalvin was heading home to Winsboro, Louisiana, to stay with his mom's widowed sister, and I figured the least I could do was keep him company till we got to New Orleans. Zeke's talk about the brotherhood of the road must have stuck with me. *You give when you can, and take when you can't.* I had nothing to offer Kalvin except camaraderie, but that seemed to be all he was looking for, and I could understand why. After Kate died, I'd relied on my friends at the Raccoon Lodge to lift my spirits. Poor Kalvin had had no one to confide in until I came along, and I could tell how relieved he was to share his story when we made camp in Mobile. Of course, Kalvin claimed it was the thick smoke from our greenwood campfire that made his eyes water, but I knew better, and my heart went out to him, like it had to Charlene back in Richmond. Which left me wondering if that wasn't why the road had brought us together. To remind me again that I still had a heart. A heart willing to reconnect with the world, if only I had the sense to let it.

The sun was going down by the time we finally caught a ride from the Mississippi Welcome Station, where we'd been stranded most of the day. The young redhead who picked us up was named Kevin, and when he mentioned that he played third base for the Mets farm team in Jackson I told him he was doing a solid for a long-time Mets fan. I'd been following the team since their inaugural season in 1962, and Kevin got a kick out of the stories I told him about the team's hapless early days when the 'Loveable Losers' were the National League's perennial cellar-dwellers. When he dropped us off at the D'Iberville exit a half-hour later, Kevin thanked me for the history lesson and advised us to hike a couple miles further up the road to the D'Iberville rest area, where he said we'd have a better chance of catching a ride. It was pitch dark, and we were deep in bayou country now, on a desolate stretch of unlit causeway flanked by gloomy swamps and creepy cypress trees draped with Spanish moss.

'Looks like a great place to dump a body,' I said to Kalvin, putting up a brave front. I could sense he was as spooked as I was.

'Or two bodies,' Kalvin observed grimly. He was right about that. I couldn't wait to get to the rest area Kevin had told us about. Even if it was deserted, at least there'd be streetlights.

A mile into our hike, to our surprise, a car pulled over to the shoulder thirty yards ahead of us. Thinking no one would stop for us on the narrow causeway, we hadn't even tried to flag it down. 'Come on, Kalvin, we just got lucky!' I said, sprinting toward the tail-lights. But as soon as we got close the car peeled out, spraying gravel in our faces.

'Eat dirt, faggots!' a teenage voice yelled out the window, as laughter erupted inside the car. Faulkner's yokels of

Yoknapatawpha, amusing themselves at our expense. Sunday night fun in the Magnolia State. *Get me out of here!*

'Assholes!' Kalvin shouted, but only after the car was safely out of range. Smart move. The last thing we needed was a bunch of rednecks backing up and breaking out the Louisville sluggers.

'I'm getting a bad vibe from this place, Kalvin.' I said. 'We're easy targets out here in the dark. I think we'd better just make camp for the night when we get to the rest area.'

Kalvin agreed, but when we reached the rest area parking lot the road had another surprise in store for us. The lone car in the lot was a beat-up old Ford Falcon, and behind the wheel sat a stocky guy with a wispy black moustache who was squinting at a road map in the feeble glow of the car's dome light. As we walked past, he rolled down his window and waved us over.

'Heading to New Orleans, are you?' he smiled, nodding at the sign in Kalvin's hand. 'Hop in if you want a lift. My name's Bear. Don't worry, I'm no psycho. Just a wayward Inuit, on my way to work an oil rig in Texas. Be passing right through New Orleans in a couple of hours, so long as this beater holds together.'

I grinned at Kalvin, and he grinned right back. Decision made. Neither of us was looking forward to camping in a swamp overnight. Now we had a shot at making it to New Orleans in time to score a bed at a Rescue Mission. Which was hard to believe, considering it had taken us the entire day to make it sixty miles down the road from Mobile.

'Sounds mighty good to us, Bear,' I said. 'I'm Pete, and that's Kalvin.'

I climbed in beside Bear, and Kalvin squeezed into the back, shifting some of Bear's toolboxes to make room. 'You boys like Red Hots? Help yourself,' Bear said, nodding at a

five-pound jumbo bag of hard candies on the seat between us
– a bag that was already half-empty. 'I been suckin' on Red Hots
all the way down here from my sister's place in Boston. They
keep me awake better than coffee.'

Which explained the rustling sound I kept hearing whenever I shifted my feet. I glanced down between my knees and,
sure enough, the floorboard was carpeted with cast-off candy
wrappers.

I grabbed a handful and passed some back to Kalvin. We'd
gone hungry all day. Any food was welcome. Even if it set our
mouths on fire.

I told Bear he was the first Inuit I'd ever met, though I'd
been curious about Inuit culture ever since my parents took us
to see Nicholas Ray's *The Savage Innocents* at the Commack
Drive-In when I was twelve. Bear let out a derisive hoot and
said, 'Yeah, I caught that movie on late-night TV at a motel up
in Anchorage years ago and laughed my ass off. Anthony Quinn
as an Inuit. Only in Hollywood.'

Quinn had played an Inuit named Inuk, who welcomes a
visiting missionary priest into his igloo and offers him the tradi-
tional tokens of hospitality – a meal of whale blubber and a
tumble in the bearskin rugs with Inuk's wife. The priest turns
his nose up at the offered food, and scoffs at the idea of having
sex with Inuk's wife. Insulted by the priest's refusal, Inuk flies
into a rage and kills him, and spends the rest of the film on the
run from a Canadian Mountie played by Peter O'Toole. It wasn't
one of Nick Ray's more successful films at the box office, but
in its own way it pursued the same theme that he'd explored
to greater acclaim in *Rebel Without a Cause* – society's intolerance
for those who won't abide by its repressive rules.

As luck would have it, a dozen years later, I had the pleasure of meeting Nick Ray one evening at the Lion's Head and he had a good laugh when I told him my parents had made me and my kid brothers cover our eyes during the scene in *The Savage Innocents* where Inuk's wife goes into labour and gives birth to a wailing infant on the igloo floor. Ray said my parents weren't the only ones squeamish about the childbirth scene. The studio had urged him to tone down its unflinching realism, but Ray had flatly refused. Back then he had enough clout in Hollywood to get away with it. Those days were long gone, however. When I met him in 1973, Ray was in his early sixties and had fallen on hard times.

Drinking and drug use had cost Nick Ray his last teaching position, leaving him without access to the equipment he needed to complete the editing of his work-in-progress, a film called *We Can't Go Home Again*. When I heard about his predicament, I thought maybe I could help. One of the authors I was working with at Harcourt Brace during those days was a documentary filmmaker named Lee Bobker, whose filmmaking textbook *The Elements of Film* was in the process of being updated for release in a second edition. Lee Bobker had a state-of-the-art film studio in midtown, with the latest word in editing equipment – a Steenbeck digital editing console. When I mentioned to Nick Ray that I might be able to get him access to a Steenbeck, his bleary eyes lit up with interest. But then he ruefully admitted he couldn't afford to pay for studio time. I told him to let me see what I could do. When I made a call to Lee Bobker and explained the situation, he graciously offered Ray free after-hours access to his editing room. Ray was delighted, of course, and I was so proud of myself for brokering the deal I'm surprised my big head didn't split my hat. Unfortunately, I never crossed paths with Nick Ray again. But six years later, when I read the sad news that he had died of lung cancer, I flashed back on our brief encounter and was glad I'd done what little I could to help him when I had the chance.

Thirty miles outside New Orleans, Bear announced that he had to stop and make a call to his union's shape-up office to find out when he was scheduled to report to his new job in Texas. He turned off the highway at Slidell, Louisiana, and pulled into a truck stop to use a pay phone. 'Sit tight, boys, I'll be right back,' he told us. Ten minutes later, he returned bearing gifts – coffee and snack cakes for both of us. But he also brought bad news. The union had switched his job assignment, and he'd been told to turn around and report to Mobile instead of Brownsville, Texas. Which meant Slidell was the end of the line for Kalvin and me.

It turned out Kalvin had once lived in Slidell, so he took the lead as we set off from the truck stop to find a campsite – New Orleans would have to wait until morning. Meanwhile, both of us were still hungry. Bear's handout had only whetted our appetites. Kalvin had an idea where to score some free food and he led the way to a Dunkin' Donuts shop about a mile down the road from the truck stop. 'The dumpster in back should have plenty of stale doughnuts we can scavenge,' Kalvin predicted. He was right, too, but as soon as we popped the dumpster's lid we nearly gagged. Some righteous Dunkin' Donuts asshole had bum-proofed the trash with a jug of Clorox. The smell of bleach was so strong it made our eyes water. Slamming the lid in disgust, we walked away cursing. Two human vermin, successfully repulsed. Then, as if that wasn't discouraging enough, the sky opened up and suddenly began pelting us with chilly rain.

Kalvin made a run for it, and I followed him through the

dark streets of a ramshackle neighbourhood until he pulled up short in front of a sagging old Victorian house with boarded-up windows and a half-collapsed roof.

'This might work,' Kalvin said. 'Looks abandoned. Let's check it out.'

The front of the place was well secured with plywood, but when we circled round back the porch door was hanging open, half off its hinges. We crept up the porch steps and dug out our lighters to look inside. The house smelled of mildew and charred wood, and there was rainwater cascading into the kitchen through a jagged hole in the roof. Skirting the edge of the big puddle beneath the hole, we worked our way warily toward the front of the house, looking for a dry spot to crash. The floors were littered with crushed beer cans and crumpled cigarette packs and empty pint bottles of Thunderbird, so it was obvious we weren't the first squatters to seek shelter there. I half-expected we'd turn a corner and scare the bejesus out of some poor wino in his bedroll, but it turned out we had the place to ourselves – at least for the moment.

The house's carpeted bedrooms all reeked of mildew, so we bedded down on the parlour's plank wood floor. I was warm enough in my overcoat, but our dash through the rain had left Kalvin shivering with cold. Luckily, the parlour's windows were hung with heavy brocade drapes. We ripped down a pair and shook the dust out so Kalvin could use them as blankets. Then we turned in for the night and let the white noise from the kitchen waterfall lull us both to sleep.

I stayed dead to the world for hours, but at some point, deep in the night, I felt something strange going on. When I jerked awake, I was shocked to find a ferret-faced wino with sour breath kneeling over me in the shadows, rummaging through my coat pockets with his greedy little hands. 'Get the fuck off me!' I shouted, and shot an elbow to his throat. I caught him square in the windpipe, and when he tumbled backwards I heard him hit the wall. Next thing I knew, he was on his feet again, clutching his throat and croaking like a gigged bullfrog as he ran splashing through the kitchen and out the back door.

Amazingly, Kalvin snored on serenely, an arm's length away, throughout the entire incident – just like my brother Steve had slept through my father's performance the night he threatened to carve me up for sandwiches. I saw no point in waking him. One of us might as well get some rest and it surely wasn't going to be me. I knew I'd be up the rest of the night, jacked on adrenaline, keeping watch in case the wino returned with a brick to collect some payback. I would just have to wait impatiently to share the blow-by-blow with my snoring sidekick. *Hey, Kalvin, you slept through all the fun!*

～

New Orleans, at last! After seven days on the road, there I was, standing in the noon rush on Canal Street, digging the sweet tropical air that Jack Kerouac said feels like soft bandanas, with a dopey stoner's grin on my face and the scent of marijuana still clinging to my clothes – and Kalvin standing right beside me, equally wrecked.

It had been quite a trip from Slidell. We'd waited all morning to catch a ride out before finally hitting the jackpot with a young welder from Biloxi, who welcomed us into his smoke-filled Ford Galaxy and plied us with Dixie beers and Oaxacan sensimilla all the way across Lake Pontchartrain. By the time we got to the French Quarter, we were slit-eyed and wasted. And hungrier than ever.

'Man, I wish we had some money,' Kalvin said. 'I could go for a big plate of rice and beans.'

'I hear you, Kalvin,' I nodded. 'Right now, I'd give my left nut for a fried oyster po-boy. Maybe we should find a blood bank and raise some quick cash selling plasma.'

Neither of us had ever sold blood before, but Kalvin said he was game, so we set off through the French Quarter, heading for Jackson Square Park to consult the experts. I knew the park was a daytime hangout for the Quarter's street people. A decade earlier, during our cross-country road trip, Kate and I had stayed at a bed-and-breakfast just blocks from Jackson Square and I still remember how relentlessly we'd been panhandled whenever we'd crossed through the park on our way to the Riverwalk. No doubt we'd find some tramp there who could give us the scoop on the local blood banks.

Cutting through the lunchtime crowds, we hustled down cobblestone streets that echoed with the clip-clop of horse-drawn carriages and the come-on calls of the Lucky Dog vendors, whose comical, wiener-shaped food carts sat steaming on nearly every corner. Ten minutes later we were huddled up on a park bench beside a white-haired old black wino, who kindly tore a scrap from the brown bag that held his pint of port so that I could jot down his directions. He told us the closest blood bank was on Canal Street, just south of the Quarter – which wasn't far. But hiking there was pure torture. We must have passed two dozen restaurants along the way and each one smelled more appetising than the last. By the time we got to the blood bank the antiseptic smell in the waiting room was actually a welcome relief. But the sour-puss receptionist promptly sent us packing when we couldn't produce picture ID, and that was the end of that.

'Let's see if I can bum us a few smokes at least,' Kalvin ventured, approaching two leather-faced tramps on the sidewalk outside the blood bank. They handed over a couple of cigarettes and we stood around bullshitting with them while we smoked.

'Haven't seen you boys around before,' the bearded one said. 'Just hit town?'

We admitted we had, and glumly told them how we'd just struck out in the plasma centre.

'You boys should head over to the Traveller's Aid office at the train station,' the other tramp suggested. 'Don't need picture ID with those folks. Just tell 'em you're broke and stranded. They'll hook you up with food and lodging vouchers for five nights at the Oz. All-expenses paid,' he chuckled.

'The Oz?' I asked. Had we reached the end of the Yellow Brick Road already?

'Yup, that's what everyone calls it. The real name's somethin' longer, don't ask me what. But the first two letters are O and Z, so we call it the Oz. Catholics run it, but it ain't a bad flop.'

The Amtrak station was out near the Superdome. We found our way to the Traveller's Aid Society office on the concourse and told our stories to the sweet little woman at the counter, who bobbed her blue-rinsed head in sympathy and gave us some forms to fill out. Then she asked if we had any ID. I had nothing to show except the hitchhiking ticket I'd been issued in Florida, but she said that was good enough. *Thank God I saved it*, I thought to myself. Kalvin followed suit and dug out a desk appearance ticket he'd been issued for shoplifting in Miami. Easy as that, we collected two vouchers for the shelter and a mimeographed map to help us find our way there from the train station.

The Traveller's Aid lady told us we were eligible for

Greyhound tokens, too, if we could contact a friend or relative willing to reimburse the society for the cost of a ticket. She said we could use her desk phone to call anyone we thought might sponsor us. Kalvin's face lit up when he heard her offer, and he immediately called his aunt in northern Louisiana, who gave the Traveller's Aid lady the go-ahead to issue him a bus ticket to Winsboro. He could finally give his thumb a rest. I was happy for the kid. And a little envious, too.

When Kalvin got off the phone, I asked if I could make a call to San Francisco to let a friend know I'd been delayed on the road. I wasn't planning to ask Tanner to spot me a bus ticket, but I figured he'd be wondering why I hadn't turned up on his doorstep yet. The Traveller's Aid lady said no problem, so I dialled information, got Tanner's number and called to break the news that I was running behind schedule. Whereupon Tanner broke some news of his own, and it wasn't good. His condo project had run into problems with the planning commission and his permits had been denied. His architect was preparing revised plans, but Tanner had no idea how long it would take to get them approved. Meanwhile, the job site was shut down and he had no work to offer me.

'Sorry, Hat,' he said. 'I didn't see this coming.'

That makes two of us, I thought, my brows knitting into a frown. But I swallowed my disappointment and told Tanner not to sweat it. I'd work something out once I got to California. This time, however, I knew better than to forecast my arrival. 'I'll see you when I see you,' I said, no longer in any big hurry.

'Bad news?' Kalvin asked, reading my face as I hung up.

'Bad enough,' I said. 'My job in Frisco just fell through.'

Kalvin shook his head. 'That's a bummer. What are you going to do now?'

'Push on to California and take my chances, I guess. But I think I'll kick back in New Orleans for a few days and rest up before I hit the road again. Anyway, don't worry about me. Let's get you on your way to Winsboro.'

At the bus station, Kalvin got lucky again – there was a Greyhound to Winsboro leaving within the hour. While we waited for his boarding call, I asked him what he planned to do once he got home.

'Not sure,' he shrugged. 'Maybe work at the bottling plant with my aunt for a while and save up some money for truck driving school. I wouldn't mind driving long-haul rigs coast to coast. Be a good way to see the country and get paid for it, right?'

'Sure, go for it,' I said. 'But if I hit you up for a ride at a truck stop one of these days, you'd better not be one of those chicken-shits who quotes the rule book and leaves me hanging.'

'Okay, you got it,' Kalvin laughed. 'Let me give you my aunt's address,' he said, and scribbled it out on the back of the Traveller's Aid map. 'Send me a Golden Gate postcard when you get to the coast.'

'I'll do that,' I promised. The kid had been good company the past three days, but I was back to travelling solo now. Off to Oz, to spend my first-ever night in a homeless shelter.

Even without the mimeographed map, I'd have found the place easily, just by following the herd. Dozens of street people were trooping through the Warehouse District toward Camp Street to join the queue for supper at the Oz. When I reached the shelter, the line in the parking lot outside the three-storey brick building was getting longer by the minute. I climbed the front steps and rang the office doorbell. A ruddy-cheeked man invited me in and introduced himself as Brother Kevin, of the

Little Brothers of the Good Shepherd. I showed him my voucher from Traveller's Aid, and he ushered me over to his desk and handed me a brochure to look at while he registered me for a bed. Scanning the pamphlet, I saw that the shelter's actual name was the Ozanam Inn, in honour of Frédéric Ozanam, who founded the Society of St Vincent de Paul back in 1833. The list of services the shelter offered included not just food and lodging, but also clothing, medical check-ups, addiction counselling — even a barbershop — all free of charge. I could see why the blood bank tramp had called the place a good flop.

There were two plaques on the wall behind Brother Kevin's desk. One said: *We give a man a fish today, we teach a man to fish for tomorrow!* The plaque beside it quoted St Vincent de Paul: *It is because of your love, and only your love, that the poor will forgive you the bread you give them.* Inspiring words, even to a seminary drop-out like me. But the good folks at the Oz didn't have to worry about me forgiving them their bread. My belly was too empty for anything but gratitude. I couldn't wait to chow down.

'All right, Peter . . .' Brother Kevin smiled. 'We've reserved you a bed for the week. The dining-room entrance is around back. Just join the line in the parking lot and our volunteers will call you in when supper's ready.'

Fifty or sixty hungry people were already queued up when I joined the line, and more kept straggling in until the crowd was nearly two hundred strong. We were a sorry assembly of the hobbling and the unhoused, burdened by backpacks and bulging garbage sacks, by duct-taped suitcases and grimy khaki duffle bags — misfortune's impedimenta, everywhere I looked. There were a handful of shopping-cart ladies in the crowd, but most of the Oz's clients were men my age and older, boozers for the most part, passing pocket pints back and forth with their buddies as they stood in line smoking hand-rolled tobacco and coughing like fugitives from a TB ward.

As I waited in line, taking in the scene, my eye was drawn to the graffiti-tagged wall of the warehouse building that over-looked the far side of the parking lot, where some sardonic joker had spray-painted in big looping silver letters: *It's never too late to have a happy childhood!* I wondered how quickly you'd get laughed out of the parking lot if you tried peddling that Peter Pan bullshit to this crowd. And yet, the truth of the matter was that all of us, whether by hard luck or our own bad choices, had been reduced to needy children. Children waiting patiently for the grown-ups at the Oz to feed us our supper. Happy childhood, my ass. 'The mother of dissipation is not joy, but joylessness' – now there's a tag that would have been more resonant under the circumstances. But how many graffiti artists read Nietzsche these days? Not enough, it seemed, or they wouldn't be wasting good paint on bad quotes from a pap-slinger like Tom Robbins.

'How's the chow here?' I asked the guy in line ahead of me, a short black man in his fifties who stood leaning on a tripod cane.

'Oh, they feed us plenty good here,' he said. 'You ain't been to the Oz before? Must be new in town then.'

'Just got here this afternoon,' I admitted. 'Traveller's Aid hooked me up with a voucher for this place. Glad they did, too. I've hardly had a thing to eat in two days.'

'Well, at supper they only feed us sandwiches, but you'll get your belly full anyway. Breakfast and lunch are the two hot meals. You a drinkin' man, son?'

'Not much any more,' I replied, with a hint of Dixie beer still bitter on my breath.

'Even so, watch your step when you're walking around town,' he warned. 'Mardi Gras is coming up soon, and the cops are doing what they always do this time of year – snatching drunks off the streets so the crooked judges can sentence them to community service. That's who gets stuck putting up most of the bleachers along the parade route.'

'That sucks,' I said. 'What a scam.'

'Slave labour, you ask me. Cousin of mine got snatched two days ago. He was fresh out of detox. Hadn't touched a drop in a week. But the cops still charged him with drunk in public when he stumbled on a rough patch of sidewalk. So, like I say, son, mind how you step.'

When the bells of St Patrick's Church up the block began to toll five o'clock, everyone on line surged forward, jostling for position as the dining-room doors swung open. I heard a loud argument break out behind me and turned around to see what was going on. Two drunken latecomers who'd tried to cut the line were being set upon by four or five other tramps intent on teaching them some manners. It was more a Punch and Judy show than a real beat-down, but it drew hoots of approval from the others in line. *The last shall not be first if we can help it!* That seemed to be the general sentiment. The crowd's solidarity was touching to see. They might be low down, but they weren't doormats – and the two line-jumpers were being taught the difference.

The Oz's low-ceilinged dining room was about the size of a basement banquet room in your average Knights of Columbus hall, with a steam-table serving line along one wall, and three long rows of picnic tables with attached benches and plastic tablecloths arranged in the centre of the room. Along the far wall, floor space had been left clear for the Oz's guests to deposit whatever baggage they were carrying before they sat down to eat. 'No bags at the table' was one of the house rules. 'No shouting or swearing' was another. 'Clear your own table' was the third. Other than that, it was a beggar's banquet, and you were welcome to eat your fill. I wolfed down three ham and cheese sandwiches and a quart of fruit punch before I was done, and relished every bite.

After our meal, one of the shelter's volunteers got on the microphone and announced that any man with a bed reserved for the night should line up outside the stairwell to the second floor. I joined the line, and after the volunteer checked off my name on his clipboard I trooped upstairs with the rest of the overnighters, where another volunteer explained the dormitory rules. Everyone had to strip down to their skivvies and put their clothes and belongings into big plastic bags, to be held in storage until the morning. After that, we were each given a bath towel and a tiny tube of shampoo and told to hit the shower room. 'Be sure you wash your hair,' the volunteer instructed us. 'Anyone comes out of the shower with a dry head won't be given a bed.'

I thought I'd seen a lot of scarred bodies in the showers at Rikers Island, but the tramps at the Oz made the gangbangers in prison look like milk-fed choir boys. There were tattooed Vietnam vets with jagged shrapnel scars, diabetic alkies with amputated toes, and more than a few bellies and chests cross-stitched with raised surgical scars like welted laces on a football – all in addition to the usual grim assortment of healed-over knife wounds I had seen often enough at Rikers. And me without a scar on my body. I suppose that was something to be grateful for, but as I stood there surrounded by so much disfigurement I couldn't help feeling conspicuous. However, my failure to blend in didn't stop me from enjoying the first hot shower I'd taken since Petersburg, and by the time I traded my wet towel for a set of clean pyjamas at the linen room down the hall I felt right at home. Which wasn't how I'd been expecting to feel on my first night in a homeless shelter, believe me, but you get a lot less picky about what passes for 'homey' after you've been roughing it by the roadside for a week. *This isn't bad at all*, I thought. *It's like a sleepover camp for prodigal sons*. What more could I ask for?

The Oz's narrow beds were comfortable enough, but once the lights were switched off I only managed a few hours of fitful sleep. All around me in the dark the dormitory reverberated with consumptive hacking and the night moans of men in the grip of troubled dreams. Even after I ducked into the men's room and fitted myself with toilet-tissue earplugs it was hard to snatch more than an hour's sleep at a time before the next coughing fit or nightmare cry woke me up again. Which made for a long night – a night I was more than happy to put behind me when the wake-up alarm came blaring over the intercom speakers at 5 a.m.

All the other overnighters looked as tired as I did as we trooped downstairs for breakfast, and when the shelter volunteers shooed us out the door at six o'clock I'd wager most of us hit the streets with the same intention – to find a quiet spot where we could sack out for just a few more hours before facing another day. That's what I had in mind, anyway, as I set off up Camp Street, looking for a likely place to catch a nap. Three blocks later, I came to an address made famous by JFK conspiracy theorists like Jim Garrison: 544 Camp Street. It was then I realised I'd spent the night on the very street where Lee Harvey Oswald had once been based during his shadowy days as an anti-Castro pamphleteer. A coincidence to which I attached no real significance, but it would add a bit of local colour to my road journal nonetheless.

Across the street, in Lafayette Square, some of the Oz tramps were already settling in beneath the trees for their morning snooze, so I joined them on the dewy grass and caught a few more hours of sleep myself – until I was awakened by a loud metallic clanking nearby. I looked around to find the source of the noise and saw a work gang of jumpsuited prisoners unloading sections of steel pipe from a public works truck in front of the Federal Courthouse, just down the block. Under the watchful eye of a uniformed guard, a second work gang was bolting the pipes together to form the framework for bleacher seats that would no doubt be reserved for the wealthy and the well-connected come next week's Mardi Gras. Apparently, the tramp at the Oz hadn't been crying wolf when he'd warned me about the local cops. I'd have to heed his advice and watch my step, or risk being shanghaied into service with a socket wrench.

I had a few hours to kill before lunch at the Oz, so I hiked across Canal Street and drifted through the French Quarter, taking in the sights, but I found myself growing sadder by the block. Everywhere I turned, I kept seeing places Kate and I had visited on our honeymoon. Pat O'Brien's bar on Bourbon Street, where we'd gotten giddy-drunk on Hurricane cocktails after a jazz show at Preservation Hall. Tujague's Restaurant on Decatur, where we'd eaten the *prix fixe* Creole dinner each night of our stay. And across the street from Tujague's, the Café Du Monde, where we'd loitered every morning on the terrace beside the levee, sharing the *Times-Picayune* while we sipped our cafés au lait and made plans for a life we imagined would be as sweet as the Du Monde's famous French beignets.

Those decade-old memories were now only bitter reminders

of how much I'd let Kate down in the end. When Kate died, I had no steady job and could barely pay the rent at the flophouse hotel in the Flatiron District where I'd been staying. There was no way I could scrape together the money to give her a proper burial. Which left me no choice but to call her mother and explain that she'd have to foot the bill for flying her daughter's body home to Alabama to be buried beside her dad. Kate's mom, a devout Baptist, had never seen much promise in me to begin with, and I hated proving her instincts right, but I swallowed what little pride I had left and did what had to be done. Though it made me feel like the world's biggest shit-heel, I might have learned to live with it if only I'd had the balls to fly down to Cullman and show my face at Kate's funeral. But even though my friends at the Raccoon would surely have chipped in to buy me a plane ticket, I didn't ask them for help. Why bother? I knew I'd never have the nerve to stand at Kate's graveside and pretend to be the dutiful husband while all her church-going relatives looked on with contempt. Of all the chicken-shit junkie moves I'd ever pulled, skipping Kate's funeral was, hands-down, the most cowardly, and as I discovered in the days afterwards, no matter how many shots I drank, or how much coke I snorted, there was no escaping the shame I felt for not manning up and doing the right thing.

A fresh start on the West Coast might save my life, but I was under no illusion it would ever ease the burden of my guilty conscience. I'd be carrying that weight to my grave, and I accepted that. Still, some days it felt heavier than others, and that morning in New Orleans was one of them. If I hadn't turned tail and fled the French Quarter, it would have brought me to my knees.

Back at the Oz, my mood improved when I learned that

Tuesday was 'clothing exchange day'. I'd put fifteen hundred miles on my tattered Reebok high-tops since leaving New York and by the time I hit New Orleans they were coming apart at the seams, so I gladly joined the line outside the exchange office after lunch. When it was my turn at the pick-up counter, I told Brother Kevin I needed a sturdy pair of shoes before I could get back on the road to California. 'Come on in and see if you can find a pair that fits you,' he said, and led me to the rear of the storeroom, where the shelves were stocked with at least a hundred pairs of dusty shoes, most of which looked like they'd been scavenged from the closets of dead husbands by pious Catholic widows. The soles of the faithful departed, on display and up for grabs.

There were enough wing-tip brogans to outfit a platoon of FBI field agents, and scattered among their stolid ranks were all sorts of shoes not likely to be claimed by even the least discriminating of derelicts. Flimsy suede moccasins, white duck boating shoes, sporty two-toned saddle shoes, and – for that exceptional tramp with a touch of *savoir faire* – even a shiny black pair of patent leather ballroom shoes. Foxtrot, anyone? Fortunately, tucked in among all these ludicrous cast-offs, I found a thick-soled pair of work boots that looked like they'd never been worn. When I tried them on, they felt about a half-size too small, but I laced them up anyway. I figured they might pinch for a while and give me blisters till I broke them in, but so what? At least they wouldn't look ridiculous on my feet. If I had to put up with a little discomfort to avoid crossing the country looking like a clown, so be it. I was willing to pay the price. Cervantes said knowledge of yourself will preserve you from vanity. Clearly, I still had a lot to learn – and down the road, those boots would teach me some painful lessons.

That night at supper I met Arne Hill, a guy about my age who said he was planning to hop a freight train west in the morning. As soon as I heard that, I asked if he'd let me tag along. 'I've never hopped a freight,' I admitted. 'But I've been dying to try it since I was a teenager. Did you ever read *On the Road*?'

'Ah, a fellow Kerouac fan,' Arne grinned. 'Not many of us left these days, sad to say.'

'You're right about that,' I agreed. 'Thumbing down here from New York, I didn't catch one ride with anybody who'd ever heard of him, much less read his books.'

'I believe it. But out in Denver, where I'm from, he's a little more well known. I guess because Neal Cassady was one of our own. When I was in high school, sneaking into dive bars on Colfax Avenue, you could still find old-timers who remembered drinking with Neal in the forties. My old man was one of them. He's the one who turned me on to *On the Road*. He said if I wanted to know what Denver was like during his misspent youth that was the book to check out.'

'Well, if you don't mind breaking in a rookie, I'm down for a train ride. What do you say?'

'Sure, why not? Where you heading?'

'San Francisco.'

'That means we'll have to split up at El Paso, but you should have the hang of it by then,' Arne said.

I woke up the next morning raring to hit the rails, but the hard rain beating against the dormitory windows put a damper on our plans. Arne said the nearest railyard was across the river in the town of Avondale, about fifteen miles outside the city, and he wasn't up for hitchhiking that far in the pouring rain. Which was a letdown, but I could see his point, so I resigned myself to another night in New Orleans and spent the rest of the day hanging out at the public library, sheltering from the weather between mealtimes at the Oz.

Maybe it was the rain that put me in an Irish mood, I don't know, but I wound up pulling a copy of *Dubliners* from the stacks and rereading James Joyce's familiar stories to pass the time. When I came to 'Grace', a sentence I'd never paid much attention to in the past suddenly jumped out at me: 'His line of life had not been the shortest distance between two points and for short periods he had been driven to live by his wits.' That was me in a nutshell, no doubt about it. Except in my case what Joyce called 'short periods' were threatening to add up to a lifetime sentence. A gloomy possibility I'd rather not have thought about, but it was that kind of day.

On Thursday morning the weather cooperated, and Arne and I caught the free ferry across the Mississippi to Algiers, the town where 'Old Bull Lee' – Kerouac's pal William Burroughs – had lived in the forties. We both agreed it would be fun to go hunt down Burrough's old house, but a side trip wasn't on the cards. We had a train to catch.

Thumbing from Algiers to Avondale took us all morning. We managed to catch a few short-hop rides, but for the most part we covered the fifteen miles on foot and we were both exhausted by the time we reached the train yard. When I'd left the Oz that morning, my new work boots were still damp from Wednesday's rainstorm and as they dried out on our hike from Algiers they got tighter by the mile, cramping my toes and chafing both my heels raw. Arne's beat-up loafers hadn't treated his feet any better and we were a sorry sight as we hobbled through the poor black shantytown that bordered the railroad tracks.

At the last shack before the tracks a white-haired black man was sitting on the front steps. To my surprise he gave us a friendly wave and invited us to fill our water bottles at the hand-pump in his yard. 'Gonna hop you a train, fellas?' he asked. We admitted we were, and he said he'd figured as much because the only white people who ever ventured into that part of town on foot were rail tramps. The old boy said he'd hopped a lot of trains himself in his younger days. He warned us to keep a sharp eye out for the white Suburban the local yard bulls drove while patrolling the tracks. 'I seen too many tramps hauled away in that Suburban already, so watch yourselves, boys. The bulls round here are all hard-ass crackers and they won't cut you any slack.'

Arne asked him where he'd recommend we lay low while we waited for a train and he pointed us toward an old cemetery across the road from the tracks. He said the best place to stay out of sight was under the weeping willow trees that bordered the edge of the graveyard, so we thanked him for the advice and headed straight to the cemetery to begin our vigil. And for the next two hours there we sat, hidden from sight beneath an umbrella of willow branches, waiting impatiently for a west-bound train to come through the yard.

While we waited, the white Suburban cruised past our hidey-hole three or four times, but thanks to the old man's tip the bulls never spotted us, and luckily when a locomotive came slowly rumbling into the yard from the east the Suburban was nowhere in sight. We grabbed our packs and made a lame-footed dash across the tracks to the far side of the yard before the locomotive passed, and when Arne spotted an open boxcar coming down the line he ran alongside the train, threw his pack through the open doorway and grabbed a handrail to swing himself aboard. I was running right behind him and, as soon as I threw my pack aboard, Arne grabbed my wrist and yanked me up into the car.

What a rush! I caught my breath and realised how close I had come to losing my footing on the trackbed gravel and stumbling beneath the killer wheels. Who knew that hopping a freight train on the fly would be even hairier than riding the Cyclone at Coney Island? Still, I had pulled it off on my first try and I was so elated I'd have whooped for joy if I hadn't been worried about attracting unwanted attention. Until we cleared the yard the railroad bulls were still a threat, so I held my tongue and saved my celebration for further down the line – little suspecting that we'd boarded a train to nowhere.

Minutes later, to our dismay, the train squealed to a halt halfway through the switching yard and then started backing up onto a siding. Arne leaned out of the boxcar for a quick peek and immediately started swearing under his breath.

'We're screwed,' he reported. 'The fucking brakeman's uncoupling the whole line of cars. We better clear out before he spots us.' Which was deflating news, but only a foretaste of the way the rest of our day would unfold.

We snuck back to our hidey-hole without being seen, and shortly after we settled in for another wait the sky grew darker and a steady drizzle began to fall. And it kept on raining throughout the long afternoon while we sat around smoking the last of Arne's cigarettes and waiting in vain for another westbound train. By four o'clock, Arne's patience had reached its limits. 'Fuck it,' he said. 'I'm heading back to town. You with me? If we hustle, we might make it in time for supper at the Oz.'

'Suits me,' I said. 'I'd sooner spend the night at the Oz than in a boneyard.'

We'd stayed dry beneath the willow tree all afternoon, but by the time we hiked back to the highway our clothes were completely waterlogged. I'm sure our sopping appearance didn't help our odds of catching a ride, and as we trudged along the shoulder of the Westbank Expressway cursing every driver that splashed past without stopping it began to seem likely our next meal at the Oz would be breakfast, not supper. Two short rides were all we could catch. The rest of the way we hoofed it, through the puddles and the darkness and the steadily increasing protests from our blistered feet. It took us nearly three hours to reach the Morial Bridge. Arne's feet were so sore by then he couldn't walk without leaning heavily on me for support. I'm surprised I could shoulder the extra weight. My feet were as torn up as Arne's, and I had to stop every quarter-mile or so and prop him against a light pole while I caught a breather.

The Morial Bridge was off-limits to pedestrians, so when we reached it we had no choice but to wait for a ride, no matter how long it took. Twenty minutes later, as we stood forlornly keeping vigil beside the approach ramp, a middle-aged redneck wearing a Marine Corps ball cap came weaving unsteadily toward us, obviously drunk, and offered us two tokens for the cross-river bus if we'd swear out loud that we hated 'niggers'.

Racist dickhead! I thought, but when Arne crossed his fingers behind his back and played along with the guy, I did the same.

'Now I know how Judas felt,' I said to Arne, after the redneck walked off into the night.

'Hey, I didn't like dealing with that scumbag either, but sometimes you've got to go along to get along,' Arne said. 'We've already missed curfew at the Oz. The Brothers lock the doors at seven. But we've still got a shot at the Gospel Mission, if we can get there before ten.'

We caught the next downtown bus to Basin Street and made it to the Gospel Mission with an hour to spare. Once again, my hitchhiking ticket from Florida came in handy as ID and the clerk booked me in for the night. But he cautioned me that I wouldn't be admitted again without a health department card that certified I'd been tested for TB, and he advised me to get tested in the morning.

Arne wasn't as lucky. His name was already in the Gospel Mission's ledger from a previous stay and he'd never bothered to get a TB card in the interim, so the clerk refused to book him a bed. I asked him what he was going to do. He said he'd just have to head back to the Oz. 'If I pound on the doors long enough, maybe one of the Brothers will take pity on me.'

And that's exactly what happened, as Arne happily informed me the next morning when I turned up at the Oz for breakfast. The Brothers had not only taken him in after curfew, they'd bandaged his mangled feet, issued him a pair of crutches and even promised to buy him a bus ticket home to Denver as soon as his feet were healed. Meanwhile, he was getting the royal treatment – the Brothers were letting him loll around the dormitory all day instead of putting him out into the streets with the rest of the overnighters. I envied him that more than the bus ticket. I was still so beat from our trip to Avondale I'd have gladly spent the day in bed. Instead, I had to settle for the grass in Lafayette Square.

After lunch, I went to see the nurse at the Oz's health clinic. She clucked sympathetically as she disinfected and bandaged my bloody heels, then gave me a fresh pair of socks and advised me to stay off my feet for a couple of days. 'I'll see what I can do,' I said with a smile, but I knew that wasn't going to happen. I was down to the last night of my vouchered stay at the Oz. Tomorrow morning, come rain or shine, I'd be back out on the highway – hobbling west toward whatever the road had in store for me next.

CHAPTER 6

When I limped out of the Oz on Saturday morning, cold rain was drizzling from a Gulf Coast sky as darkly clouded as my mood – and I felt every bit as miserable as the weather. The Ibuprofen tabs I'd downed with my breakfast hadn't yet kicked in, and my blistered feet were so sore all I could manage were baby steps as I hobbled through the empty streets of the Warehouse District, heading for the interstate. The nearest on-ramp was behind the Superdome, only a mile down Poydras Street from the Ozanam Inn, but at my painfully slow pace it took me nearly an hour to cover the distance. I was wincing the entire way. Of course, the irony of my situation did not escape me. After all, hadn't I fled New York to avoid being crippled by Bobby Bats? And yet here I was, crippled just the same. I couldn't help wondering if there'd ever come a day when I'd get far enough down the road to escape my own stupidity.

The stretch of I-10 behind the Superdome was elevated highway, with a narrow on-ramp that made it a tough spot to thumb a ride. I wagged my thumb in vain for hours, and as I watched car after car pass me by I remembered the old story about Diogenes begging alms from a marble statue. When a curious passer-by questioned his odd behaviour, Diogenes explained that he was 'practising'. 'Practising what?' the stranger asked. To which Diogenes replied, 'Being ignored.'

By noontime, I was so sick of being ignored I decided to switch over to the eastbound ramp, just to see if I could change my luck. I wasn't thrilled about doubling back in the wrong direction, but I figured the truck stop in Slidell was bound to be a better place to catch a ride than the luckless spot I'd been stuck in all morning. It certainly couldn't be any worse. My change in tactics paid off minutes later when my losing streak was ended by a mud-splashed Ford pick-up with Louisiana plates.

As soon as I climbed into the cab and got a look at the beefy guy behind the wheel I thought I'd been time-warped back to the fifties. The double-chinned driver looked so much like the old kiddie TV host Andy Devine I wouldn't have been the least bit surprised if the first words out of his mouth had been, 'Plunk your magic twanger, Froggy!' I took this as a good omen. *Andy's Gang* had been one of my favourite Saturday morning shows when I was in grade school. To me, the best part of the show was when Devine would pronounce that five-word command and suddenly, in a puff of smoke, Froggy the Gremlin would appear, croaking his familiar catchphrase: 'Hi yah, kids! Hi yah! Hi yah!' Whereupon, as always, Froggy would immediately start cracking wise and causing trouble. Naturally, being six or seven at the time, I found Froggy's knack for insti-gating mischief appealing. What kid that age wouldn't? But, even more than his mischievous nature, it was Froggy's power to teleport himself from place to place that impressed me most. Imagine it, plunking your magic twanger and popping up anywhere you felt like going! How cool would that be? A lot cooler than trying to hitchhike across the country without a penny in your pockets, that much I knew for certain. *Sans* magic twanger, the best I could hope for was a long-distance ride that would keep me off my feet for the rest of the day. When we got to the Slidell exit and I saw the westbound entrance ramp already crowded with a half-dozen hitchhikers waiting for rides, I began to doubt whether Andy Devine's doppelganger was really the lucky charm I'd imagined.

Rather than join the queue on the ramp as the seventh man in line, I decided to station myself near the fuel island in the truck stop parking lot, where I'd have a shot at intercepting a westbound driver at the pumps before he got back on the interstate. It seemed like the easiest way to jump the line at the ramp. All I needed now was to make up a sign.

Scrounging a scrap of cardboard from the dumpster behind the coffee shop was the easy part. Coming up with a way to letter it took more ingenuity. Too bad I hadn't asked Kalvin to hand over his stolen Magic Marker before he left for Winsboro. But I'd missed my chance, and now I was forced to improvise. Channelling my inner kindergartener, I decided to go with finger painting. I squatted beside one of the truck stop's ornamental boxwoods, dipped my forefinger in the wet dirt beneath it and began printing out the words 'WEST COAST' on the cardboard in strokes of dark mud. *The moving finger writes, and having writ, moves on.* Isn't that what it says in the *Rubáiyát*? I hoped to hell Omar Khayyám was right about that. After five days in New Orleans, I was overdue to get a move on.

Luckily the morning's rain clouds had blown over, or my mud-lettered sign wouldn't have held up for long. But even though the weather stayed dry and the sign remained legible, hours passed before it did me any good. It was late afternoon when my sign finally caught the eye of a bearded guy in a shiny silver Audi, who pulled up beside me and asked if I felt like joining him in the restaurant for a cup of coffee so he could 'run an idea' by me.

What's this guy up to? I wondered, a little leery. Still, I figured it was worth a cup of coffee to hear him out, so I said sure, and he told me to wait by the entrance while he parked his car. When he got back, he shook my hand with a powerful grip and we swapped names before stepping inside the coffee shop. Gino Cardello looked to be about my age, but he stood two inches taller than me and had the build of a middle linebacker. His bulging forearms reminded me of Popeye the Sailor, and his close-cropped beard was as black as Bluto's. However, there was nothing comical about the confident way he carried himself, or the probing gaze with which he sized me up when we settled into a booth at the back of the restaurant.

'So, where you from, Pete?' he asked, after the waitress had poured our coffee. When I told him New York, he asked what part, and as soon as I said Brooklyn he grinned and told me he'd been stationed at Fort Hamilton for a while when he was in the service.

'I think the neighbourhood was called Bay Ridge,' he said. 'Anywhere close to where you come from?'

Once again, the road had taken me by surprise. A Bay Ridge connection? In Slidell, Louisiana? What were the odds?

'Can't get any closer,' I grinned back. 'I was born in Victory Memorial Hospital, right behind the base. Fort Hamilton's where

I took my draft physical, back in '67. Small world, right? When were you stationed in Brooklyn?'

'Must have been 1970,' he said. 'After I got back from Nam, I spent six months in Brooklyn, doing recruitment for the Corps, and I'll tell you what – I thought the French Quarter had a lot of bars until I got to Bay Ridge. Man, did I have some wild times in your neighbourhood!'

'You and me both,' I smiled, flashing back to the night I'd spent in Elena's bed on my farewell visit to Bay Ridge. Had it really been only two weeks since she'd bum-rushed me out of her apartment after our Super Bowl hook-up? So much had happened since then, it already felt like ancient history.

'Anyway, here's the deal,' Gino said, getting down to business. 'I'm moving out to Tacoma, Washington, to open a foreign car repair shop and I need someone to drive my other car out West with me. Otherwise I'll have to lay out big bucks to ship it to the coast by truck.'

'Can't you just rent a trailer and tow the extra car behind your Audi?' I asked.

'Yeah, if I was a dumbass and didn't care about fucking up the Audi's transmission by towing that much weight for two thousand miles, sure I could,' he replied, in that condescending tone mechanics everywhere employ when explaining the obvious to those of us less mechanically inclined. 'Besides,' he said, 'I've got my shop equipment in a storage unit I leased in Tucson. Once I get there, I'll have to rent a U-Haul box truck for all my gear. Then I'll be towing the Audi behind the truck the rest of the way to Washington. So, either someone drives my Fiat and follows me out there, or I'll have to ship it by truck. Those are my only options. Can you drive stick?'

'Sure,' I said. 'No problem.'

'Good, because the Fiat's a Roadster turbo, with five on the floor. How's your driving record?'

'Clean,' I said. 'Except, here's the thing, Gino . . . I lost my wallet last week back in North Carolina, so I don't have my licence. But if we stick to the speed limit, I shouldn't have to show my licence to any cops, right? What do you think? I'm game if you are.'

Gino frowned and rubbed his beard as he considered this new wrinkle. I was afraid I had queered the deal. But to my relief, after a moment's pause, he nodded and said, 'Okay, what the fuck, let's do it.' I can't say for sure it was the Bay Ridge connection that tipped the scales in my favour, though I'd wager it didn't hurt. In any case, I could hardly believe my luck. *Plunk your magic twanger, Froggy!* In no time at all now, I'd be popping up on the West Coast – not in a puff of smoke, but a Fiat Roadster! I was so psyched, if it had been up to me we would have hit the road immediately. But Gino said he still had some packing left to do at his parents' place in Slidell, where he'd been crashing temporarily while he organised his move to Tacoma, so I throttled back my enthusiasm and resigned myself to spending one more night on the wrong side of Lake Pontchartrain.

Gino's parents lived in a modest ranch-style house on a cul-de-sac in a sixties-era development on the outskirts of Slidell. When we got there, Gino said he was sorry, but I'd have to wait outside in the car. It was suppertime, and he said he wouldn't feel right turning up at the dinner table with a stranger he'd just picked up in a truck stop. I could see his point and told him not to sweat it.

'Sit tight. I'll bring you out a sandwich after we're done eating,' he promised, and true to his word he came back out forty-five minutes later with a roast beef sandwich and a can of RC Cola. He also brought out a pillow and a blanket, so I was comfortably set for the night. I thanked him for the room service and told him to get on back inside to his folks.

'Okay, then, I'll leave you to it,' Gino said. 'Get some rest. I'll see you in the morning.'

There was plenty of room to curl up in the back seat of the Audi, and the silence that settled over the neighbourhood once the stars came out was a big improvement over the nightly racket in the dorm at the Ozanam Inn, so when I finally nodded off it was the best night's sleep I'd enjoyed in more than a week, and I was well-rested and ready to go when Gino came out in the morning to check on me.

Gino was carrying two mugs of black coffee with him when he arrived. 'Here, I brought you an eye-opener,' he said, handing me one of the steaming mugs. 'Mom says to invite you in for breakfast, but let's hang outside here for a while. I need a cigarette first.' He fired up an unfiltered Camel, then passed me the pack.

'Can't smoke in the house, I take it?' I said.

'No way,' Gino said. 'My pop's got emphysema. He's always after me to quit. Says if I don't wise up I'm going to end up sucking oxygen from a tank just like him.'

'Was he a heavy smoker before he got sick?' I asked, thinking of my parents. Both of them Raleigh smokers. Two packs a day each, for as long as I could remember.

'Nope, that's the bitch of it,' Gino said. 'My old man never smoked a cigarette in his life. But he played jazz clarinet in the Quarter for more than thirty years, and I guess all the second-hand smoke in the clubs finally got to him. It's a damned shame. Pete Fountain called Pop one of the best clarinetists in New

Orleans. Now his lungs are so shot he can't blow three notes without getting winded.'

'Jesus, that sucks,' I said. 'What a lousy break.'

'Yeah, it sucks all right. Even though he never complains, I can tell it's killing him that his playing days are over. Once in a while he'll take his clarinet out and finger the keys while he's listening to one of his Sidney Bechet records, but he never puts the mouthpiece to his lips any more, and that's a fucking sad thing to see.'

'If your father's so sick, aren't you worried about moving all the way to Tacoma?' I asked, without thinking. And immediately regretted it. Who the hell was I to ask such a question? The last time I'd visited my parents, they were still smoking Raleighs. How many years had that brand been off the market now?

'Sure, of course I am,' Gino frowned. 'I offered to stick around, but my parents say there's no need. I guess if Pop takes a turn for the worse I can always fly back to New Orleans quick enough. At least, that's what I tell myself. Anyway, come on, we'd better get inside before Mom burns the bacon.'

If you've ever seen an oversized cowbird chick in a nest full of fledgling sparrows, you'll have some idea how incongruous Gino looked when we joined his parents at the breakfast table. They were both so tiny it was hard to believe they'd spawned such a hulking son. Still, there was no mistaking Gino's paternity. Take away the nasal cannula that snaked down from his nostrils to the portable oxygen tank parked beside his chair and Gino's father's face was as Italian as a jug of Chianti — even Gino's wiry beard couldn't hide the family resemblance.

I'd been unsure what kind of reception I'd receive as an unexpected guest at their table. It turned out I needn't have worried. They treated me as if I were an old friend of Gino's, and once I got used to the novelty of hearing two pure-bred Italians speaking with Southern drawls I soon relaxed and enjoyed their company as much as the heaping portions of scrambled eggs and bacon Gino's mom dished up.

After breakfast, Gino and I tag-teamed the dishwashing, while his parents got dressed for Sunday Mass. They invited us to join them at church, but Gino begged off, claiming he still had a lot of last-minute stuff to take care of before hitting the road – and the first thing on his list was to take me out for a test drive in his Fiat to let me get a feel for how it handled.

The Fiat was parked beneath a tree in the side yard. When we pulled off the protective tarp, it was such a beautiful machine I immediately had second thoughts about driving it cross-country. It was a Fiat 2000 Spider Turbo convertible, vintage 1981, without a single blemish visible anywhere on its cherry-red paintwork. Driving such a pristine car all the way to Tacoma suddenly seemed like a daunting challenge. Nonetheless, I gamely played along and took the wheel as Gino put me through the paces on the local backroads. It took me a few bucking false starts to get used to the Fiat's tight clutch, but by the third stop-and-go I was shifting smoothly and, as far as I could tell, Gino was satisfied with my performance.

Everything seemed fine when Gino had me pull into a gas station to fill the Fiat's tank for the road. However, by the time we got back to his parents' house he'd had a change of heart. To my surprise, he announced he'd decided to ship the Fiat out to Tacoma by truck after all. He swore his decision had nothing to do with my driving skills. I wasn't so sure about that. But I took him at his word when he said it was only my lack of a driver's licence that had him worried.

'God forbid, some asshole gets you into a wreck, how am I going to explain it to my insurance company? They'll shit-can any claim I put in once they see there was an unlicenced driver at the wheel. Sorry, man, I don't think that's a risk I want to take. But don't get pissed. You can still ride along with me in the Audi and help spell me at the wheel. Okay?'

'Better than okay,' I admitted. 'Tell you the truth, soon as I saw there wasn't a scratch on it I started sweating the whole deal myself. I think shipping it by truck is the smart play, Gino. Go for it.'

'Yeah, that's what I think, too. Except now we'll have to wait another day to hit the road. I'll need to do some scrambling in the morning and find a trucking outfit to come pick the car up. My parents have enough to deal with already. I'm not dumping another problem in their laps on my way out the door.'

'I hear you,' I said. 'Makes no difference to me what time we leave. I'm just happy to have a ride.'

It was mid-morning on Monday by the time we finally made our getaway – and not a moment too soon, either. I doubt I could have survived one more gorge-fest at Mama Cardello's table. The woman's favourite Italian imperative verb seemed to be: *Mangia!* And, bless her heart, she just wouldn't take no for an answer. I was feeling fat and happy when we hit the road, but Gino was in a grumpy mood and hardly spoke a word all the way to Baton Rouge. Thanks to my snoring, he'd been up half the night, and every time I saw him yawning at the wheel I was sorry I'd accepted his offer to bunk on the floor of his bedroom instead of sleeping in the Audi.

Not wanting to poke the bear, I kept silent and just stared out the window at the roadside advertising. Judging by the signs, the economy of southern Louisiana seemed to be driven by two main engines – shops selling guns and ammo, and sea-food shacks offering boiled crawfish and baby-alligator fricassee. Which made sense, I supposed. After a hard day's hunting on the bayou, spraying swamp critters with lead, nothing says *laissez les bon temps rouler* like a heaping plate of mud-bugs and gator, *n'est-ce pas?*

After a coffee stop in Lafayette, we pushed on toward Lake Charles, and as the caffeine kicked in Gino livened up and broke his long silence by asking me a question I'd been asking myself for longer than I cared to admit:

'No offence, Pete, but what the fuck happened to you?'

'How do you mean?' I asked, surprised more by the blunt way he'd put it than the question itself. Then again, what did I expect from a graduate of Parris Island? Conversational politesse? Tell it to the Marines!

'Come on, get real,' he snorted. 'You know exactly what I mean. You tell me you went to Dartmouth, and talking to you I can believe it. What I can't figure out is how a guy with an Ivy League degree ends up out on the street, living like a bum. Tell me to fuck off if it's none of my business. I'm not trying to bust your balls here. I'm just curious, that's all. How did it happen?'

'Ever make it to the '64 World's Fair in New York, Gino?' I asked.

'The World's Fair? Yeah, I stood in line two hours for a Belgian waffle. So what?' he replied. 'The fuck's that got to do with anything?'

'Remember the slogan at the DuPont Pavilion – *Better Living through Chemistry*. There's your answer, Gino. The secret of my success. Booze and cocaine. I couldn't have done it without them,' I said, with a half-assed grin. 'Even with an Ivy League degree.'

'Well then, I don't care how smart you are, you're still a moron,' Gino scowled. 'You make like it's a joke, but what's so goddamned funny about pissing your life down the drain? Or pissing on everyone that's close to you while you're at it? Because that's what junkies always do, isn't it? Piss on everything and pretend it's just for laughs!'

'Jesus, Gino, this is you not busting my balls?' I objected. His questions were a painful reminder of how shabbily I'd treated Susan and Danny and Bobby Bats. Everything Gino had just said was true – and I'd be lying if I said it didn't sting.

'Sorry, man,' Gino said, though he didn't sound sorry in the least. 'I've got no sympathy for junkies. I made the mistake of marrying one.'

That explains it, I thought. The sudden note of bitterness in his voice had caught me off guard. But as Gino's story spilled out over the next fifty miles, I realised he had every right to be bitter.

He'd been working as a mechanic at a Mercedes dealership in Albuquerque when he met his future wife, a barmaid named Cindy who had just moved to town from Minnesota and landed a job on the day shift at the roadhouse where Gino did his after-work drinking. Cindy was ten years younger than Gino, so he'd been hesitant at first to ask her out, but they were soon making wedding plans. After they tied the knot, they started saving every dollar they could spare for a down-payment on a house, so when a bartending slot on the night shift at the road-house came open, Cindy had jumped at the chance to change shifts and double her earnings. That's when the trouble started, according to Gino.

'The night crowd was full of cokeheads, and the stupid bitch couldn't resist temptation,' Gino said. 'She started using, but I didn't notice at first. With the two of us working opposite shifts, it wasn't hard for her to hide what she was up to, and she managed to keep me in the dark for months. She was already hooked by the time I wised up, and when I confronted her and started ripping her ass for being such a dumb fuck she burst into tears and told me she'd just found out she was pregnant. Can you believe that shit? If she hadn't been carrying our baby, I think I'd have strangled the bitch.'

After Gino's tirade, Cindy had vowed to clean up her act for the baby's sake, but like most junkies' promises it lasted no longer than her next opportunity to score. Claiming they needed money now more than ever, Cindy had insisted on keeping her job at the bar, and Gino had reluctantly agreed. 'More fool me,' Gino said. Having been caught once, Cindy took greater pains to keep her coke habit hidden from him this time around, and it wasn't until a few weeks before her due date that she finally slipped up and got sloppy, walking into their apartment one night after her shift with pupils like saucers and a telltale white crust around her nostrils. It was her bad luck that Gino, usually asleep when she got home, had gotten up only minutes before to use the bathroom. Even half-asleep, he couldn't miss the evidence, and he went batshit.

'I gave the bitch an ultimatum,' Gino said. 'Either she quit her job immediately and kicked her coke habit for good, or I was filing for divorce and sole custody of the baby. She knew I meant it, too. And no judge was going to side with a druggie parent in a custody case, so she stayed at home and kicked cold turkey. But by then the damage was already done. Two weeks later, she gave birth to our son, Dominic, and he was born with a deformed skull. The doctors said he had a condition called craniosynostosis.'

'Craniosynostosis? What's that?' I asked.

'It's when the gaps between the skull bones in a baby's head merge prematurely,' Gino explained. 'The gaps are called sutures, and they're not supposed to close up until your brain has stopped growing. If the fibres between sutures turn to bone before the brain is done expanding, you get too much pressure on the brain and all kinds of complications.'

'God, that's terrible. Is it treatable?' I asked.

'It *would* have been,' Gino said bitterly. 'If Dominic had lived that long.'

'Christ, Gino, what happened?'

'Two days after his christening, his worthless cunt mother killed him, that's what happened. I was working at the shop when I got the call from a nurse at the hospital telling me to get over there right away, that my son was in critical condition with swelling of the brain. I jumped in my car and blew every red light on the way, but I was still too late. Dominic was gone. When I showed up, Cindy was already being questioned by the cops. The ER doc had called them in. He'd seen shaken-baby syndrome before and suspected Dom had been throttled. Of course, Cindy denied doing anything wrong, but I knew how short-tempered she'd gotten after kicking her coke habit and I had no doubt the doctor was right. And, sure as shit, when the pathology report came in, it confirmed his suspicion.'

'I'm so sorry, Gino,' I said. 'Did they arrest Cindy?'

'Yeah, the county DA brought manslaughter charges against her. Which was a fucking joke. She should have been charged with murder. The bitch knew Dom's condition made him extra vulnerable to brain injury. He was scheduled to have corrective surgery at the end of the month, but until then the doctors had warned us to be especially gentle with him, so she knew better.

She just didn't give a fuck. No matter how much she cried about it afterward. At her trial, her defence attorney tried pleading post-partum depression. The jury didn't buy that bullshit. They convicted her of first-degree manslaughter, and the judge sentenced her to five years in prison. She got off easy, you ask me. But there was nothing I could do about it. Except file for divorce and hope sooner or later some prison dyke gives her the punishment she deserves. You understand now why I've got no sympathy for junkies?'

'Sorry, Gino, I had no idea. But I get it, believe me.'

'Then do yourself a favour and start owning your fuck-ups instead of playing them for laughs. I'm just sayin'.'

'Point taken,' I replied, duly chastened. What else *could* I say? He was right. Still, that didn't make his criticism any easier to swallow. I hoped this wasn't a foretaste of what he had in store for me in the miles ahead. If so, it was going to be a longer trip than I'd bargained for. Nevertheless, Gino's horror story gave me plenty to think about and, as we pushed on toward the Texas border, I couldn't help reflecting that I'd treated those I loved with no more care than Cindy had treated little Dominic.

Like Gino said, that's what junkies do. When you're an addict, you live in the moment, because that's where the rush is. You never think about the collateral damage until it's already done. Of course you're appalled afterward, but that only makes you hate your-self for being such a selfish prick. Eventually, you begin to doubt you're even capable of loving anyone. Or worthy of being loved in return. Which is too depressing to contemplate, so you turn around and get high again and the regrets keep piling up.

I could understand Gino hating Cindy for what she'd done, but I doubt he hated her any more than she hated herself. Like me, she probably thought prison was where she belonged. That's how I felt when I got arrested and sent to Rikers Island a few months after Kate's death. Like I deserved to be punished. Not for selling cocaine, but for betraying Kate and my family. Though it was too late to redeem myself with Kate, I'd written to my parents from prison and begged their forgiveness, promising I'd come see them after my release. But it was too little, too late. My parents' hearts had hardened just like Jack's, and my father brushed me off with a terse reply. He said he hoped for my sake I'd get my life together one day, but he couldn't forgive me for treating my mom – the woman he loved – with so much disrespect.

What did you expect? I thought. *You made yourself a stranger, and now you're being treated like one.* Even so, I took the news hard. If I'd been locked away in solitary confinement instead of a cellblock, I couldn't possibly have felt any lonelier than I did the night my father's letter arrived. I hoped for Cindy's sake her parents hadn't disowned her, too, because though Gino might think she'd gotten off easy I knew better. Like me, she'd be paying for her mistakes long after her sentence was up.

It was mid-afternoon when we reached the Sabine River and crossed over into the Gulf Coast oil town of Beaumont, Texas, where the brown air was acrid with the stench from the refineries' cracking plants. If I had closed my eyes, I would have thought we'd just taken Exit 13 off the Jersey Turnpike – the only other place I'd ever been to that smelled as bad was Elizabeth, New Jersey, another refinery town no one drives through with their windows down. We'd been travelling for nearly six hours, but Gino showed no signs of tiring and he pushed on through to Houston, where we got mired in the start of the evening rush hour and slowed to a crawl as we worked our way past a three-car pile-up in the eastbound lanes.

The traffic reporters from the local radio stations were out in full force above the wreck, their helicopters circling like buzzards over roadkill, and whenever a copter came into view Gino would give it the finger. I assumed his contempt for helicopters stemmed from his time in Vietnam. Over the weekend, he'd briefly mentioned that he'd spent his tour as a helicopter mechanic. But he hadn't said more than that and, despite being curious, I hadn't pressed him for more details. Most Vietnam vets I'd known were similarly reticent about their wartime experiences, rarely sharing their stories with people who hadn't been to war themselves. I was one of those people – part of the fortunate majority who'd spent the war years safely shielded from service by a college deferment – so I knew better than to pry. Nevertheless, it wasn't hard to imagine why Gino was still flipping the finger at helicopters so many years later. As I sat there silently beside him, refraining from comment, I pictured a helicopter all shot to shit, returning to base with casualties after taking fire from Viet Cong machine guns. Then I pictured a nineteen-year-old mechanic tasked with patching it up – and having to hose out the blood of his fellow Marines before repairs could even be started. If I'd been through what Gino had, I'm sure I'd have given those traffic copters the finger myself.

Two hundred miles later, we rolled into San Antonio, and Gino stopped for gas and more coffee at a Flying J truck stop. I got out to stretch my legs and to use the restroom. On my way back outside, I paused for a moment to check out the 'You Are Here' road map posted in the restaurant's lobby and was disheartened to see that we were still five hundred miles from El Paso and the New Mexico border. Fucking Texas was endless.

We'd been travelling for nearly ten hours by that point and I figured Gino must be getting worn out. But when I offered to take over the driving for a while he wasn't ready to give up the wheel yet. He told me to go ahead and sleep for a few hours, he'd wake me when he felt like taking a break. We were halfway to El Paso when he finally pulled over and shook my shoulder. After we'd swapped places, Gino warned me to keep a sharp eye out for mule deer because the Diablo Mountains up ahead were full of them. He said he'd almost clipped one the last time he'd crossed Texas. I told him not to worry. I was well rested after my four-hour nap and promised I'd keep a close watch for deer on the road. Minutes later, he was snoring softly, slumped into the pillow he'd grabbed from the back seat and propped between his head and the window.

As soon as I was sure Gino had nodded off, I switched off the radio and took a break from the country music he'd been playing non-stop since we'd left Slidell. I could tolerate Johnny Cash and Willy Nelson in small doses, but everyone else with a Nashville pedigree just made me wish I were deaf. When I was fourteen, just before I entered the seminary, my parents had gone through a country and western phase that completely baffled me at the time. How could two native Brooklynites fall for such cornpone music? But for months on end that's all they played on the car radio – no matter how relentlessly I mocked the songs' predictably rhymed lyrics from the back seat.

I imagine my beleaguered parents were looking forward to my departure to St Mary's, just so they could enjoy their cowboy music in peace – though that wasn't how things worked out. In my absence, my younger brothers had carried on the anti-country and western campaign till my parents finally caved in; to my surprise, when I returned home four months later for Christmas break the car radio was tuned to a much hipper station: WMCA, 'Home of the Good Guys', where DJs like Jack

Spector played the latest rock-and-roll releases. To a music-starved teenager just emerging from four months of cloistered life in the seminary, where students had no access to radios (or television, or even a daily newspaper), this was a welcome change. Before starting at St Mary's, I'd been a Beach Boys fan, but, thanks to Jack Spector, by the time my holiday visit was over I was hooked on the Beatles.

It was the week after Christmas in 1963 when Spector started spinning the Beatles' debut single, 'I Want to Hold Your Hand', and as soon as I heard it I joined the hordes of American teenagers who were rushing out to their local record stores to buy the 45. Though radios were banned in student quarters at the seminary, we had occasional access to a hand-crank record player in the classroom where Father Artie Wendel taught his music lessons, and I couldn't wait to get back to St Mary's at the holiday's end so I could introduce my classmates to the Fab Four – little suspecting that most of my friends would be returning to campus already avid Beatles' fans themselves, with copies of the selfsame 45 safely tucked between sweaters in their luggage.

We were certainly an incongruous-looking bunch of Beatlemaniacs whenever we gathered in the music classroom in our free time that winter, and I used to wonder what the boys from Liverpool would think if they could have seen us jiving around in our full-length black cassocks, singing their tunes with far more enthusiasm than we ever mustered during Father Wendel's snooze-worthy lessons in Gregorian Chant. I suspect John Lennon would have been especially tickled. After all, he was a man who would later claim that the Beatles were bigger than Jesus. What better proof could he point to than a room full of seminarians fervently singing the Fab Four's latest hit?

Neither Jesus nor John Lennon would have condoned the mean-spirited prank some of us pulled off later that semester, however, when we callously used that same Beatles song to publicly shame one of our classmates on the night of the annual Spring Carnival. The target of our cruelty was a fellow freshman – a homesick, pimple-faced Midwestern kid who was known behind his back as 'Master Bates', a nickname earned by his frequent, and embarrassingly audible, bouts of self-gratification in the attic dormitory after lights-out. In truth, there were few of us in that dormitory full of hormone-driven teenagers who weren't guilty of the same so-called mortal sin, myself included. But, unlike Master Bates, we were more scrupulous in adhering to the rule of silence. Which is why we turned against him, I imagine. Our own failures in the chastity department were already the cause of much self-loathing, and Master Bates' un-stifled moans were unwelcome proof that the flesh is weak – a painful truth we didn't appreciate being reminded of on a nightly basis.

The Spring Carnival, intended as a night for letting off steam after midterm exams, was staged in the gymnasium and featured an assortment of carny-style games on which we could squander the stack of Monopoly money each of us was issued with upon entering the gym. The Carnival was also the only event at which the students were given free rein to choose the music. Would-be DJs put their names on a sign-up sheet, and when they were called to the turntable they got to play whatever tunes they liked from their personal record collections. One of our co-conspirators in the plot against Master Bates had signed up to DJ, and when he dropped the needle on 'I Want to Hold Your Hand' he gave a nod to his accomplice, who was manning a roving spotlight up on the balcony that overhung the gym floor. The roving spotlight was meant to enhance the carnival atmosphere, but, as the Beatles sang, its beam skimmed the crowd in search of prey, and with perfect timing swooped down on the face of Master Bates, right at the start of the third verse's lyrics about touching and feeling happy.

The light's accusatory beam stayed hotly trained on the poor kid's squinting face the entire time, while the rest of us who were in on the prank snickered knowingly and watched for his reaction. He stood alone at the back of the gym, slouched against the padded wall behind the basketball hoop, with one hand dangling a can of Orange Crush, the other trying to shield his eyes. It took a moment, but when it eventually dawned on him why he'd been singled out he burst out crying and sagged a little further into the wall, before quickly pushing back off and rushing out of the gym in shame. Meanwhile, we sniggered some more as we watched him flee, too heartless in victory to realise that we should have been sobbing with shame ourselves.

Of course, we felt guilty the following weekend when his parents arrived from Ohio to collect him. He was crying then, too, and I overheard his mother trying to console him on the staircase as they hauled his baggage down from the dorm. She was telling him there was nothing to cry about. That his dropping out of St Mary's must be God's will. But how could I believe that? Surely the cruelty we'd shown the poor kid couldn't really be God's way of culling the priestly herd? Or could it? And if so, why would I want to serve such a God?

My complicity in the humiliation of our classmate was without doubt the unkindest thing I'd ever done in my short life, and the questions it raised about my fitness for the priest-hood would continue to trouble me long after my initial remorse over the Carnival incident had faded. In fact, it was still troubling me eighteen months later when I finally joined Master Bates in the ranks of the drop-outs.

It was the week before Thanksgiving, three months into my junior year, when I made the decision to leave St Mary's. Though I was firm in my resolve to drop out, I still dreaded breaking the news to the seminary's rector, Father Murphy, who was an old friend and former seminary classmate of my Uncle John's. But one night after dinner I screwed up my courage and presented myself with a timid knock at the door of his office in the priests' quarters. My downcast eyes were already brimming with tears as I entered the room, and I'm sure Father Murphy knew at a glance what was up. Drop-outs are an unfortunate fact of life for a seminary rector. Less than twenty per cent of each entering class at St Mary's would graduate and go on to the Novitiate House in Maryland, where novices spend a year in prayerful reflection before taking their vows of poverty, chastity and obedience. Still, despite his long experience, Father Murphy seemed genuinely surprised by my confession that I'd 'lost my vocation'. Mine was a defection he hadn't seen coming. Not from his friend John's promising nephew, who'd just been awarded the Rector's Prize for academic excellence and selected to serve as editor of the annual literary anthology, a post traditionally reserved exclusively for a member of the senior class.

Father Murphy tried his best to dissuade me from acting rashly, urging me to hold off on my decision until I'd had a chance to sit down with my parents to seek their advice over Christmas break, but my mind was made up and I wouldn't be swayed. The following morning I wrote home asking my mother for bus money.

I was sad to say goodbye to my seminary friends when they

gathered around the taxi cab that was about to take me out of their lives forever. And sadder still as I passed through the tall wrought-iron gates of St Mary's for the final time. But by the time the cab dropped me off at the bus station and I was dragging my heavy steamer trunk across the concourse, rushing to catch the Greyhound that would carry me back into secular life, my sadness had given way to excitement. I was sixteen years old, embarking on my first-ever solo road trip and the novelty of anonymous travel on a Greyhound was so thrilling it made me giddy. And the best part was, now that my life was my own again, I had a world of thrilling 'firsts' to look forward to, no matter where the future might take me next.

My euphoria lasted only as far as Buffalo. As soon as the bus turned onto the Thruway and started pushing downstate toward New York City, reality began to set in, and I realised I had no idea how I was going to explain my change of heart to my family. My letter home had been terse. No more than a simple plea for a bus fare, with the promise I'd explain later. Well, later was fast approaching and I still didn't know how I'd explain myself. In my exit interview with the rector, I'd offered only the vague explanation that I no longer felt called to the priesthood. Though Father Murphy had pressed me to be more specific, I had steadfastly resisted his probing questions. The answers would have been too painfully personal. I just couldn't bring myself to say them out loud.

If I'd had the courage to be candid, I would have told him about the Spring Carnival incident, and how the cruelty I'd been party to had undermined not only my faith in my worthiness to serve as a priest but my faith in God himself. When you feel that way, it's hard to envision a priestly future.

And if I'd been honest, I would have told him, too, how

much I'd grown to hate the humiliating experience of kneeling in the Confessional box every Saturday afternoon, confessing to the same sorry teenage sins of the flesh – knowing full well that my confessor was undoubtedly one of my classroom teachers, who could recognise my voice even through the so-called privacy screen, no matter how softly I mumbled. 'Were these impure deeds, or impure acts, my son?' *My son?* What a laugh! They might as well have come right out and asked me by name. I don't know why I squirmed through so many of those dreaded Saturdays before I finally got the message, but in the end I figured out what my confessors had probably long since concluded: I wasn't cut out for the celibate life.

As if those weren't reasons enough to abandon any hope for a future in the priesthood, I'd recently added another, and oddly enough it resulted from my appointment as editor of the literary annual. One of the perks of the job was a private office and, though it wasn't much more than a converted broom closet, it turned out to be harbouring unexpected treasure: a boxy old tabletop Emerson radio, with oversized Bakelite control knobs and a gut full of cathode tubes – tubes which, by some miracle, were still in working order. Suddenly, I had access to music again! And news from the outside world! I began spending most of my free time in the office, pretending to be doing editorial work, when all I was really doing was listening to the latest tunes – and wondering why I'd ever thought enrolling in a school that bans radios was a good idea.

One of the songs in heavy rotation on the rock stations in the autumn of 1965 was Bob Dylan's 'Positively 4th Street'. Every time I heard it I couldn't help taking the lyrics personally. When Dylan insisted that you can't lose your faith if you have no faith to begin with, it was like hearing the voice of my own conscience finally admitting the truth. Ergo, it was time to go back to the world.

Throughout the long night, as the Greyhound rolled steadily south toward my reunion with my parents, I tried to picture myself telling them the full truth and realised in the end I could never do it. Though my mother might have been sympathetic to my reasons for quitting, I knew my father well enough to know he'd find them flimsy, and I had no trouble anticipating how he'd dismiss each one in turn.

The cruel prank at Spring Carnival?

'Simple, quit being a dick.'

My struggles with celibacy?

'Simple, quit playing with your dick.'

My radio-inspired conviction that cloistered life was not my calling?

'Simple, quit listening to that dick Bob Dylan.'

None of which I had any desire to hear face-to-face, so when the time came I took the easy way out and kept the truth to myself. The only explanation my parents got was as vague as the one I'd given the rector. All I told them was that I'd prayed on the matter a lot in the past few months and God had let me know I didn't have a calling to the priesthood after all. Case closed. End of story.

I could tell my parents were disappointed, and I couldn't blame them. First, I'd made a life-changing decision without bothering to consult them. Which was bad enough. But then I'd compounded their justifiable confusion by offering an explanation which was hardly forthcoming. Yet what could they do? By characterising my decision to drop out of St Mary's as a purely spiritual matter, I'd effectively ducked all the awkward questions I'd have faced otherwise, which left my parents still squarely in the dark – but at what cost?

I told myself I hadn't really lied to my parents, yet by evading the truth I'd deceived them just the same, and deep down I knew it. Still, I never came clean, and the longer I lived with the lie, the easier it became to start thinking of the truth as something malleable. Without realising it at the time, I had set a fateful precedent, and in the years ahead I would become a master at massaging the truth to suit my needs whenever honesty would have proved embarrassing or inconvenient. And, as any liar soon discovers, the lies you tell others are far outnumbered by the lies you wind up telling yourself. One day you wake up and realise you no longer know what the fuck the truth even sounds like any more. But by then your future has turned into a series of car rides with strangers – strangers you can only fob off with flippant answers when they ask: 'No offence, Pete, but what the fuck happened to you?'

～◦～

Gino was still sleeping soundly when we reached the Diablo Mountains, where the first warning signs began to appear – not just for deer, but for rockslides too. *Okay, Pete, stay sharp,* I thought, and lowered the side window, letting the cool night air wash over my face. I felt wide awake and alert, but as the road climbed steadily higher I also began to feel more and more hemmed in and claustrophobic. On my left, steep, rocky slopes now divided the eastbound and westbound lanes of the highway, and I could no longer see the lights of oncoming traffic. On my right, beyond the low steel guardrail, the mountainside dropped away even more steeply, into the shadowy maw of a deep canyon.

Faced with danger on both sides, I played it safe and straddled the centre line, giving myself extra room to manoeuvre if a hazard suddenly materialised around the next bend. But my vigilance was no defence against what happened moments later, when a suicidal mule deer buck came crashing down the hillside on my left and bolted directly into the beam of the Audi's headlights. *Oh, shit!* If I had veered sharply to my right, I might have dealt the deer only a glancing blow, but my fear of the sheer drop beyond the guardrail kept my hands frozen on the wheel. Before I even had a chance to hit the brakes I struck that mulie head-on. Two sickening thumps followed in rapid succession, as first the front wheel then the back wheel rolled over the animal's thick neck.

'What the fuck?' Gino exclaimed, as his body heaved forward when I belatedly slammed on the brakes. 'Tell me you didn't just hit a mule deer,' he groaned, while I pulled to a stop beside the guardrail.

'Sorry, Gino,' I admitted guiltily. 'There was nothing I could do, I swear! The fucking thing must have had a death wish. It came barrelling off the hill and jumped right in front of me before I even saw it coming.'

'Jesus, you're unbelievable. It's not like I didn't warn you,' Gino griped, as he climbed out of the car to assess the damage. I was so amped up on adrenaline I felt like snapping back at him: *There's nothing you could have done any different if you'd been behind the wheel, you jarhead jackass!* But I held my tongue. Mad as he was, I didn't want to provoke him further and wind up being dumped by the side of the road in the middle of nowhere.

The damage appeared to be confined to the wheels on the driver's side. The front and back rims had been bent out of shape by the force of the collision. Luckily, the tyres were run-flat radials and hadn't yet deflated. Which was more than you could say for the carcass of the mule deer that lay open-eyed on the road behind us.

'What do you think, Gino? Is it still drivable?' I asked, fearing the worst. We were still at least a hundred miles east of El Paso. I had no idea how far we'd have to hike to find a phone if we needed to call for a tow truck.

'We'll soon find out,' Gino frowned.

For the next few hours, as Gino nursed the Audi through the mountains at a cautious twenty-five miles per hour, I sat listening to his muttered curses and wondering if he'd send me packing once we reached El Paso. Gino must have been considering the idea, too, because when we finally pulled into the lot of a Goodyear service centre at 7 a.m. — a half-hour earlier than the shop was scheduled to open — he told me to take a hike.

'So this is it?' I asked. 'I'm on my own?'

'I don't know,' Gino said. 'I haven't made up my mind yet. But I damned sure don't want to sit here looking at your face right now. See that taco stand down the block? Go wait for me in the parking lot. If I don't turn up by noon-time, you'll have your answer.'

At the taco stand, my grade-school Spanish lessons came in handy in a way my fifth-grade teacher, Miss Diaz, would never have anticipated, as I spent the next hour panhandling spare change from the mostly Mexican locals until I'd collected enough money for a breakfast burrito and a cup of coffee. I'm sure the sight of a *blanco* begging alms in their mother tongue was quite a novelty for everyone I accosted, and it was a novelty for me as well. Since leaving New York I'd occasionally bummed spare change from drivers I'd thumbed rides with, but until that morning in El Paso I'd never had the nerve to panhandle money out on the street. I'd always told myself I'd rather starve than suffer the humiliation of begging in public. But there was something about begging in a foreign language that made it less embarrassing than I'd expected – as though the humiliation I'd feared had somehow gotten lost in translation. Of course, dealing with naturally generous Mexicans made it that much easier. Even those who couldn't spare any change wished me '*buena suerte*' and smiled apologetically when they turned me down. *Bienaventurados los pobres de espíritu, porque de ellos es el Reino de los cielos.*

By the time Gino showed up at the taco stand, I'd been sweating it out beneath the desert sun for four hours and had just about concluded I'd been dumped. 'I was starting to think you'd written me off, Gino,' I said. 'Wouldn't have surprised me if you did, but I'm glad you didn't.'

'Believe me, I thought about it,' Gino frowned. 'But that would have been letting you off too easy. Much as you've cost me, I might as well get some work out of you. I've got a ton of shit to load out of my storage unit in Tucson and I can tell you right now who's going to be humping most of it into the U-Haul truck. If you bust your ass and earn your keep, I'll consider taking you the rest of the way to Tacoma. That's the deal. Take it or leave it.'

Naturally, I took it, and promised Gino that once we got to Tucson he wouldn't have to lift a finger. And with that settled, we hit the highway again and were soon crossing the state line into New Mexico. For once, I was glad when Gino fiddled with the radio and tuned in a country station. Mindless music was better than the brooding silence Gino had lapsed into since we'd got back on the road – a silence he sullenly maintained for the next hundred miles. But as we approached the town of Deming,

Gino spotted signs for a western wear outlet and his mood suddenly brightened. Next thing I knew, he was pulling off the highway to find the place. When we got to the warehouse-sized outlet, Gino left me outside in the sweltering parking lot while he took his time shopping for a new pair of cowboy boots. When he finally reappeared an hour later, he was all smiles as he opened the big shoebox he was carrying and showed me his new boots – a gaudy pair of hand-tooled snakeskin Tony Lamas. I whistled appreciatively and quipped that they must have set him back a few bucks. Gino admitted he'd laid out three hundred for the pair – and then couldn't resist adding, 'Which means they cost me only half as much as you did when you ran over that fucking mule deer.'

Six hundred dollars for new rims and tyres? I'd been wondering what the Goodyear bill had totalled but hadn't dared ask. Now I knew. No wonder Gino was so pissed at me. I made a show of looking sheepish, but my heart wasn't in it. I'd apologised enough already. It was hard to work up much sympathy for a guy who'd just spent three hundred dollars on custom boots, while my poor feet were still crammed into dead man's shoes from the Oz. But at least Gino's newly acquired finery had put him in a better mood, and he sounded almost civil when he proposed we grab something to eat and call it an early night.

Two exits down the interstate from the western wear outlet we found Deming's fast-food strip and pulled off the highway for an early dinner at Burger King. Then Gino drove across the street to a Best Western motel and told me to stay out of sight while he registered for a single room.

The long Texas crossing had left me beat, and I was looking forward to nodding off the minute I had a place to lie down. But when Gino came back to the car with his room key he told me to make myself scarce until after sundown. *What the fuck?* I knew Gino was planning to save money by sneaking me into his room. I just didn't expect he'd be too squeamish to try it in daylight. It pissed me off, but what could I say? His money, his rules. Which left me wandering the streets of Deming for the next three hours, until it got dark enough for the cottontail rabbits to emerge from their burrows in the sagebrush lot behind the motel.

When we left at first light, Gino was in a foul mood again. He'd had to wake me three times during the night to complain about my snoring. I couldn't wait to get to Tucson, just so I could finally do something Gino wouldn't find annoying. Fortunately, he seemed to be in as big a hurry to start the load-out as I was, and he kept the Audi cruising at seventy the entire way. An hour down the road, we crossed the Continental Divide, and I was cheered by the thought that the Pacific Coast was now only a two-day ride away.

After a quick stop for gas and coffee in Lordsburg, we pushed on across the Arizona border and into the Sonoran Desert, where the sagebrush and creosote bush were dwarfed by monumental saguaro cacti, many of them thirty to forty feet high. I knew their multiple upraised branches were called 'arms' but, seeing them in person for the first time, they seemed to me more like giant fingers, and every time we passed one with its middle digit towering above the rest, I thought of Gino and his helicopter salute – a salute I was certain would soon be aimed at me, if I didn't pull my weight once we got to Tucson.

It was late morning when we pulled up to the U-Haul depot across the street from Gino's storage unit. The temperature must have been in the low eighties already, and over the next two hours, while I loaded hand truck after hand truck with mechanic's tools and heavy boxes of household goods, it got so hot I had to strip to the waist. Meanwhile, Gino stood beside the truck's roll-out ramp barking orders like a gunnery sergeant and gleefully watching me sweat. But I kept my head down like a good little slave and didn't complain, and by the time the truck was finally loaded even Jarhead Gino was impressed.

'Under two hours, start to finish. Not bad,' he said. 'I didn't think you had it in you. Let's get the Audi on the trailer and we're out of here.'

Apparently, busting my ass on the loadout had gotten me back on Gino's good side, because on our way out of Tucson he pulled into a Dairy Queen and treated me to a jumbo root beer float. I was so thirsty after my workout I chugged the first two gulps like an idiot and immediately gave myself a brain freeze. While I sat there moaning and clutching my throbbing forehead, Gino had a good laugh at my expense. Which was fine with me. Better to be a source of amusement than a target of scorn.

As it turned out, Gino had more laughs in store a few hours later, when a construction detour in Phoenix took us off the interstate and onto the local streets. At one point, we stopped for a red light in front of a gated retirement community whose sidewalks were lined with orange trees heavily laden with what looked to be ripe fruit, and I asked Gino if he'd mind me jumping out of the truck to snatch a few oranges. He told me to go ahead and grab as many as I wanted, so I hopped out and quickly picked a bunch before the traffic light changed. When I got back in the truck, I offered one to Gino, but he said he wasn't hungry.

'You think they're ripe?' I wondered.

'Only one way to find out,' Gino said, with a sly grin that

should have tipped me off that something was fishy. But I was so pleased with my unexpected score I just blundered into his trap and peeled the rind from one of the oranges. Then I took a big juicy bite – and nearly gagged. I immediately spat it back out through the open window. Sweet Jesus, I'd never tasted anything so bitter!

Gino was laughing so hard at my puckered face I thought he'd piss himself. 'Didn't you wonder why all that fruit was hanging there unpicked? Those are ornamental orange trees, you dummy. They're just for show.'

'*Now* you tell me,' I griped. What did I know about oranges? Betty Smith said 'a tree grows in Brooklyn', but I can guarantee you she wasn't talking citrus.

'Sorry, man,' he grinned. 'I was going to warn you. Then I thought, fuck it, why spoil the show?'

Leaving Phoenix, Gino turned onto I-93, heading northwest toward Las Vegas, and my long run on Interstate 10 finally came to an end – two thousand miles down the road from Baldwin, Florida. We were travelling through high desert country now, with the silhouettes of flat-topped mesas looming purple in the distance. As I stared out the window into that empty landscape, I saw nothing but sagebrush and boulder-strewn fields – and an endless montage of roadkill jackrabbits gathering flies and ravens along the roadside. On every long uphill stretch the overburdened U-Haul truck whined in protest, and our progress was dismally slow. The truck was a gas-hog, too, and before we got halfway to Vegas, Gino started looking for someplace to refuel.

We soon spotted a sign for a trading post ten miles up the road and, as we got closer, more signs appeared, all of them touting the trading post's big attraction: ARIZONA BABY RATTLERS! I was curious to check them out – I'd been a great collector of garter snakes and milk snakes in my Long Island youth. So while Gino was filling the truck's tank, I followed the arrow signs to a teepee behind the trading post building, where the 'Baby Rattlers' Cage' was housed. I had to laugh when I saw that the rattlers were like the orange trees in Phoenix: not what I'd expected. Oh, they were rattlers all right, but none of them were snakes. Instead, the wire cage perched on cinder-blocks inside the teepee held dozens of cheap plastic baby's rattles, all dangling from strands of fishing line and rattling softly as they swayed in the draught blowing in through the open doorway. I had to admit, it was a clever ploy for luring gullible tourists to the trading post. A bait-and-switch with a sense of humour. Desert humour. Dry as the sunbaked landscape.

The sun had been down for hours by the time we approached the Nevada border and my eyes had grown accustomed to the dark – which made what happened next even more dazzling. We rounded a bend in the road and suddenly there it was, Hoover Dam, radiant in the megawatt glare of a hundred flood-lights. Even the water cascading from the spillways far below the dam's massive face was brightly lit. I was glad Gino was doing the driving so I could just sit there and gawk at the spec-tacle as we descended from the hills onto the causeway that crossed the dam.

The last time I'd seen anything so impressive was on a whirlwind trip to Niagara Falls with my family when I was in grade school. The trip was my mother's idea, but my father was the only driver in our family, and he seemed anything but enthusiastic as we all piled into his Studebaker early one Saturday morning for the five-hundred-mile trip from Long Island to Niagara. For the next twelve hours, my dad drove like a man possessed, allowing us only two five-minute pit stops along the way, and when we arrived in Niagara after dark we were treated to a twenty-minute stop at the illuminated Falls before he hustled us off to the cheapest motel he could find – a motel located next to a chemical plant, whose acrid fumes permeated the motel's rooms and no doubt explained its low-budget rates.

My brothers and I christened it 'The Stinky Motel', and we were all complaining of sore throats when we checked out at dawn the next morning and hurried back to the Falls for one last visit. In daylight, they were still awesome, though not as magical as they'd seemed under the coloured lights the night before. My father posed us all by the overlook and took a few snapshots to prove we'd been there, and then quickly herded us back into the Studebaker for the long drive home. By the time our 'family adventure' was over, we'd spent twenty-four hours on the road and less than an hour visiting Niagara Falls. But I was glad I'd gotten to see it, and I felt the same about Hoover Dam that night.

We rolled into Las Vegas – another dazzling light show – a little after eight o'clock. Gino stopped for gas and snacks at a service station on the north end of town, and I got out of the truck to use the bathroom. When I stepped inside the convenience store, I was surprised see the entire back wall lined with slot machines, all of them being pumped with quarters by travellers who looked just as road weary as Gino and me. I knew Vegas was a gambling town, but I'd never imagined the prevailing vice was so pervasive that its reach extended even into the gas stations. Gino had told me the locals referred to the town as 'Lost Wages'. Now I understood why.

We were thirty miles out of Vegas, still travelling north on I-93, when Gino's energy gave out. He'd been doing all the driving since we'd left Deming and now he was finally tired enough to risk turning the wheel over to me so he could catch a few hours of sleep. When we swapped places, Gino instructed me to just keep going straight on I-93 and to wake him when we reached the town of Ely, two hundred miles up the road. This time, he didn't warn me to watch out for deer. I guess he figured the rental truck was heavy enough to mow down any mulies that might cross our path.

Not long after Gino nodded off, snowflakes began drifting through the headlight beams, and I cursed my luck. Still, I wasn't really worried. The snow seemed to be melting as soon as it hit the roadway, and there was hardly any traffic to contend with, so I kept my foot on the gas and we lumbered on steadily through the pitch-dark night. I drove for the next three hours without incident, but thirty miles outside of Ely, as we began climbing into the Ely Springs Mountain Range, the snowfall got heavier and now it was definitely sticking to the road surface.

Soon I began to feel the truck's tyres losing traction on the mountain's switchback curves and out of caution I slowed down to twenty miles per hour and flipped on the hazard lights to warn anyone coming up from behind that we were travelling slower than the posted minimum speed. Meanwhile, Gino continued sleeping peacefully beside me, oblivious to the deteriorating road conditions, and I was reluctant to wake him. I was still confident I could make it over the pass and down into Ely on my own, but my confidence disappeared a thousand feet short of the summit, when the truck's tyres began to slip so badly that I had no choice but to stop on the highway and wake Gino for help.

'What's going on?' Gino demanded. 'What'd you hit this time?'

'Nothing,' I said. 'But the road's too slick, and the truck's too heavy to climb this grade. I think we'd better unhitch the Audi to lighten the load or we're not going to make it to the top of the pass.'

Predictably, Jarhead Gino was too gung-ho to take my word for it and insisted on getting back behind the wheel himself so he could prove I was just being a pussy about driving in snow. I had set the parking brake when I stopped, but, despite that precaution, the instant we jumped out of the cab to swap places the truck began sliding slowly but inexorably downhill, and the two of us went into panic mode.

'Holy shit, you weren't kidding!' Gino shouted. 'Quick, grab some big rocks! We need to chock the wheels before this sucker goes over the edge!' Both of us started frantically scrabbling for rocks in the snow beneath the guardrail and managed to chock the truck's rear wheels before it could gain any more momentum. Then Gino jumped behind the wheel of the Audi and immediately backed it off the trailer and parked it beside the guardrail. Disaster averted.

My hands were shaking as I climbed back into the truck, but as soon as Gino kicked aside the rocks we'd used to chock the wheels I was able to drive the lightened load safely the rest of the way over the pass and down into Ely, with Gino tailing cautiously behind in the Audi.

'Talk about a close call!' I said, as we hooked up again in the parking lot of an abandoned gas station on the edge of town.

'Yeah, that was some hairy shit all right,' Gino agreed. 'Good thing you woke me when you did or it could have been a lot worse.'

'Now aren't you glad you didn't dump me in Tucson?' I grinned. For a change, I'd given him no reason to bitch.

'I suppose,' Gino conceded. 'But when you're done patting yourself on the back, how about giving me a hand loading the Audi back on the trailer so we can get the fuck out of this snow and find someplace to bed down. There must be a motel in this hick town.'

Unfortunately, the only two motels we spotted on the way into town were already flashing 'No Vacancy' signs, and in the end Gino had to settle for a room in the Hotel Nevada, a six-storey red brick relic from Ely's pre-Depression glory days. Gino left me out in the parking lot while he registered for a room, and when he returned to the truck to grab his overnight bag he gave me the bad news. The lobby's layout was too open, and there was no way he could sneak me in past the night clerk on duty at the desk. I had no choice but to rough it outside in the truck.

'Don't worry, you won't freeze,' Gino assured me. 'I've got plenty of extra moving pads you can use as blankets, and there's room enough for you to bed down in the box if we shift a few things around.'

I wasn't looking forward to bunking in the back of the U-Haul, but it was one in the morning and I was too tired to argue, so I said nothing as Gino unlocked the roll-up door and fished out a flashlight to light my way. Once I'd cleared enough space to lie down at the front of the box, I spread some moving pads out on the cold steel floor. As soon as Gino saw I was settled, he handed me the flashlight and rolled down the door. Hours later, when my bladder woke me, I tried pulling the door up so I could jump out and take a piss, but the fucking thing wouldn't budge! The paranoid bastard had locked me in the box without my realising it! Now I was trapped until he deigned to return. Cursing Gino did nothing to relieve my bladder, though, and I started scanning the contents of the truck with the flashlight, looking for any kind of empty can or bottle, with no success. Then I spotted a chainsaw whose plastic gas well had been drained for transport. I had my solution. And felt the satisfaction of imagining the unpleasant surprise Gino was in for the next time he tried to cut firewood.

Unavoidably, my situation in the truck triggered flashbacks to Rikers Island, where I'd spent many hours locked in a box of nearly identical size while I'd worked in the prison laundry. Every weekday morning I'd report to the CO and he'd unlock the room that contained the big steam press machine used for ironing out wrinkles in the freshly washed guards' uniforms, which accounted for the bulk of my workload. It would have been a serious threat to security if any of those guards' uniforms were to fall into the hands of the inmates, so I was always locked in by myself when I worked. The CO only unlocked the door when one of the other inmates arrived to drop off another rolling laundry cart full of clothes for pressing. The pedal-operated pressing machine threw off so much steam it was like working in a sauna, but I still considered it a lucky job assignment. There was a small transistor radio in the room, and a barred window that offered a view of an interior courtyard planted with lilacs and forsythia, so five days a week I at least got a minimal glimpse of nature, which was more than most inmates could say.

The truth is, the pressing room was the one place in Rikers where I ever felt reasonably safe. Compared to the open-plan cell block, where I slept at night with eighty other prisoners free to wander where they pleased once the lights went out, that locked room in the laundry was a fortress of solitude, and oddly enough I used to miss it on weekends. Besides the temporary security it offered while I was locked in, my job also proved to be a source of revenue — over and above whatever few cents an hour I was making from the Department of Corrections for my labour.

Within days of my taking over, I was approached by another inmate in the laundry, an Italian guy who worked the counter in the exchange room, where prisoners came once a week to trade in their dirty uniforms for clean ones. The guy had a scheme going — at Rikers they called it 'working a contract' — and he offered to cut me in if I was willing. I asked what it involved and all he wanted me to do was put sharp creases in certain inmates' uniforms, which he would smuggle into the pressing room with the help of his accomplice, the Puerto Rican kid who delivered the laundry carts to my door every shift.

'What's in it for me?' I asked.

When he told me I'd be paid half a pack of cigarettes for every uniform I pressed, I told him to count me in. Apparently even in prison catering to vanity is a lucrative business. You'd be surprised at how many inmates were willing to shell out their commissary money just for the privilege of strutting around in a sharply creased uniform. It was a status thing. In their minds, it set them apart from the losers who served their time in rumpled clothes. Which was fine with me. For the rest of my sentence, I never had to buy a pack of smokes.

When Gino popped the lock and finally set me free at a little past seven, I scowled at him and snarled, 'About fucking time!' And without another word I jumped down from the box and dashed away to relieve myself between two cars that were parked beside the U-Haul. When I came back to the truck, I resumed venting my anger, and I laid such a guilt trip on Gino for locking me in the box overnight he ended up making amends by stopping at a McDonald's on the way out of town and treating me to a big breakfast – which was exactly the result I'd been angling for with my complaints. By the time we had finished, my anger and my growling stomach had both been appeased, and when we got back on the road again we lapsed back into the same uneasy truce we'd been maintaining ever since Gino had decided not to ditch me in El Paso.

It was a grey, misty morning, with drizzle in the valleys and light snow falling on the upper slopes of the surrounding peaks. We pushed north toward the Idaho border through alternating tracts of Buereau of Land Management land and private ranches, where large herds of sheep and Black Angus cattle dotted the rocky hillsides, grazing placidly amid the sagebrush and pinyon pines. There were quite a few thermal hot springs in the area, and we kept passing rustic-looking spas whose signs advertised the therapeutic powers of their mineral waters. What I wouldn't have given to soothe my achy joints with a long soak in one of those pools! Bedding down overnight on the steel floor of the cargo box had left me sore all over. But even if I'd had money to pay the entry fee, I knew Gino would never agree to interrupting our trip for a spa session. He was intent on making it to Boise by nightfall. With four hundred miles of road still ahead of us, we had no time to spare.

Five hours north of Ely, we reached the last town on the Nevada side of the border with Idaho and rolled through the one-street town of Jackpot, a tourist trap whose five or six casinos appeared to be a thriving destination for gamblers from neighbouring states. Nearly all the cars I saw parked in the casino lots bore licence plates from Idaho or Wyoming or Montana. If I ever passed through Jackpot again, I knew which casino would get my business – the biggest of the bunch, a sprawling place called Cactus Petes (for some reason, spelled with no apostrophe – was punctuation a lost art in Jackpot, or were there several Petes behind the operation?).

The sky had begun to brighten by the time we got to Jackpot, and as we crossed the Snake River into Twin Falls, Idaho, we were greeted by the first triple rainbow I'd ever seen. Naturally, I took it as a promising omen. After seventeen days on the road, I was within striking distance of the West Coast at last, and the rare spectacle of a triple rainbow seemed to me nothing less than a sign that my luck was about to change for the better. *From your lips to God's ear*, as my Irish nana was fond of saying.

We reached Boise in late afternoon, and by that time I'd had ample opportunity to see the Snake River justify its name. The stretch of I-84 between Twin Falls and Boise was riddled with bridges that spanned the river's meandering switchbacks, and I lost count of how many we crossed before we finally arrived in the capital city.

The golden dome of the statehouse building was gleaming so brightly in the late-day sun it hurt my eyes to look at it when Gino pulled off the interstate at the city centre exit. Maneouvring our long load cautiously through the traffic, he headed for an industrial area on the northwest side of town and eventually turned onto á busy side street, where his Vietnam buddy, a guy named Bob, had an auto repair shop. The plan was to spend the night in Boise with Bob and his wife Ellen, who'd invited Gino to stop by on his way to Washington so they could show off the new house they'd bought since his last visit.

As soon as Gino pulled up in front of the shop and climbed out of the U-Haul, Bob came trotting out to greet him, and as I watched the two of them bear-hug, they were certainly a mismatched pair. Gino, with his strapping build, was the perfect picture of a fighting leatherneck, but Bob was short and wiry, built more like a VC tunnel rat, and it was almost comical to see him trying to wrap his short arms around Gino's hulking frame.

When they were done embracing, Bob hustled back into the shop to let his mechanics know he was leaving for the day and then hopped into his Ford pick-up to lead us to his new house, which turned out to be a fixer-upper on a quiet rural road a few miles outside the city limits. Ellen, his wife, came out to the driveway to greet Gino when we arrived, and though I could see by her puzzled expression that she hadn't expected him to turn up with a guest in tow, she smiled pleasantly when Gino introduced me, and then excused herself so she could go set an extra place at the dinner table. Ellen proved to be quite a good cook. The spaghetti and meatballs she served us were delicious, and when I finished my first plate and she graciously offered me a second helping I happily accepted. It was only after she'd refilled my plate that I noticed the angry glare Gino was aiming at me from across the table, and I realised I'd somehow just pissed him off.

When the meal was over, Gino and Bob went outside for a smoke, and I stayed behind to help Ellen clear the table and load the dishwasher, hoping this might get me back in Gino's good graces. But, as I quickly discovered, Gino was far too angry to be so easily mollified. The second I stepped out of the house Gino excused himself from his conversation with Bob, grabbed me by the arm and quick-marched me to the U-Haul, which was parked kerb-side out in the street. He kept his voice down, but he was seething as he ripped me for embarrassing him in front of his friends by being such a greedy pig at the dinner table.

'I didn't ask for seconds, Ellen offered them,' I replied in defence.

'She was just being polite, you dumb fuck!' he spat back. 'In case you hadn't noticed, these aren't rich people. The extra helping you just ate was probably tomorrow's lunch for Bob. Well, that's it, I'm done with your sorry ass. Help me get the Audi off the trailer, then grab your pack from the truck. I'm taking you back to the highway right now.'

The worst thing about Gino's tirade was that I knew it was justified. Poverty had turned me feral, and like a stray cat who never knows when the next meal is coming I had slipped into the needy habit of eating anything that was put in front of me, even when I could have done with less. My mother had raised me better than that. And I'm sure she'd have been as mortified by my behaviour as I now was. And yet, for all my embarrassment, when I was done mouthing lame apologies to Gino on the ride back to the interstate, I still had the unbelievable nerve to hit him up for a handout before he dropped me off at the Oregon border forty-five minutes later. Desperation knows no shame, I guess.

'Jesus, you're some piece of work,' Gino said, shaking his head in disbelief. But to his credit, he handed me two dollars anyway, and when we parted company I had to admit he was a better man than me.

The idiot wind had blown through Gino's life, too, yet he'd survived.

I could only pray that out here in the West I'd find some way to do the same.

CHAPTER 7

You're a pain in the ass, Pete, but good luck, I guess. I hope for your sake you get your act together soon.

Gino's parting words were still ringing in my ears as he pulled away and left me shamefacedly clutching the two dollars I'd just cadged from him. Of course, I was grateful for his generosity, but that didn't stop me from sighing with relief as I watched him go – four days of travelling with Gino had worn me out, both mentally and emotionally.

I suspect if we hadn't been the same age Gino's prickly personality and withering candour might have been easier to shrug off. But the fact that our lives spanned exactly the same years, and had been plagued in their own way by the same destructive drug, gave Gino's criticism a validity that sharpened its edge and made it cut deeper. Then, too, there was the matter of Gino's imposing size and gruff demeanour, which were so similar to my father's that they made his remarks even harder not to take to heart. Though it pained me to admit it, Gino had been right when he'd said it was high time I started 'owning' my fuck-ups. Facing up to the hard questions I'd been ducking for so long was the only way I'd ever turn my life around. There was no getting around it. But soul-searching is an exhausting business, and for the moment I was glad to be free of Gino and the constant reminder of my shortcomings he'd come to represent as our time on the road dragged on.

The highway rest area where Gino had dropped me off was just over the Oregon border, in the small farming town of Ontario, and the only amenities it offered were the usual block-house with public toilets and a few tin-roofed informational kiosks clustered on the sidewalk outside the restrooms. After Gino pulled away, I walked over to one of the kiosks and spent a moment checking the posted roadmap to get my bearings. According to the map, Interstate 84 would take me straight into Portland, 375 miles down the road. I figured with any luck I could cover the distance in ten or twelve hours of hitchhiking. But I'd never been to Oregon before, and I thought it would be a shame not to check out the scenery, so I decided to post-pone my departure until the morning.

Before looking for somewhere to bed down at the rest area, I made a cautious dash across the highway to a roadside diner on the eastbound side and spent the better part of Gino's two dollars on a pouch of Bugler tobacco and a small cup of coffee to go. I took my coffee outside to the diner's gravel parking lot and sat down on a kerbstone to roll a cigarette. Then, as I relaxed in the chilly twilight, enjoying a leisurely smoke, I noticed a dark mass of clouds sweeping in from the west and had a bad feeling the weather was about to change. Fearing I would get caught in a downpour, I hurried back across the highway and immediately started scouting the shadowy pine woods at the back of the rest area for a spot to make camp.

But, as I quickly discovered, the pine woods wouldn't do. The ground between trees was overgrown with dense thickets of some sort of bush that was bristling with needle-like thorns, sharp as tiny icepicks, which poked right through my socks and drew blood from my ankles before I realised what I'd stumbled into. Cursing in pain, I retreated to the parking lot and pulled down my socks to assess the damage. It was hard to see in the dusky half-light, but what I could see wasn't pretty. Suffice to say, the word pincushion came to mind. Hunched over, plucking thorns from my skin, I couldn't help thinking that my first night in Oregon had gotten off to an inauspicious start. Which, as it turned out, was merely a foretaste of the miseries in store for me in the hours ahead.

I had hardly finished pulling out the last of the thorns when suddenly the parking lot got ominously dark. An instant later, the storm clouds gusting overhead opened up and began pelting me with rain and sleet, a mixture I was sure would soon turn to snow as the night air got colder. I ran to the restroom building to escape the downpour. As I stood in the open doorway of the men's room, wondering how I was going to survive the night in such weather, I spotted a pile of construction sand near the parking lot exit and found my answer. The big blue plastic tarp atop the pile was meant to keep the sand dry, but I definitely needed it more than the sand did, and as soon as the rain let up a little I ran over to the pile, kicked away the concrete pavers that were anchoring the tarp's edges and dragged the tarp back to the shelter of one of the map kiosks.

The Plexiglas-sided kiosk was maybe twice the size of your average phone booth, but there was room enough on the concrete pad beneath it for me to hunker down in the foetal position, and that's where I wound up bedding down, wrapped up like a mummy in the sandy tarp's gritty embrace – and watched over throughout the long night by Meriwether Lewis and William Clark, both pictured on the Oregon Trail poster which hung above my head. Every time I glanced their way, their intrepid gazes seemed to be mocking my tenderfoot's discomfort. I just flipped them one of Jarhead Gino's helicopter salutes and went on shivering.

The sleet soon turned to snow as the temperature dropped into the twenties, and the three-sided kiosk offered no protection from the biting winds that swirled through its open end. Even swaddled in the tarp, I could only catch ninety minutes of sleep before the cold drove me inside to the restroom, where I spent the next fifteen minutes punching the start button on the hot-air hand dryer until I was thawed out enough to brave trudging back out to the kiosk and wrapping myself in the tarp again. And that's how it went for the rest of the night, with me shuttling back and forth between the kiosk and the men's room – though the intervals of sleep got shorter and shorter as the temperature continued to drop.

The only break in my routine came sometime after midnight, when one of my sessions at the hand dryer was interrupted by a tap on my shoulder. I spun around to see what was up and found myself face-to-face with a smiling old queen in a cracked leather bomber jacket and cashmere scarf, who sheepishly ran a hand through his slicked-back silver hair and politely enquired if I'd care for a blow job. When I just as politely declined, he simply shrugged and headed for the door. But as he stepped back outside into the snowy night, I heard him mutter, 'Never hurts to ask.' Which left me wondering if the guy didn't have a screw loose. Ask the wrong person that question, it could definitely hurt. Then again, maybe the old boy lived a charmed life. If so, I hoped he'd left some of his luck behind, because hypothermia and frostbite were starting to seem like real possibilities before the night was over, and I'd need all the help I could get to make it through till dawn.

The next few hours were by far the worst I'd suffered since leaving New York, and I'd venture to say there was nobody in that sleepy town of Ontario any happier to see the sunrise than I was. I was stiff all over, and the teeth-chattering cold had left me with an achy jaw, but I'd survived to see another day – a day which (as if I needed further cause for celebration) just happened to be my birthday. My thirty-eighth. I was now three years older than Dante was when he wrote '*Nel mezzo del cammin di nostra vita, mi ritrovai per una selva oscura, ché la diritta via era smarrita*' ('Midway upon the journey of our life I found myself within a dark wood, for the straightforward pathway had been lost'). I had a strong hunch the year ahead would determine my future. Unless I found my way back to the straight path, and soon, I'd be stuck in Dante's dark wood forever.

The frosty air fogged my breath and I was shivering with cold as I dragged the tarp across the parking lot and returned it to the sand pile, which was now covered by a thin skiff of snow. All I could think about at that point was getting my hands on a hot cup of coffee. However, after bedding down on cold concrete all night, my joints were too sore to risk a dash across four lanes of traffic, so I took the prudent course and hiked half a mile back up the road to use the overpass bridge. The exercise did me good, though, and by the time I reached the diner I was no longer moving like a stiff-legged zombie.

At the diner, I counted out my pocket change and was

upset to discover I was a nickel shy of the price for a small cup of coffee. 'No problem,' smiled the kindly woman at the cashier counter, plucking five pennies from the 'take one, leave one' cup beside the register. Thanking her, I remarked that she'd just given me the only gift I was likely to receive for my birthday, and when she heard that sob story she gave me a jumbo coffee instead of the small cup I'd ordered. Score!

After the previous night's ordeal it was nice to see Oregon showing me a softer side, and though I was penniless once again when I left the diner I was smiling as I hiked back to the highway. My birthday was off to a good start. Now if I could just make it to Portland by nightfall, in time to claim a bed at a homeless shelter, I'd really have something to celebrate . . . With that hopeful thought in mind, I got busy wagging my thumb.

The coffee was long gone, and my hands and feet were frozen numb by the time I caught my first ride an hour later, with a sheep rancher heading home to Baker City, seventy-five miles up the road. My first impression of the sandy-haired little guy was that he looked like he'd had an even rougher night than I'd had. His skin was sallow, and the bags beneath his eyes were puffy and as dark as ripe plums, so it didn't surprise me when he confessed that he'd just spent the weekend getting chemo-therapy treatment at the VA hospital in Boise. 'Liver cancer,' he said, before I could ask. 'Agent Orange took its time, but it finally caught up with me.'

His name was Elvin, and he'd been drafted into the army as soon as he'd finished high school, back in 1965, during the heyday of Operation Ranch Hand, the US military's campaign to chem-ically defoliate Vietnam's jungles and deprive the Viet Cong of their hiding places. Back then, Elvin said, our troops were given little warning about the risks of the chemicals they were handling.

'Whenever we set up a new base camp, we had to strap on backpack sprayers loaded with Agent Orange, and then our dip-shit looey would march us out into the jungle to poison all the bush on the perimeter. Nobody bothered to tell us we were poisoning ourselves in the process. Which was typical. Everything over there was FUBAR, if you know what I'm saying.'

'Fucked up beyond all recognition'. I nodded knowingly. Though I hadn't served, I'd read enough war memoirs to recognise the acronym. But I'd always wondered why the defoliant was nicknamed Agent Orange, and out of curiosity I asked Elvin. He explained that there were a number of herbicides being used during Operation Ranch Hand and the fifty-five-gallon drums the chemicals were shipped in came marked with different colour codes so you could tell them apart. 'We called it Agent Orange because the barrels it came in were painted with orange stripes.'

'Makes sense,' I said. Which was more than you could say about most things connected with that tragically senseless war.

Hoping to steer our conversation into less painful territory, I asked Elvin if he enjoyed raising sheep. He laughed at my question and grinned as he replied, 'If I didn't enjoy it, I'd be crazy to keep at it. 'Course, there's some would say I'm crazy just the same. There's a lot easier ways to make a living, no question. But I like being my own boss and working outdoors, so sheeping suits me fine.'

'I'm from Brooklyn, so all I know about sheep ranching is what I've seen in the old Westerns,' I confessed. 'Seemed like in the frontier days the cattlemen were always picking fights with the sheep ranchers for fencing their pastures. Do you still get hassled by cattlemen?'

'Nah, those feuding days are over, but cattlemen still look

down on us – that much will never change. You know what the cattle ranchers round here call sheep?'

'What?' I asked.

'Meadow maggots,' Elvin chuckled.

'Jesus, that's harsh!' I replied. Still, I have to admit, the cattlemen's slander made it hard to sustain my idyllic view of the sheep I saw dotting the hillsides of the alpine meadows as we approached the Baker City exit.

After Elvin dropped me off, I soon caught a ride to the town of La Grande with an elderly gent in a Chrysler Le Baron. The back seat of the car was crammed with open boxes full of King James Bibles and I wondered if he might be a preacher, but he turned out to be a travelling salesman who specialised in religious books, and for the next hour, as the road climbed steadily higher into the Blue Mountains, he bemoaned the dwindling prospects in his line of work. Apparently, in recent years, his sales territory in Eastern Oregon had been overrun by Mormons relocating from Idaho and Utah, and as a result the demand for 'true Christian' reading material had plummeted. When I asked why he didn't just broaden his base by stocking books the Mormons would buy, he scoffed and said I obviously didn't know much about Mormons. Which was certainly true enough, so I asked him to explain.

'Mormons will only deal with their own, son,' he replied. 'Doesn't matter what you're selling, if you don't know the secret LDS handshake you'll never get your foot in the door.'

I couldn't tell whether the salesman's explanation was the truth or just sour grapes, but his bitterness was definitely genuine, and I was glad to get away from it and back out into the fresh air when he dropped me off at La Grange.

By now it was mid morning, and the bright sunshine had

warmed the air considerably. Which was fortunate, because it took me nearly two hours to flag down my next ride. Still, it was a picturesque spot to be temporarily stranded, and as I stood gazing west at the evergreen slopes of the Umatilla National Forest and the snow-capped peaks of the Blue Mountains I was thrilled to spot a white-tipped black speck tracing spirals high above me – the very first bald eagle I'd ever seen in the wild. It was a sight I'd have missed if I hadn't postponed my trip until daylight, and it made me feel a lot better about the frigid night I'd just suffered through in Ontario.

As noon-time approached, my growling stomach kept reminding me that I hadn't eaten anything since last night's spaghetti dinner, and I could feel a case of the hypoglycemic shakes coming on. I was reluctant to leave the highway to go foraging for food in La Grande, so I made do with the only source of sugar I had handy – a McDonald's ketchup packet I found burrowed down like a plump little tick in the furry lint at the bottom of my overcoat pocket. Ripping the packet open, I stuck out my tongue and slurped up every drop. It was a pretty pathetic birthday Happy Meal, but at least that squirt of ketchup kept my shakes at bay until an old Chevy pick-up with dealer plates pulled over to pick me up a short while later.

The pick-up's young driver, a blue-eyed blond named Jakob, turned out to be a fellow Norseman, and as soon as we were back on the road he pointed to a baggie of homemade cookies on the seat between us and told me to help myself. 'Norwegian butter cookies,' he said with a smile. 'Cherry-almond. My sister Ingvild baked them last night. When our grandma passed away back in December, Ingvild inherited all the old family recipes and she's been baking like a fiend ever since. I guess it helps her cope. Grandma pretty much raised us on her own after our parents got killed in a car wreck when we were young, so losing her was like losing a second mom.'

'Well, I'm sorry for your loss, but tell your sister she's done your grandma proud,' I said, after wolfing down one of the buttery, rich wafers. The pastry chefs at Ebinger's famous Scandinavian bakery in Bay Ridge had nothing on Ingvild, that was for sure. I couldn't have asked for a tastier – or more timely – birthday treat.

When I told Jakob I was heading to Portland, he said he could take me as far as Pendleton before he had to turn north into Washington to drop the truck off at an auction lot in Pasco. He worked as a detailer for a car dealership in Boise and occasionally they'd have him drive one of their trade-in vehicles to Pasco and then return to Boise by bus. It was cheaper than shipping the vehicle by truck, Jakob said, and he enjoyed the trips because they gave him a break from his everyday routine. 'The only hassle is when they stick me with an old beater like this one and I have to worry about it holding together long enough for me to make it to the auction lot.'

Maybe Jakob should have knocked on some Norwegian wood before sharing that thought. Before we'd gone twenty-five miles up the road, the truck's engine began to sputter and cough like an asthmatic climbing stairs and he was forced to pull over onto the shoulder, where he began pounding the steering wheel in frustration and cursing out someone named Tommy.

'Out of gas, sounds like,' I observed. 'Didn't you gas up before you hit the road?'

'I would have,' Jakob frowned. 'But Tommy at the shop swore he'd filled the tank last night. The gas gauge on this piece of shit is busted, so I just took his word for it. But I guarantee you, the kid's ass is grass when I get back to Boise tonight!'

'So, what next?' I asked.

'Guess I'll have to hike back to Meacham and pick up a can of gas. I hate to ask, but would you mind hanging out with the truck till I get back? I'm afraid some highway patrol cop will ticket it as an abandoned vehicle if there's no one here keeping watch.'

'Don't worry, I've got you covered,' I told him. 'Any cops come by, I'll let them know what's up.'

'Thanks, man. Meacham's only a couple of miles back, so I shouldn't be gone long. Help yourself to all the cookies you want while you're waiting.'

It was a good thing Jakob left me to mind the truck because, just as he'd feared, a highway patrol cop came cruising by a half-hour later and pulled up on the shoulder behind me to ask what the problem was. When I told him Jakob should be back soon with a can of gas, the cop said he'd sit tight and escort us across the median to the eastbound lane so we could get back to the Meacham exit to finish filling the tank. According to the cop, the nearest gas station on the westbound side was too far to reach on a gallon of gas, and he didn't want us going through the same drill again a few miles up the road.

Fifteen minutes later, Jakob came trudging back with a gallon can of gas, and while I emptied it into the tank the cop went through the motions of checking Jakob's licence and registration. Unlike me, Jakob had his papers in order, and as soon as we got the truck started the cop hit the cruiser's lights and led us across the grassy median to the eastbound lanes.

'Pretty cool cop,' Jakob grinned. 'I was thinking I'd have to back up two miles on the shoulder to get to the westbound exit, which would have gotten me a ticket sure as shit if I'd been spotted. Lucky thing you stayed behind to mind the truck.'

'Yeah, he was cooler than most,' I agreed, thinking of the redneck cop who'd tried to run me out of Lumberton. 'We were shooting the breeze while you were gone, and he told me the stretch of road up ahead is pretty hairy. Good thing we ran out of gas where we did.'

'Yeah, we'll be climbing two thousand feet to Deadman Pass. Supposedly, it's one of the most dangerous mountain passes in the country – six per cent grade, and nothing but double hairpin curves all the way.'

'Then let's hope the brakes on this beater are in better shape than the gas gauge,' I remarked uneasily.

Jakob grinned and told me not to worry, the brake pads had just been replaced that week. But I worried anyway as we climbed steadily out of Meacham toward the grimly named heights of Deadman Pass, staying cautiously in the slow lane, while a succession of maniac drivers went flying by in the fast lane, making suicide passes on blind curves to overtake the two massive log-hauler trucks we were sandwiched between. When we reached the crest, however, my uneasiness gave way to amazement as I looked down at a sun-splashed panorama of farmland and forest that stretched clear to the gorges of the Columbia River and, far to the west, the blurry, jagged line of the Cascade Range. And, once again, I was glad I'd decided to cross Oregon in daylight.

Twenty miles later, I parted company with Jakob at the Pendleton exit and started hoofing it along the shoulder toward a rest area Jakob said was five miles up the road. Down in the valley now, it was warm enough to shuck my overcoat and I worked up a sweat (and a fresh set of blisters on my heels) as I hiked past wheat fields and cattle pastures and a string of faded billboards hawking the town's big rodeo, the Pendleton

Round-up. *Whooee, pardner!* I thought. *You're in the West for sure now!*

Though I kept flashing my thumb whenever I heard a car coming up behind me, I couldn't get anyone to stop, and I ended up hiking all the way to the rest area, which turned out to be more like seven miles down the road than the five Jakob had estimated. But it proved to be a lucky spot. I'd just finished gulping a quart of water from the outdoor fountain when a dusty white Ford Falcon pulled in beneath one of the rest area's two scruffy shade trees, and a pony-tailed old hippy climbed out and began doing yoga stretches beside his car. He was easing into the salutation to the sun pose when I walked over and complimented his car, which, except for its white paint job, looked to be an exact replica of my buddy Kenny Brown's high school party mobile, 'Fanny Falcon'.

'Sweet ride,' I grinned. 'Man, did I have some wild times back in the sixties in a Falcon just like this one.'

'Didn't we all,' the hippy grinned back. 'My pops bought it new back in 1960. Been in the family ever since. She's on her third rebuilt engine now, but she still runs great. Can't beat a Ford.'

'Any chance you could give me a lift toward Portland?' I asked.

'Sure, dude, no problem,' he said. 'I'm heading to Hood River. That'll get you most of the way. Just give me a minute to drain the lizard.'

The hippy's name was Nate, and as soon as we got back on the road he reached beneath his seat and pulled out a baggie full of pre-rolled joints and fired one up.

'Check it out, bro',' he said, passing me the joint. 'Strawberry Mountain homegrown. Me and my partner have got a grow spot up in the Malheur National Forest. I was just up there helping him clear our patch for spring planting.'

'Nice,' I coughed out, after sucking down a big hit.

The stuff tasted like dirt, but I kept that thought to myself, and after a few more tokes I was too mellow to care how it tasted. Next thing, I was telling him stories about my time as a freelancer for *High Times* magazine, and how the staff used to congregate in the mail room at delivery time, vying to be the first to get their hands on the sample buds that marijuana growers like Nate would submit in hopes of seeing their handiwork selected for display as one of the magazine's pot-porn centre-folds. Which was certainly a perk no other publisher could offer its staff – until the postal inspectors started cracking down and the magazine had to caution its readers to submit only photos of their buds, not the buds themselves.

'Dude, you're not going to believe this, but I know a guy in Corvallis whose Sativa bud got picked for a *High Times* centre-fold. He took the picture to a commercial photo lab and had them make a wall-size blow-up for his downstairs den. Cost him a bundle, but he didn't care. The publicity tripled his busi-ness. Till he got busted, anyway. That's why my partner and I don't sell our shit. We grow strictly for our own heads. Who wants to worry about some snitch setting you up for a buy-and-bust? Defeats the point of smoking weed, you ask me.'

I couldn't argue with that. In fact, before long I couldn't argue with anything. I was so high, my half of the conversation was reduced to nodding at whatever Nate said, and for the rest of the trip I mostly just gawked out the window at the amazing scenery, as we cruised deeper and deeper into Columbia River Gorge country, where every bend in the river seemed to offer another rainbow-making waterfall or fern-covered cliff to catch my eye. A few hours later, just as darkness was falling, we passed the huge hydroelectric dam at The Dalles, and Nate announced we were getting close to his exit in Hood River, the end of the line for me.

'Thanks for the mellow ride,' I said, as he pulled onto the shoulder a short while later. 'You sure made my birthday a lot more festive.'

'No shit, it's your birthday?' Nate replied in surprise. 'Why didn't you tell me! Hold up a minute, let me give you a little something for the road.'

'That's okay, Nate, you've done enough for me already,' I said, but he climbed out of the car anyway and motioned me back to the trunk. He popped the latch to reveal a big Hefty bag half-full of dried marijuana plants that hadn't yet been trimmed. Before I knew it, he had filled a small baggie with a couple of handfuls of loose pot from the bottom of the garbage bag. 'Strawberry Mountain shake,' he grinned, tucking in a pack of Zig Zag papers before passing it to me. 'Should hold you for a while, till something better comes your way. Portland's only about eighty-five miles up the road. Good luck the rest of the way.'

Watching the Falcon's tail-lights recede, I found myself remembering what Jack Kerouac said about heaven: if you show kindness to everyone you meet, you'll find that paradise is right here on earth. The real gift Nate had just given me wasn't the pot but the reminder of a truth I'd been neglecting for far too long, and I was more thankful for that than anything. Oregon was turning out to be full of pleasant surprises, and as I waited for my next ride I began to wonder if I shouldn't just stick around Portland for a while and take my chances in the Northwest. With no job waiting for me in San Francisco any more, there seemed little reason not to give Portland a shot. But first I had to get there, and that turned out to be harder than I'd figured, given the smooth way the rest of my day had gone.

I was stranded in the dark in Hood River for nearly two hours and had long since given up hope of catching supper at a Portland rescue mission by the time a college kid in a Subaru wagon finally stopped to pick me up. His name was Jed, and he was on his way home to Portland from Eastern Washington University to spend the weekend with his girlfriend. I asked what he was studying, and when he said he was majoring in geology I laughed and told him about the only geology class I'd ever taken at Dartmouth – a dumbed-down intro course that was nicknamed 'Rocks for Jocks' because it attracted so many football players who needed an easy way to pick up part of the required minimum credits in math and science. 'The funny thing is, quite a few of the jocks got hooked on geology and ended up majoring in it,' I said. 'Which was fine with the volcanologists on the faculty, I'd imagine. Every spring they'd take a group of geology majors down to Central America to do fieldwork and it must have been handy to have a few muscular athletes around for the heavy lifting.'

'Yeah, the fieldwork's tougher than most people imagine, but I love it,' Jed said. 'I'm hoping to land a job as a field geologist with one of the big oil companies once I finish graduate school.'

'Good money in that line of work, I'd imagine,' I said.

'Yeah, the salaries are good, but the money's not what I'm after so much as the travel and the fieldwork and the chance to discover a big deposit where nobody else has thought to look. Long as I get a shot at that kind of rush, they could pay me minimum wage for all I care. What line of work are you in?' he asked.

'I'm a freelance writer,' I said, taking the safest tack. I was still feeling mellow from my ride with Strawberry Mountain Nate and had no desire to spoil the mood by rehashing the sorry details of my true situation. Instead, I trotted out my fall-back story about hitchhiking cross-country to gather stories for an updated version of Kerouac's *On the Road*.

'Cool book,' Ned said. 'We read it for English class my senior year in high school. I wanted to hit the road myself after I read it. In fact, a buddy of mine and I were planning to hitch out to the East Coast during summer vacation before we started college, but my parents thought it was a crazy idea. Said if I went bumming across the country, they'd take back my tuition fund and make me pay for college on my own. That ended that. But sometimes I still wish I'd said "fuck it" and done what I wanted. When you think about it, field geologists and freelance writers aren't so different. Both jobs let you travel and do fieldwork, right?'

'True enough,' I agreed, as my stoned brain began spinning its wheels in the soft sand of free-association. 'You could take the comparison even further than that, if you consider the similarities in method,' I added.

'Not sure I follow,' Jed said. 'How so?'

'Well, look at it this way. Don't geologists study the world for clues to what lies hidden beneath the surface? Writers do the same thing, really, when you get right down to it,' I grinned. 'You deal with rocks, I deal with people, that's the only difference. Hell, some of the people I meet might as well be rocks, but that's a different story.'

It was nine o'clock when Jed let me out on Burnside Street in Old Town, the heart of Portland's skid row district, which Jed said was the likeliest place for me to find a place to crash for free. On first impression, the neighbourhood seemed remarkably like the Bowery in Manhattan. I saw the same cast of bag ladies and grizzled winos haunting the sidewalks, and the same mix of cheque-cashing shops and cut-rate liquor stores and pawnbrokers. Even the air in the neighbourhood smelled the same as the Bowery's, with a faint hint of wok-fried Chinese cooking overlaying the prevailing stench of urine-splashed dumpsters and diesel smog. Oddly enough, I found all these similarities comforting – I might be a stranger, but this was no strange land. Not to me.

The block where Jed dropped me off had a multi-storey Salvation Army centre on one corner and the Portland Rescue Mission directly across the street, but both shelters turned me away for arriving past curfew when I tried to book myself in for a bed. Apparently, 9 p.m. was an unacceptable hour to arrive penniless in Portland. Who knew? Certainly not me, or I wouldn't have been wandering the streets of Old Town on a cold and misty February night.

At a loss for where to try next, I approached a white-haired old tramp who was nursing a mickey of Tokay in the doorway of a boarded-up storefront. He was within pissing distance of the Salvation Army shelter, so I figured he'd know the score. But when I asked him where I might find a free bed for the night, his response left me doubting I'd picked a reliable source.

'Baloney Joe's is your best bet,' the wino replied without hesitation.

'*Baloney Joe's*?' I repeated skeptically, not sure I'd heard him right. His voice was so raspy you could have grated hard cheese with it.

'That's right. Baloney Joe's, you got it,' he said. 'Most all the other flops around here lock down at seven. You miss curfew, you're SOL. Only Baloney Joe's and the Gospel Mission stay open this late. You could try the Gospel, I guess, but I steer clear of the place myself.'

'Why's that?' I asked him.

''Cause it's run by Baptists, and they're too damned preachy. A little ear-beating's fine, but that bunch don't know when to quit.'

'I hear you,' I nodded, just to be agreeable. I had no idea whether his jaundiced opinion of the Gospel Mission was justified, but he'd been right about the early curfew at the Sally and the Rescue Mission, so I decided to take him at his word.

'Okay, I'll bite,' I shrugged. 'Where do I find this Baloney Joe's place?'

'Over the river,' he said, and leaned out of the doorway to point me in the right direction. 'You take the Burnside Bridge, right up the block there.'

'How far is it?' I asked warily. My blistered heels were still throbbing from the long hike I'd made to the Pendleton rest stop and I was too beat to tackle more than a ten-block trudge.

'Not far at all,' the wino assured me. 'Once you cross the bridge, it's just a few blocks down on your left. There's a big sign out front. You can't miss it.'

That remains to be seen, I thought. You could miss an awful lot in a fog as thick as the one that was rising up off the Willamette River. It had already swallowed most of the Burnside Bridge, and when I reached the river it swallowed me, too. Dim halos floating in the mist were all I could see of the bridge lights, and their fuzzy glow was too weak to light the walkway, so I had to cross the bridge by feel, like a blind man, with one hand skimming along the catwalk's clammy railing, and as I shuffled through the fog toward a destination I still suspected might be nothing but a bad joke I suddenly broke out laughing in the dark. Maybe I was loopy from fatigue, or still feeling the effects of Nate's Strawberry Mountain homegrown, but blindly crossing a bridge in the fog seemed such a comically apt metaphor for the current state of my life I couldn't help but laugh. It was all too crazy. After eighteen days on the road, I was now three thousand miles from anyone who gave a shit whether I was still alive or buried in some roadside ditch. But, by God, I *was* still alive, and for the moment that seemed reason enough to celebrate – if not with a birthday cake, then at least with laughter, no matter how rueful.

The fog was still thick when I reached the Willamette's east bank, but a block beyond the river it began to thin out. Up ahead on Burnside I soon spotted a floodlit 7UP sign emblazoned with black lettering, and as I approached through the mist the letters gradually resolved into the words: Baloney Joe's Junction – a name that struck me as even more ludicrous than the shortened version the wino had given me. *Petticoat Junction* and the Shady Rest Hotel immediately came to mind, and I couldn't help wondering what twisted logic had inspired someone to give a homeless shelter a name that conjured a sitcom spin-off. But it didn't really matter what the place was called, as long as they'd take me in from the cold.

It was after nine-thirty when I walked through the doors of the storefront shelter, and when I stepped up to the reception window in the lobby area the young volunteer behind the counter informed me that all the cots in the dormitory were already full for the night. But he said I was welcome to flop with the rest of the overflow crowd in the rec room down the hall, or I could try my luck at one of the other shelters in the neighbourhood.

'The rec room's okay with me,' I told him. It was already well below freezing outside and I had no desire to go searching through the streets of an unfamiliar city for another shelter at such a late hour.

Once again, the flimsy carbon copy of the hitchhiking ticket I'd been carrying since Florida came in handy as ID, and while the clerk was signing me in I asked if there was any chance I could get something to eat. Except for the few butter cookies I'd mooched from Jakob that morning, I hadn't eaten anything in more than twenty-four hours. I figured it was going to be a long night if I couldn't scrounge up something to take the edge off my hunger pangs.

'Sorry, the kitchen's closed,' the clerk said. 'Supper's at six. You missed it.'

'Come on, brother, cut me some slack,' I pleaded. I was way too hungry to let him brush me off that easily, so I tried softening him up with my story about just hitting town after hitchhiking all the way from Boise, and finally, much to my relief, he relented and said, 'Okay, wait a minute. Let me look in the back and see what I can find.' A few minutes later, he returned to the counter and handed me a baggie with a peanut butter and jelly sandwich in it. I thanked him for hooking me up and tried my best not to show my disappointment – I'd hated peanut butter ever since I'd first tried it at a friend's house when I was a little kid. Considering the shelter's goofy name, I'd been hoping for something meatier.

'What happened?' I grinned. 'You run out of baloney?'

The clerk rolled his eyes to let me know it was a stupid question, and said, 'Believe me, we never run out of baloney around here. Rec room's just down the hall on your right. Have a good night.'

I followed the muted sound of a TV down the hallway and as soon as I stepped into the rec room I could see what the clerk had meant about the 'overflow' crowd. The low-ceilinged room was maybe sixteen feet square and crammed with more losers than a bullpen cell in Manhattan Central Booking on a three-day weekend. Which wasn't really surprising. The colder the night, the bigger the turn-out. I didn't care about the cramped quarters, though. After the freezing night I'd spent at the rest stop in Ontario I was just grateful to have a warm place to crash.

All of the ratty couches and armchairs in the room were occupied, and most of the space on the painted concrete floor was already taken by men with bedrolls and sleeping bags. But across the room I spotted a narrow opening on one of the locker room benches that were mounted along the back wall and I cautiously tiptoed toward it through the maze of sprawled bodies, knowing from past bullpen experience that one misstep is all it takes to start a beef. I was far too road-weary for that kind of drama. Thankfully, I managed to cross the minefield without incident, and once I settled down on the hard pine bench I unbagged my sandwich and began stuffing my face.

While I was making a pig of myself, I noticed the guy sitting next to me on the end of the bench giving me wary, sidelong glances. He was a middle-aged tramp, probably mid-forties, wearing thick-lensed glasses with a tortoiseshell frame, and the adhesive tape that held his glasses together at the bridge was the same grimy shade of grey as the curly hair on his head. Seeing him eyeing me, I offered him half of my sandwich. It occurred to me that he might be as hungry as I was. But he shook his head no, and then stammered, 'A-a-anyway, I already ate supper at the Rescue Mission.'

'You sure?' I asked. 'Hell, I don't even like peanut butter. You'd be doing me a favour.'

Again, he shook off my offer with a wag of his curly head and then, to my surprise, he added, 'A-a-anyway, you shouldn't talk with your mouth full.'

What a pisser! I thought to myself. *I'm getting lectured on table manners by a bum in a homeless shelter!* It was hilarious. Even with my mouth full, I couldn't help smiling. Leave it to me to sit down next to Emily Post's most dishevelled disciple. The guy was a gem too rich to pass up, and I decided I had to make his acquaintance.

'Name's Pete,' I said, offering my hand.

He sized me up with another wary look before deciding it was safe to shake. 'A-a-anyway, I'm John,' he said, smiling shyly.

And that's how I met John Anyway, my improbable guide to Portland in the days ahead.

After hearing John start three straight sentences with the word *anyway*, I could tell I was dealing with someone who had a few scrambled wires in his control box, but that didn't put me off. He seemed harmless enough, and I was happy to spend the next half-hour pumping him for information about Portland until we both started yawning and nodded off for the night.

At five the next morning, one of the shelter's volunteers turned the rec room's lights up full, and the harsh glare chased all of us out of Baloney Joe's and into the chilly predawn darkness. 'Who the fuck is out on the street at this hour except cops and burglars?' I heard one of my fellow tramps grumble, and I thought, *Who the fuck indeed?* It's certainly a confusing, and degrading, way to start your day. One minute you're a lost soul worth helping, the next you're pushed out to the kerb like a bag of garbage.

What's the point of turning a horde of unemployed men loose in the streets before daylight, when there's nothing for them to do but huddle in doorways or hunker down on park benches until the rest of the city opens for business? I suspect it's the national abhorrence of idleness that underlies these premature evacuations. And once you realise that the so-called 'social safety net' gets its tensile strength from that most durable of American fibres – the Protestant work ethic – the perverse logic of such a misguided policy begins to come clear. The brothers' keepers who make the shelter rules would no doubt tell you they're just trying to build character – *Early to bed, early to rise, etc., etc.* – but as far as I could tell, all they really built was resentment. Which explained why so many of the homeless men I'd met in my travels refused to stay in shelters. (Other shelter policies, such as the ban on alcohol, and the mandatory communal showers, kept even more away.)

'Anyway, we need to get over to the Rescue Mission now for breakfast,' John said, taking me in tow as we set off towards the river. 'Anyway, this is the Burnside Bridge. Portland has seven bridges. Anyway, the Food Stamp office is over by the Steel Bridge, that's the next one downstream. Today's Saturday, so the Food Stamp office is closed. On Monday, you can go sign up for your stamps. Anyway, all you need is your Social Security card.'

'That's going to be a problem, John. I lost my wallet back in North Carolina a few weeks ago. I need to find a Social Security office and apply for a replacement.'

'Anyway, the Social Security office is downtown by City Hall. I can take you over there on Monday if you want.'

'That'd be great, if you can spare the time,' I said.

'Anyway, I can just hunt for cans when we're downtown,' he replied, and that seemed to settle the matter.

When we came down off the bridge, a few dozen men were already gathered in front of the Rescue Mission, their faces bathed in blue light from the big neon cross above the entranceway, and for a second I had the weird impression I was looking at a pack of grizzled Smurfs. John and I joined the crowd, and at six o'clock a Mission worker opened the big double doors and we all filed inside to the chapel for the mandatory morning prayer service before breakfast. The shelter's overnighters were already slumped in the chapel's pews when we arrived. Up on the stage at the front, a white-haired, hawk-nosed preacher in a white button-down shirt and tweed sport coat was pacing back and forth, Bible in hand, waiting for the last of the walk-ins to settle in before starting his sermon. I'd never attended a Protestant 'ear-beating' before, and had no idea what to expect, but John had assured me that the Mission preachers usually kept the morning service brief. Hungry as I was, I hoped he was right.

After welcoming us and introducing himself as Pastor Floyd, the preacher opened his Bible and read a passage from Psalm 118 – *This is the day which the Lord hath made; be happy and rejoice in it* – and followed it up with a brief exhortation: 'When you leave here this morning, take the Lord with you into the streets, and I promise you, He'll give you the strength to resist temptation and keep your steps on the righteous path. Now, before we go in to breakfast, let's start our day with the Lord's Prayer.' The entire service took less than five minutes and seemed no different than I'd have expected from a Catholic priest in a similar setting. I only felt out of place when we got to the end of the Lord's Prayer and I betrayed my Catholic roots by pre-maturely saying 'Amen' before the rest of the congregation had finished reciting the extra verse that Protestants tack onto the prayer ('For thine is the kingdom . . .').

As soon as the final 'Amens' were properly muttered, we all trooped next door to the refectory for a hurried breakfast of oatmeal and watery coffee, and in no time at all we were back on the street, with John Anyway leading me on a tour through the still-sleepy streets of Old Town. Despite his peculiar verbal tic, John's running commentary on the local homeless scene was not only fluent but practically encyclopedic, and as I tagged along and tried to get my bearings on the unfamiliar streets he pointed out every shelter and rescue mission in the neighbourhood, while rattling off a barrage of information about each one. Check-in times. ID requirements. Number of beds. John had it all down pat. Want to know which shelters make you sing for your supper? Whose showers have the hottest water? Whose day-old doughnuts are the freshest? John Anyway's your man.

What John Anyway didn't tell me about the neighbourhood, I picked up on my own, just by reading the signs in the shops we passed along the way. 'Restrooms for Customers Only!' 'We Accept Food Stamps'. 'Loose Cigarettes – Ten Cents Each'. 'NO LOITERING!' 'Government Checks Cashed Here'. I didn't need one of Bob Dylan's mystery tramp decoder rings to decipher the signs' real message: *Welcome to Desolation Row.* But I was okay with that. If I was going to turn my life around, the end of the line seemed like a logical place to start. 'Anyway,' as my stoic guide John would say, 'here I was.'

With street-savvy timing, John's tour brought us to Glisan Street, a few blocks from the bus depot, just in time to join the line for lunch at a Catholic soup kitchen called the Blanchet House. There must have been at least a hundred hungry locals milling around on the sidewalk in front of the place, despite the steady rain that had been falling. By the time John and I joined the line it snaked all the way down the block and around the corner. A few minutes later, a volunteer in a rain poncho stepped out of the two-storey brick building with a fat roll of paper tickets in hand and started working his way down the line, issuing everyone a numbered chit. John told me it was a good system, because it cut down on all the line-jumping that went on at a lot of the other shelters. I could see his point, and wondered why the Brothers at the Oz, down in New Orleans, hadn't installed the same system.

When the kitchen doors opened, the line surged forward and the first forty or fifty people filed into the dining room. The line then stuttered to a halt, and John told me that was all the people the place could handle in one sitting. Those of us left out in the rain had to wait our turn for an empty seat at the tables. After about twenty minutes, the first wave began to trickle back outside and, as they did, the burly staff member stationed at the door started barking out numbers, and by dribs and drabs the rest of us were called inside.

It took us nearly half an hour to reach the head of the line, but as soon as we stepped inside, I could tell the wait was worthwhile. One whiff of baked ham and boiled potatoes was all it took to trigger instant flashbacks to Christmas dinners at my Irish grandmother's tiny two-bedroom apartment on 81st Street in Bay Ridge. To this day, I still remember those impossibly crowded family gatherings with a certain residual awe. How Nana managed to shoehorn two dozen of us into such a tight space was nothing short of amazing. Whenever a fresh batch of relatives would arrive at the door, one of the grown-ups would always shout, 'Get out the room-stretcher!' Though none of us kids ever got to see this mythical tool in action, we didn't doubt its existence. After all, if reindeer could fly, anything was possible.

'Anyway,' John said, interrupting my reverie, 'the Blanchet House has the best free lunch in Portland. Everybody eats here.'

Everybody? By the look of things, I'd say that was an under-statement. *Everybody and his cousin* would be more like it. Even a logistical genius like my grandmother couldn't have wedged another body into the Blanchet House dining room. The crowd at the tables was elbow-to-elbow, filling the room with the syncopated rhythm of silverware clicking on hard plastic plates, and to me it was a siren's song. My mouth was watering and I couldn't wait to get in on the action.

When I saw one of the volunteers waving us toward a table in the back, I nudged John and told him, 'Let's get to it!'

'Anyway, hold up a second. I've got to drop this first,' he said, shucking off his rope-tied bedroll and adding it to the pile of duffle bags and backpacks that lined the baseboard beneath the front window. The Blanchet House had the same rule as the Oz: no baggage at the dining tables.

'Take those two seats in the corner,' the volunteer told us, and pointed to two empty chairs at a two-top table that was tucked against the pony wall dividing the dining area from the cook's line. The table we were assigned to was right next to the dishwashing station, and from where we sat we had a close-up view of a tattooed guy with junkie-thin arms running dishes through a vintage two-door Hobart washer.

The noisy old dish machine looked as hard-used as its operator, and every time he popped the doors to load a rack of dishes I saw a cloud of steam escape and billow up to the pressed-tin ceiling. When the steam hit the tin, it condensed into raindrops, and we happened to be sitting right under the leading edge of the squall line. The ceiling above our table was weeping like a Mexican Madonna, and as the warm drops sprinkled down on us I couldn't resist razzing John about it.

'Check it out, John,' I grinned, catching a droplet on my upturned palm. 'They put us by the water feature. You must really have some pull around here.'

John looked baffled by my attempt at humour, and for a moment he just stared at me like *I* was the one with the scrambled control box. Then he calmly replied, 'Anyway, so what? We're already wet, aren't we?'

'Can't argue with that,' I had to concede, chastened by John's humble outlook. Like most veterans of the streets, he knew better than to sweat the small stuff. We were hungry, and there was a hot meal coming our way. At that moment, what else really mattered?

Fortunately, the Blanchet House staff was well-drilled and quick on their feet, and we didn't have to wait long for our share of the feast.

'Here you go, fellas,' our waiter said, slapping down two plates of baked ham, mashed potatoes and green beans. I dug right in, and every bite brought a pleasant shock of recognition. Incredibly, everything tasted just the way my nana used to make it: the ham was overbaked and slightly dry, the mashed potatoes were lumpy and the greyish-green beans were perfectly rubbery – and as I sat there cleaning my plate, I couldn't remember a meal I'd ever enjoyed more.

'You were right. This place puts out quite the spread,' I said to John on the way out. 'I can see why it's so popular.'

'Anyway, the Blanchet is closed on Sundays. Tomorrow you have to go across the river to St Francis Church. The food there's pretty good, too.'

'St Francis Church on Sundays? I'll have to remember that.'

Despite the cold drizzle that had been falling most of the day, Portland was beginning to grow on me. After scraping by on short rations for the past few weeks, it was a comfort to realise I'd landed in a town that wouldn't let me starve. A big comfort. Especially to someone like me, born with a metabolism that burnt through calories like they were jet fuel. I'd always been called skinny as a kid. In recent years, though, my coke habit had left me looking practically emaciated, and if Portland could help me pack on a few pounds, so much the better.

'Anyway, after lunch I mostly go can-hunting till suppertime,' John said. 'You can come with me if you want, and I'll show you where the recycling centre is.'

Rooting through dumpsters right after lunch didn't sound very appealing, so I told John I'd take a rain check. Now that my belly was full, all I really wanted was to find a warm place to dry out and I asked John if he could point me in the direction of the public library, but he insisted on walking me there so I wouldn't get lost. With John on point, we cut through Old Town's narrow Chinatown, crossed Burnside Street and headed south into downtown Portland, bound for the library's main branch at Tenth Avenue and Yamhill Street. Along the way, John pulled a plastic grocery bag from his coat pocket and started checking every trash bin we passed for cast-off treasure. Any aluminum can he found went right into his wrinkled Safeway bag. He ignored the returnable bottles. Too heavy to haul around, he said. 'Anyway, I leave the bottles for the shopping-cart guys.'

Even while he was foraging for nickels, John kept up his

tour guide's patter, and by the time we reached our destination I'd already learned a thing or two about the Portland Public Library. According to John, it's the oldest public library in Oregon, and a fairly bum-friendly place to hang out. He told me that as long as you didn't talk to yourself too loudly or nod off in your chair, the library's security guards wouldn't usually hassle you – and in John's considered opinion, this made them finer human beings than the goons who patrolled the bus station and the Galleria shopping mall.

'Anyway, it's a pretty nice library,' John said, and when we got there a few minutes later I saw he was right, as usual. The library's three-storey Georgian-style building was clad in weathered sandstone and took up the entire block between Tenth Avenue and Eleventh Avenue on Yamhill Street. I was eager to get inside and out of the rain, but before we parted company John took my elbow and asked me if I thought I could find my way back to the Rescue Mission on my own. When I assured him I could, he told me he'd meet up with me there at six for supper. 'Anyway,' he added, 'come early, so you can sign up for a bed before supper. The Rescue Mission lets you sleep there three nights per month. Anyway, ask them to sign you up for a mailbox slot, too. Then you'll have a place for Social Security to send your new card.'

'Always thinking, aren't you, John?' I smiled. I thanked him for showing me around and wished him good luck can-hunting, then bounded up the wide front steps and got my first look at the library's beautifully crafted interior, an open-plan space gleaming with polished marble floors and burnished walnut woodwork. Suddenly, I was back in familiar territory. My mother's love of books when I was growing up was infectious, and throughout my childhood her weekly visits to the local public library were a lot more faithful than her sporadic attendance at Sunday Mass. So loitering with intent among the stacks of a well-stocked library has always been my favourite way to while away a rainy afternoon. Which was serendipitous, I supposed, now that I found myself in such a famously rainy town as Portland.

Hoping to get a better feel for the neighbourhood that was now my adopted home, I spent the next few hours rummaging through the local history section, digging for information about the Burnside District. My sleuthing took me back to the decades after the Civil War, when the popular nickname for Portland was 'Stumptown' and Burnside Street was one of the busiest skid roads in the Pacific Northwest. During its heyday as a vital conduit for transporting timber from the forests to the docks, Burnside Street was clogged day and night with teams of draught horses pulling massive logs over its skid-lined surface (the wood skids were greased with fish oil) in an endless, slow procession toward the Willamette River. It must have been an impressive spectacle. But once the railroads expanded west, the iron horse pushed the draught horse out of the logging business, and by the end of the century the big show was over.

Even in its most prosperous phase, however, the Burnside District was never the sort of place you'd take the family for a Sunday stroll. By all accounts, in its wild youth Burnside Street served as a kind of moral Mason–Dixon line that separated the God-fearing folks on the south side of town from the Satan-lovers to the north. In those days, the neighbourhood north of Burnside was considered dangerous territory, full of saloons and brothels and gambling houses frequented by hard-drinking, hard-fighting loggers and merchant seamen. In short, it boasted all the parasitic vices you'd expect to find in a frontier boom town, and then some.

If you were lucky enough not to get maimed in a bar fight, or swindled in a gambling hall, or dosed with the clap by a woman of easy virtue, there was still the chance you could find yourself dropping through a trap door into the secret tunnel system that ran beneath Burnside Street, where a shanghai gang would be waiting to snatch you up and bundle you off through the subterranean passageways to the docks. And before you knew whose blackjack had hit you, you'd find yourself in the hold of a ship, taking a trip you never saw coming.

The neighbourhood's unsavoury reputation persisted even after the skid road was dismantled and paved over, and decades later, when the Great Depression hit, the Burnside District naturally became a catch-basin for the steady stream of down-and-out drifters who poured into town on the freight trains that passed through the Old Town yards. Jobless and broke, they wandered the streets of Portland, hoping (like me) that this would be the place that changed their luck – but for most of them, all Portland offered was a change of scenery.

A fortunate few found jobs on the Works Progress Administration's big project to widen Burnside Street – a major feat of engineering at the time. The old skid road was only twenty feet wide, too narrow for a major thoroughfare in a modern city. The WPA's plan was to expand the street by forty feet, but first the engineers had to figure out how to carve out the extra space without demolishing the buildings that already lined both sides of the street. The solution they came up with was to surgically remove twenty feet from the rear of each building before jacking up the façade, lowering it onto rollers, and then pushing it back to rejoin its truncated body (had my nana's room-stretcher actually existed, it would have been the perfect tool for the job).

The Burnside expansion project took years to complete, and it put a lot of men to work, but for every drifter who was lucky enough to land a job with the WPA, there were hundreds more who struck out. The unlucky ones wound up sleeping in hobo jungles on the banks of the Willamette and standing in line at free soup kitchens to keep from starving. It was during this bleak period in the thirties that the term *skid row* was coined, and Burnside Street, the former 'skid road', is the prototype – the stubble-faced, pissed-his-pants granddaddy skid row of them all.

It was nearly sundown when I left the library, and I was glad to see that the rain had let up because my clothes were finally dry after the hours I'd spent in the overheated reading room. Retracing John's route, I hiked back down Yamhill to Burnside Street and then cut east to the Rescue Mission, where my trusty guide was already saving me a spot on the dinner line. But before I joined him in the line, I stepped inside to register for a bed and a mail slot, just as John had suggested. Everything went according to plan, and when I stepped back outside I felt more hopeful about my future than at any time since I'd fled my troubles back in New York. For the next three nights, at least, I had a warm, dry place to sleep, and food was no longer a problem, so things were definitely looking up. Come Monday, I'd start the process of restoring my ID papers by filing for a replacement Social Security card, and once I had my new card in hand I'd be eligible for Food Stamps, and – as John pointed out – I'd be able to register at the plasma centre, too, and start selling my blood for pocket change. I'd been living minute-to-minute for so long I'd forgotten what a pleasure it is to make a plan and see it through. Portland had reminded me of what I'd been missing. Which was one more reason to be grateful that my trip to San Francisco had taken a detour into the Northwest.

Unlike the abbreviated chapel service we'd breezed through before breakfast, the evening service at the Rescue Mission that night was a full-blown example of the sort of 'ear-beating' I'd heard so many tramps complain about during my time on the road. Preacher Floyd was up on the stage again and beside him at the dais stood a young married couple who'd been brought in as guest speakers. It was a Saturday night, but the couple were dressed in their Sunday best. After Preacher Floyd started us off with a group singalong of 'Amazing Grace', he introduced the husband and wife and invited them to tell us their story – and, as soon as they began, I had the eeriest feeling that God was fucking with me.

I mean, what were the odds that my very first experience of a true Mission ear-beating would turn out to be delivered by two former coke addicts? I'd never given much credence to the Protestants' claims that theirs was a 'personal Savior', but listening to that young couple describe the depths they had sunk to while hooked on cocaine certainly felt like a personal message aimed squarely at me, and to keep from squirming in my pew I had to keep telling myself it was just a coincidence that they'd shown up that night to 'testify'.

The couple claimed that near the end, before they admitted they were powerless without God's help, their habit was costing them twenty thousand dollars a year. They lost their jobs. The bank foreclosed on their house and left them homeless. Their families disowned them. Of course, none of the harrowing details they recounted came as any surprise to me. In fact, it was all too painfully familiar, and it was a relief when their twenty minutes at the podium finally ended with their testimony that they'd been lifted up out of the pit by the hand of God. Which prompted a grudging round of 'Amens' from the hungry congregation. Like me, all the other tramps in the room were probably hoping we'd heard enough ear-beating to earn our supper.

But Preacher Floyd wasn't done with us yet, and to our dismay he launched into what promised to be a lengthy sermon about the miracles God performs every day in the lives of those who pray for the gift of His grace. Five minutes into the preacher's sermon, however, one of the winos in the pew behind me nodded off and, as he slumped over in his seat, his mickey of Mad Dog slipped out of his overcoat pocket and shattered on the chapel's concrete floor, sending glass shards flying everywhere, like shrapnel from a Claymore mine.

Immediately, two of the Mission's sharp-eyed ushers descended upon the offender, hauled him out of the pew and hustled him toward the exit at the back of the chapel. As he was escorted out, the poor bastard just kept moaning, 'I broke my mickey! I broke my mickey!' Which naturally prompted scattered snickering from his fellow tramps. Fortunately, the interruption seemed to fluster Reverend Floyd and he cut his sermon short. Next thing we knew, he was telling us to open our songbooks to the closing hymn. After we'd all mumbled through a less-than-rousing rendition of 'Bringing in the Sheaves', our ear-beating finally came to an end – leaving us free at last to follow our noses toward the aroma of fresh-baked lasagne that had been wafting into the chapel from the adjacent kitchen and tormenting us all for the past forty-five minutes.

John and I found two seats at the same table and enjoyed our meal together before he said goodnight and hit the streets for the hike to his 'secret campsite' beneath an overpass somewhere in the industrial area out on the northwestern fringe of Old Town, where he chose to sleep on nights when it wasn't too cold. 'Anyway, I can show you where it is once you've used up your three nights at the Mission. Then if you need to camp out, you'll have a spot. Look for me at breakfast time. I'll be back in the morning.'

The remainder of the evening followed much the same routine I'd been through while staying at the Ozanam Inn in New Orleans. I got to take my first shower in over a week and, later, one of the volunteers at the Clothing Exchange window hooked me up with a complete set of clean clothes – brand new tube socks and cotton boxers, plus a decent pair of used blue jeans and a faded green sweatshirt emblazoned with the logo of the Oregon Ducks. I particularly appreciated the sweatshirt, figuring there might be advantages to passing for a local somewhere down the line. If only I'd been able to score a better-fitting pair of shoes, I'd have been totally set. But the clerk said I'd have to hit the St Vincent de Paul thrift shop for footwear – the Mission exchange didn't have enough room to stock used shoes.

Except for the fact that the Rescue Mission issued ass-draughty hospital gowns instead of pyjamas to its overnight guests (a cringe-worthy fashion faux pas that exposed more of God's handiwork than anyone was happy to see), the biggest difference between the Oz and its Portland counterpart was the size of the crowd in the dormitory. The Mission dorm was set up with bunk beds, automatically doubling its capacity. Which also, unfortunately, meant doubling the amount of coughing and snoring and night cries that echoed all around me in the darkness after lights-out. But I'd learned my lesson in New Orleans, and I made sure not to climb up into one of the sagging upper bunks until I'd fitted myself with a set of toilet-tissue earplugs.

Even with my ears plugged, I still had a hard time nodding off, though I suspect my sleeplessness had less to do with the noise than with the hopeful scenarios my mind kept spinning, as I tried to wrap my head around the new prospects Portland would offer me in the coming days. I lay awake for hours that night, pondering possibilities, until the muffled cries of a troubled sleeper seeped through my earplugs, repeating the same words over and over.

'Let go!' he cried out in the dark. 'Let go! Let go!'

And, finally, too tired to hold on, that's just what I did.

CHAPTER 8

M$_y$ *first weeks* on the streets of Portland reminded me a lot of my first weeks at college. Twenty years after heading off to Dartmouth, I was once again facing the challenges of making my way in a strange environment, far from home and totally on my own. And that wasn't the only similarity, either.

Strangely enough, though I was now thirty-eight, I still felt the same mixture of nervousness and exhilaration I'd felt as an insecure teenager. I'd wake up on skid row each morning acutely aware of how much I had yet to learn, and then, with the same curiosity that animated me as a college freshman, I'd eagerly get on with it. Which was a good thing, because I was now confronting the same daunting task that Jay McInerney's coke-head alter ego faced at the end of *Bright Lights, Big City*, when he concludes that everything he knows will now have to be relearned from scratch.

Even the little things had to be learned anew. Such as, how

to pronounce *Oregon* without sounding like a clueless New Yorker – or like Steely Dan in 'Don't Take Me Alive', crossing their old man in *Ore-gawn*.

Listening to the locals during my first few days in Portland, I quickly realised there is no *gone* in Oregon, and I soon found myself mimicking their pronunciation, which to my ears sounded more like *Origun*. I knew I'd never be able to pass for an Oregonian, with my Brooklyn accent, but I figured it couldn't hurt to show the locals a little respect by pronouncing their state's name correctly. Reliant as I was on their charity, it seemed the least I could do to express my appreciation, so when the pinch-faced woman at the Help Desk in the Social Security offices actually noticed my correct pronunciation and complimented me for it, I had to smile. Did it help speed the processing of my application? Not likely, but who can say? All I know is that my replacement card arrived in the mail before the week was out – much sooner than I'd expected.

Having cleared the first hurdle on the way to restoring my identity – if not yet my respectability – I followed John's advice and immediately took my card to the Alpha Plasma Center's nondescript storefront building on Fifth Avenue to register as a new donor. John said if I could pass the required physical, they'd issue me a free photo ID card that I could use as my second piece of identification when I applied for Food Stamps. And the bonus was, as a new donor I'd receive a ten-dollar sign-up fee in addition to the standard eight dollars they paid for a pint of blood.

How John knew so much about the 'Stab Lab' was a mystery, given the fact that he claimed to be deathly afraid of needles. As usual, though, his information was accurate in every detail and before the afternoon was over I walked out of there a pint of plasma short, but eighteen dollars to the good.

I'd donated blood to the Red Cross Bloodmobile a few times while I was in college, so I wasn't a total rookie at having a vein drained. But my Bloodmobile experience in no way prepared me for the impersonal, factory-like operation I encountered on my first visit to the vampires at the plasma centre.

The formidable middle-aged nurse in charge of the intake desk had the build of a Russian shot-putter and the withering demeanour of Louise Fletcher in *One Flew Over the Cuckoo's Nest*. Beneath her heavily lacquered helmet of blonde hair, her facial features hinted at Slavic origin – as did the tongue-twisting string of consonants that were engraved on her name badge.

'Don't even bother trying to decipher her name,' the twitchy meth-freak in line behind me advised. 'We all just call her Nurse Ratched. Not to her face, of course. We're not crazy. But, dude, look at her. She's got the whole scary Nurse Ratched vibe down cold, don't you think?'

'Yeah, I can see it,' I agreed. 'I wouldn't want to arm-wrestle her, that's for damned sure.'

'Shit, she could beat down everybody in this room if she felt like it,' the tweaker grinned, and I didn't doubt it. Which was likely why the bosses had her working the intake desk. Judging by the motley collection of druggies and winos that appeared to comprise the majority of the centre's clientele, a deterrent force in the waiting room was definitely necessary. Nobody seemed to pay much mind to the tubby rent-a-cop who patrolled the restrooms for illicit activity. He was little more than window-dressing. Nurse Ratched was the true deterrent in the room, and if her intimidating presence failed to have the desired effect on an unruly donor, she wouldn't hesitate to reach for the jumbo-size aerosol can of Glade air freshener she kept handy on her desk – which, as the motor-mouth tweaker informed me, does as good a job as Mace when sprayed in your face at close quarters.

Forewarned about Nurse Ratched's intolerance for anyone who dilly-dallied at the desk or slowed the line down in any way, I made sure to be quick about it when I stepped up to the counter and presented my completed application form and my Social Security card. 'This is all the ID you have?' Nurse Ratched asked, giving me an icy once-over with her pale blue eyes.

'Sorry, ma'am, that's it,' I replied. I was about to explain about my lost wallet but thought better of it. Just in time.

'All right, then,' she snapped, before I had time to get another word out. 'Bring your application down the hall and take a seat outside the doctor's office. When he's ready, he'll call you in for a physical. If you pass, you come back to see me and we'll take a picture for your Alpha ID card. While we're printing your card, you'll take a specimen cup to the men's room and then bring me back a urine sample. Any questions?'

'No, ma'am,' I said.

'Then get a move on,' she said, before barking, 'step up!' to the next man in line.

The frail, rheumy-eyed doctor who performed my physical looked like he'd been abducted from a geriatric ward. I couldn't help wondering what kind of money the Alpha Center's owners had to offer to lure him out of retirement. No matter how much they paid him, however, spending three afternoons per week giving alkies and drug addicts medical clearance to use their bodies as ATM machines had to be a depressing way to supplement your pension, and I felt sorry for the old guy. But to his credit, there was nothing slipshod about the basic exam he gave me, and nothing false about the kindly smile he wore throughout the process.

After my physical revealed no problems that would keep me from donating plasma, the doctor called in one of the nurses to draw a sample of my blood to screen for adverse protein levels (which can disqualify you as a donor) and also to determine my blood type (which would later be printed on my donor ID card). While the nurse was busy jabbing me, the doctor peppered me with questions from a questionnaire meant to assess my possible exposure to the AIDS virus. Had I travelled to Haiti or Africa within the past six months? Did I engage in anal intercourse? Had I ever been tattooed or shared a needle with anyone using intravenous drugs?

Rampant as the AIDS epidemic was in the eighties, I'd expected those kinds of questions, naturally. But when he asked if I'd spent time in prison in the past year I was taken by surprise. I don't know why I'd never thought to consider incarceration a risk factor for AIDS – it made perfect sense, when you thought about it – but until the doctor popped that question I'd never made the connection before, and it left me momentarily flustered. I had to do a quick mental tally of how many months had passed since my release date from Rikers Island before I realised I could truthfully answer, 'No'. Whereupon the doctor pronounced me fit to be drained and then sent me on my way with a wave of his liver-spotted hand and a kindly, 'Good luck, young man.'

Back at Nurse Ratched's station, one of her assistants had me toe the line taped on the floor in front of a tripod-mounted camera, and I had no trouble mustering a smile as she snapped my picture for the photo ID that would now give me access to Food Stamps. Everything was working out just the way

John had predicted. And that was surely something to smile about.

All I had to do now was to provide a urine sample, so I retreated to the men's room with my plastic specimen cup. When I emerged minutes later with the warm cup cradled in my hands, I found myself adopting the same cautious, flatfooted shuffle all the other donors employed when they were ferrying their golden offerings to Nurse Ratched. As I quickly discovered, keeping the piss from sloshing over the edge of the uncapped cup was no easy feat, and for some of the shakier alkies it was a hopeless endeavour – those were the guys you had to give a wide berth while you were standing on the intake line.

Once I'd submitted my sample, I was told to take a seat in the waiting room until my urine had been tested, and as I sat there in one of the plastic bucket seats that had obviously been chosen for their uncomfortable design ('NO SLEEPING!' signs were posted all around the waiting area), I overheard a couple of tramps complaining about Nurse Ratched's iron-handed control over the ceiling-mounted TV in the waiting area.

'Doesn't the bitch realise we already get all the ear-beating we can take at the Rescue Mission? Why do we have to listen to the same preachy bullshit from that phony Pat Robertson? Every time I come in here, she's got the box tuned to *The 700 Club*. Does she really think anyone comes to the Stab Lab to find Jesus? Give me a fucking break!'

'I hear you, brother,' the second tramp agreed. 'Why don't you go ask her to change the channel?'

'Forget that,' the first tramp replied. 'I've seen guys try it and it never works. She just says no, then buries their paperwork at the bottom of the pile. It takes long enough to get out of here with your blood money already. Cross that bitch and you'll be sitting here forever. I've got better things to do with my time.'

By the time the afternoon was over, I discovered the tramp was right about how long it took to walk out of there with cash in hand. Donating plasma turned out to be a much more involved process than pumping out a pint of blood in your local Red Cross Bloodmobile. First off, it took nearly twenty minutes before my urine was tested and my donor ID card was ready for pick-up. After that, I was escorted back to the donation room, where a couple of dozen hospital beds were lined up in tightly spaced rows. Except for the few beds that were being sanitised and lined with paper top-sheets before being put back to use, the rest of the beds were filled with glum-faced donors, who sat propped up by pillows, with plastic tubing snaking from one arm to a portable vacuum pump machine on a rolling cart parked at their bedside.

'What's with all the rubber balls?' I asked the nurse who was leading me to an open bed. Almost every donor in the place was rhythmically squeezing one of those sponge-rubber balls you see in the doggy-toy aisle at Walmart, and my first impression was that I'd stumbled into some sort of weird workout class. Loser Calisthenics, maybe. But the nurse explained that squeezing a ball with the hand of your 'bleed arm' helped speed the flow of blood, allowing you to fill your collection bag more quickly.

'It's your choice, of course,' she said. 'You don't have to use a ball if you don't want to. Some donors prefer to just open and close their fist. But if you want a ball, I'll go grab one for you.'

What the hell? I thought. *Might as well get this over with as soon as possible.* So I asked for a ball, but it still took me nearly forty minutes to pump out a full bag of blood. Then I raised my hand as I'd been instructed, and one of the roving nurses came over to my bedside and disconnected me from the vacuum machine, before collecting my bag of blood and hustling away to the onsite lab that was set up behind a glass wall at the front of the donation room.

According to the information pamphlet I'd been given with my application forms, the whole blood is then run through a special high-speed centrifuge that separates the plasma from the platelets. The process is called *plasmapheresis*, Greek for 'taking away plasma'. Once the plasma has been extracted, the remaining blood goes back into your original bag and is brought back to your bedside to be reinfused into your bloodstream, along with a saline solution to replace the fluids lost during the plasma extraction.

Reinfusion is a slower process, dependent solely on gravity, and there is nothing you can do to speed it up. It must have taken nearly an hour before the last red droplets worked their way down the clear tube into my vein, and by then I was more than ready to get out of there. But I still had to wait another quarter-hour before one of the harried nurses on the under-staffed crew got around to removing the needle-tipped tube from the crook of my arm – and it wasn't until she finished bandaging my puncture wound with a smiley-face Band-Aid that I was finally free to head for the cashier's window with the chit I'd been given to collect my pay.

Even when I got to the cashier at last, I had to jump through still more hoops before I could get paid. First, I had to sign a ledger acknowledging payment for my donation. Then the cashier wrote out a receipt she said I'd need as proof of income if I was enrolled in the Food Stamps programme. This was a wrinkle John Anyway hadn't mentioned, but I pocketed the receipt she gave me and then held out one hand as instructed, while the cashier rubber-stamped the Alpha Center logo on the back of my hand with ultraviolet-sensitive ink.

'The ink stays visible under a black light for three full days,' she explained, in answer to my quizzical look. 'Three days is the minimum safe interval allowed between plasma donations. The ink keeps donors from cheating the system by selling their blood at a different plasma centre before their three-day waiting period is up.' *Ah, that explains it.* I'd been wondering why Nurse Ratched had examined my hands with a black-light wand before she'd issued me a specimen cup.

By the time I finally collected my cash and walked back out to the waiting room, I'd been at the Stab Lab for nearly three and a half hours, and the eighteen dollars in my pocket no longer seemed like easy money. But at two hundred dollars per pint – the amount I'd heard plasma centres like Alpha charged the big pharma companies who bought the bulk of the plasma collected from down-and-outers like me – it was definitely easy money for the vampire elite. As always, the rich get richer. The rest of us just roll up our sleeves for the needle.

Perhaps because I felt ripped off as I walked back out into the drizzling rain on Burnside Street, I suddenly recalled an old Brazilian proverb that Henry Miller liked to quote: *Quand merda tiver valor, pobre nasce sem cu.* 'When shit becomes valuable, the poor will be born without assholes.'

Still, it was hard to stay disgruntled for long. For the first time in weeks, I had money in my pocket that I'd earned instead of panhandled, and I was eager to go spend some of it. The hours I'd spent sitting around the Stab Lab had given me plenty of opportunity to plan my shopping list, and as I hobbled west down Burnside Street I knew exactly what I wanted to pick up before heading out to John Anyway's campsite, where I'd been crashing ever since my allotted nights at the Rescue Mission had run out.

At the local bodega around the corner from the Stab Lab, I picked up mouthwash, Bugler tobacco, a box of Devil Dogs and two quarts of milk. Then, side-stepping the usual cluster of winos trolling for change outside the bodega's doorway, I headed down the block to one of the neighbourhood's ubiquitous pawn shops. This particular shop had an old pocket transistor radio displayed in its window that I'd been eyeing every time I passed. I figured a little music would go a long way toward relieving the Spartan dreariness of John's camp in the evenings, so I stepped inside to see how much they wanted for it. After a little haggling with the owner, I got the price down to two bucks instead of the three he'd quoted and left the shop smiling, feeling like I'd gotten my blood money's worth.

The last stop on my shopping spree was further west on Burnside, at Portland's famous bookstore, Powell's City of Books, where I picked up fresh batteries for the radio and a dog-eared paperback copy of George Orwell's hardship memoir *Down and Out in Paris and London*. It's the first book Eric Blair published under his famous nom de plume, and I'd been meaning to read it for years but had never gotten around to it. Now seemed the perfect opportunity, given my situation. And what better companion could you ask for in an Orwellian setting like the Stab Lab than George Orwell himself? If there'd been plasma centres back in his tramping days, he'd no doubt have rolled up his sleeve for the needle too. I was curious to see how much, or how little, life on skid row today resembled life at the bottom of the barrel back in the late twenties. It would make for interesting reading at my next session with the bloodsuckers at Alpha.

Loitering beneath the entrance awning as I left Powell's, I sheltered from the rain for a moment and rolled a smoke before setting off into the steady drizzle that seemed to be Portland's default weather setting in winter. Now came the hard part – the hike to camp.

Because John Anyway valued his privacy, he'd chosen a campsite further from Old Town than most tramps were willing to hike. It was out beyond the Pearl District, on the fringe of an industrial area on the northwest side of town, beneath one of the 405 Freeway's overpass bridges. Normally, hiking a mile and a half wouldn't have fazed me, but with my blistered heels still in such bad shape, hobbling out there at night was a painful exercise. Nonetheless, like John, I was willing to put in the extra effort just for the peace of mind of knowing we weren't likely to be hassled by cops or attacked in our sleep in such an isolated spot – which made it easier to relax your guard and close your eyes at night. (Guys on the street were still talking about the two tramps who'd been stomped half to death in a riverside campsite several months before I hit town, so John's seemingly paranoid insistence that we keep our campsite's location a secret actually made good sense.)

John had acquired a good supply of discarded appliance boxes from the dumpster of a freight-hauling business a block from the campsite and we stacked the flattened boxes on the hard-packed dirt beneath the overpass and used them as makeshift mattresses. They weren't soft to sleep on, but at least they gave us a layer of insulation between our bodies and the cold ground. John also had a couple of quilted pads that he'd pilfered from the back of an empty removals van. He'd been using them both as extra cushioning before I moved into camp, but when I arrived with no bedroll of my own he graciously gave me one to cover myself. With the removals blanket wrapped around my overcoat, I was usually warm enough to sleep for a few hours at a time. When the cold woke me, I'd get up and do a bunch of lame-footed jumping jacks to get my body heat back up again, and that's how I'd make it through the night.

Much of our discomfort could have been easily avoided if we'd been able to build a small campfire. But John said that was a sure way to bring the cops down on us and he wouldn't allow it. So we put up with the cold as best we could, and on the really frigid nights we'd stay in Old Town and crash on the hard pews in the Gospel Mission.

'Anyway, it looks like you made out all right at the Stab Lab,' John said, when I arrived at camp toting my shopping bags.

'It all went just like you said it would, so tonight the party's on me, John,' I grinned.

John's eyes lit up when I pulled out two quart jugs of milk and the box of Devil Dogs. Fresh milk is something you learn to live without on skid row, since none of the soup kitchens can afford to serve it. Sometimes they'll serve a powdered milk mix, but most of the time you get Kool-Aid or watery coffee or weak iced tea. So when you get a chance to down a quart of fresh milk at one sitting it's a treat you appreciate – especially if you're washing down Devil Dogs instead of a crusty day-old doughnut. John appeared to appreciate it as much as I did, because he didn't make a peep for the next ten minutes, till he smacked his lips and belched when the milk and cake were finally history.

After our pig-out, I showed John the radio and that brought a gleam to his eyes as well. 'Anyway, the Blazers are playing tonight. Can you tune in the game on that thing?'

'I'll give it a try, John, sure,' I said, a little surprised by his request. I wouldn't have taken him for an NBA fan. The Trail Blazers were the only professional sports franchise in Portland (in all of Oregon, for that matter), so rooting for the home team was probably more closely tied to civic pride here than in most places. The funny thing was how many tramps you'd see in the Burnside District wearing scarfs and knit caps with the Blazers' logo. At first, I'd wondered how the NBA had made such inroads into the skid row market, until I figured out that the team loyalty displayed by my fellow bums was more likely just a reflection of what Portland's charitable citizens saw fit to deposit in the Goodwill bins outside their local Safeway super-market. And, no doubt, also a telling indicator of how many could afford to replace their team gear on a yearly basis.

'Anyway, there you go, you found it,' John exclaimed, as the sound of a cheering crowd crackled from the radio and the announcer's voice gave the first-quarter score. The Blazers were up ten points on the Utah Jazz. John grinned and pumped his fist as we settled down side-by-side on our cardboard mattresses, with the radio propped between our heads, and gave our full attention to the game.

Even with the radio's volume cranked, it was impossible to hear the play-by-play whenever a heavy tractor-trailer crossed the overpass above our heads, and we cursed in unison every time we heard a big rig approaching. But the radio was a real hit with John, and I got a kick out of hearing him cheer the Blazers on to victory. 'Anyway, go Clyde!' he'd chant, every time Clyde 'the Glide' Drexler swooped past the Jazz defenders for another fast-break lay-up.

John's childlike glee was infectious and reminded me of all the nights I'd lain awake listening to Knicks games as a kid, a transistor tucked against my ear and pillows piled over my head to muffle the sound so my parents wouldn't hear me breaking curfew. I hadn't listened to a game on the radio in years, but that night beneath the bridge all the old thrill of watching a game in my imagination instead of on a TV screen came flooding back. By the time the final buzzer sounded, I felt like a kid again.

The following day, after my now customary lunch stop at the Blanchet House, I set off down Glisan Street to put in my application for Food Stamps at the shiny new DHS headquarters that had just been built on a razed lot in the no-man's-land beneath the Steel Bridge entrance ramps. I'd wager not one in ten of Portland's locals could tell you where the Department of Human Services was located – which is likely what the city planners had in mind when they chose such an out-of-the-way site (a clever way to neutralise the NIMBY crowd, I had to admit). But the Portland cops knew the address all too well: the DHS centre is a place where frustration frequently boils over into the sort of violent behaviour that requires police intervention.

Everyone forced to turn to the DHS for help has some kind of chip on their shoulder. Many are mad at the world. Others, like me, are simply mad at themselves. Either way, none of us are happy to be humans who require 'servicing', and it doesn't take much bureaucratic sleight-of-hand to turn our disgruntlement into disorderly conduct. When that happens, all the centre's elderly security guard can do is call 911 and take cover behind his desk until the cops arrive.

In fact, there was a PPD squad car pulling up in front of the building when I arrived that afternoon. Two young cops piled out of the cruiser and hustled toward the entrance, unsheathing their nightsticks as they ran. I knew better than to follow them inside. I was there for Food Stamps, not collateral damage, so I hung back and waited for a few minutes until the cops reappeared, herding two handcuffed men out of the building ahead of them.

Both of the men in custody were Native Americans, and they were both unsteady on their feet. When I got a good look at their faces, I realised I'd seen them before. Two wino drinking buddies named Leonard and Bear. I'd slept beside them at the Gospel Mission one night when the cold drove so many men in off the streets that some of us were forced to crash downstairs on the dusty concrete floor of the church's boiler room. I didn't get much sleep that night. Bear, the stocky one with a pock-marked face, was snoring louder than the racket from the furnace, and his partner, Leonard, a pony-tailed Vietnam vet about my age, kept jerking awake with the night terrors, kicking my back in the process.

The two buddies must have gotten an early start on their drinking that day. It was barely one-thirty in the afternoon and they were already glassy-eyed and slurring their speech. I gave them a comradely nod as the cops marched them past me, but they were too preoccupied to notice. Bear was busy serenading his handler with a tone-deaf rendition of the old Cher tune 'Bang, Bang (My Baby Shot Me Down)'.

'Whatever you say, Cher. Just watch your head,' the cop muttered, as he wrangled Bear into the squad car.

Leonard wasn't going quietly either. I could hear him ranting at the cop who had him in tow. He seemed to be claiming that he was a Vietnamese refugee. 'Here to get my shit like everyone else, goddamn it!'

'Hear that?' Leonard's cop asked his partner. 'This Gallo Brother thinks he's a Veet-namese refugee.'

'Better lay off the sauce for a while, Chief,' the other cop laughed. 'It's pickling your brain.'

Leonard's brain might very well have been pickled, but it made me angry to hear the two young cops belittle him. They were probably playing dodgeball in grade school gym class while guys like Leonard were being shipped across the Pacific to risk their lives in the jungles of Vietnam. So they had no clue, and couldn't see the sad logic underlying Leonard's argument. Because, from his point of view, he really *was* a refugee from Vietnam. And so were all his comrades in arms who were part of the lost battalion of homeless vets that I'd met since I'd hit the road. Twelve years after the fall of Saigon, they were still haunting the streets of America – trying, but mostly failing, to get their shit like everyone else.

Bear's off-key singing sounded almost melodious compared to the banshee wailing that assaulted my ears when I stepped into the DHS centre. Everywhere I turned, I saw welfare moms pushing collapsible strollers, doing laps around the perimeter of the spacious waiting area in the vain hope that steady motion would soothe their little screamers and give everyone's ears a break.

I'd thought a Rescue Mission bunk room was noisy until I heard those angry little Kool-Aid kids. To my ears, there was something almost prescient about their wailing. As if they could already tell where all those laps around the DHS centre were leading – and were letting the rest of us know exactly how they felt about starting out life on the dole. I couldn't help sympathising with their protests, but that didn't make their crying any easier to take. By the time I finished filling out my application form I had a throbbing headache – a side-effect John Anyway had neglected to mention when he'd told me how easy it was to sign up for Food Stamps.

The young mothers and their noisy infants were the most conspicuous DHS clients that afternoon, but they were just a small minority of the crowd assembled in the waiting area. Scanning the room, I spotted a handful of twentysomething skateboard slackers and a few muttering bag ladies, but the majority of the crowd was made up of ragged-looking men, ranging in age from their early thirties to their late sixties. The predominantly male crowd seemed to support John Anyway's claim that Portland was a popular destination for homeless men in the wintertime. He'd told me lots of guys from colder states like Montana and Colorado and Wyoming would turn up in Portland, winter after winter, because the city's social services agencies had a reputation for being much less nit-picky than their counterparts in sunny California.

If my experience at the DHS that afternoon was at all typical, Portland's liberal reputation was well-deserved. The cheerful caseworker who reviewed my application, a middle-aged Latina with greying bangs and a bright toucan-patterned scarf around her neck, quickly checked my ID cards and my paperwork and pronounced them all in order. But then she pointed out that I hadn't provided proof of local address with my application, and I thought, *Oh, Jesus, here comes the deal breaker! How the hell does someone who beds down under bridges prove where he resides?*

I really expected to be turned down as soon as I explained my situation, but it turned out I'd underestimated the flexibility of the good-hearted souls who staffed the Portland DHS. After hearing me out, the caseworker simply swivelled on her chair and snatched a new form from the wall shelves behind her, which she slid across the counter to me. 'This should solve your problem,' she smiled.

Glancing down at the Xeroxed sheet she'd passed me, I

was surprised to see it was a simplified map of the downtown bridges and freeway overpasses, crudely hand-drawn, like those throwaway maps they hand out at campgrounds to help you find your way to your assigned site.

'What am I supposed to do with this?' I asked.

'Find the spot where you've been camping and mark it with an X,' she said, handing me a pen. 'Then sign and date the bottom and you're all set.'

'That's it?' I asked, in disbelief. 'X marks the spot?'

'Simple as that,' she replied. 'If you change camps, or move to a permanent address, let us know and we'll update your file. In the meantime, since you have no permanent address, you'll have to report to the centre in person to pick up your Food Stamps.'

I studied the map for a moment, and when I spotted the 405 Freeway I traced its path with my finger until I came to the overpass where John and I had been camping. Assured by the caseworker that my information wouldn't be shared with the police, I marked my X, signed the form and suddenly I was officially a resident of Portland.

Next came the business of snapping my mugshot and printing my photo ID, and once that was done the caseworker explained that it would probably take about two weeks before my application worked its way through the system and my Food Stamps arrived.

'In the meantime,' the caseworker said, 'here's a twenty-five-dollar book of "emergency stamps" to tide you over. Make sure you take your ID card with you when you go shopping. The store cashiers aren't allowed to accept Food Stamps from anyone who doesn't show a DHS card. Any other questions before I let you go?'

'Just one,' I said. 'How do you stay so cheerful in a place like this?'

'That's nice of you to say,' she smiled. 'But it's not hard, really. Not if you enjoy helping people.'

Clearly, this was a woman who shared Kerouac's view on practising kindness. She'd certainly given me the help I'd been hoping for, and except for the wailing babies the whole process had been so painless that I couldn't help raving about it when I got back to camp that night. John grinned as I told him how surprised I'd been when the caseworker handed me the Xeroxed map – and his response cracked me up.

'Anyway, most guys call that the Troll Map.'

Of course they do! I thought. What could be more perfect? Isn't that how most people see the homeless? We're hairy, we're scary, we live under bridges – and just like the trolls in the old fairy tales, we demand to be paid our toll.

Food Stamps Accepted Here.

❦

The longer I hung around Portland, the more I was impressed by the variety of assistance programmes the charitable locals made available to the city's street people. The storefront 'drop-in centre' on West Broadway in Old Town was a prime example. Its modest reading room, stocked with donated paperback books and comfortable old couches, was a popular place for transients to kill a few hours between mealtimes at the various soup kitchens, but it was more than just a warm, dry hangout. The volunteers who staffed it also offered help with job counselling and résumé preparation, as well as assistance in filling out applications for the federally funded Low Income Energy Assistance Program (LIEAP), which provided financial subsidies in the winter months to those who needed help with their home heating bills (on the street, this subsidy was known as a 'leap cheque'). For those of us with no homes to heat, the centre did the next best thing by distributing warm winter coats they solicited from local corporate donors.

A few days after I'd signed up for Food Stamps, John Anyway heard a rumour that a new supply of 'leap coats' was about to be given out at the drop-in centre that afternoon, and he urged me to get over there right away so I wouldn't miss out. Which was good advice, because when I hiked over to West Broadway there was already a long line forming outside the drop-in centre, with dozens of tramps eagerly waiting for the doors to reopen once the volunteer staff's lunch break was over.

Inside, the grandmotherly woman who served as the LIEAP liaison was handing out coats from a big pile of boxes that filled most of the cramped corner where she had her desk. The boxes all bore the logo of the Columbia Sportswear Company, one of Portland's biggest corporate success stories, and though at first I cynically assumed the donated coats would be defective goods, palmed off on the poor for the sake of a tax deduction, I couldn't have been more wrong. The insulated parka she handed me was sturdily made, with a waterproof Gore-Tex shell, a handy draw-string hood and plenty of Velcro-seal pockets (a definite plus for anyone living on the streets). I couldn't believe my luck! The new parka was a big improvement over my vintage wool overcoat, which soaked up Portland's incessant rains like a tweed tampon, getting heavier and heavier as the day wore on.

Besides being lighter and more waterproof than my old overcoat, the new parka was certainly a lot less seedy-looking and as I wandered around town that afternoon I kept checking my reflection in the storefront windows, delighted by the newly respectable image I presumed I now presented to the world. More than just a warm coat, the parka seemed to me a welcome bit of camouflage that would let me blend in with the well-adjusted majority, and, for a change, go happily unnoticed.

Alas, my illusions of respectable anonymity faded all too quickly the following morning when I hiked back to the Burnside District from Camp Anyway and discovered, to my dismay, that the streets of Old Town were now swarming with homeless people sporting brand new parkas exactly the same as mine.

Needless to say, this was a deflating development – and disheartening proof that even charitable intentions are subject to the law of unintended consequences. With a little foresight, perhaps the Samaritans at Columbia Sportswear might have realised that donating coats that were all the same colour wasn't such a good idea. But, apparently, no one had considered the repercussions. And now that slate-blue had become the official colour of 'Team Homeless', those of us who'd made the roster and donned the new uniform found ourselves suddenly more visible than ever.

Naturally, our enhanced visibility now made us easier to target, and it wasn't long before the random indignities of life on skid row became noticeably less random if you happened to be a 'Bluecoat'. Restroom keys would go missing more often – and stay conveniently 'lost' until I left the premises. And at night, when I'd hike back to camp, bored cops looking for amusement would shadow me in their squad cars, busting my balls with the kerbside crawl.

Of course, the cops weren't the only ones getting in on the action. It took no time at all for Portland's swastika-tattooed skinheads to realise that slate-blue was the new black, and now when I cut through Pioneer Square, where the young cretins in black denim and Doc Martens bum-stompers hung out in packs, they'd flick their cigarette butts at me and shout, 'Get a job, you lazy fuck!'

Even the earnest young clowns in clip-on ties who managed the local McDonald's jumped on the bandwagon. Now, any Bluecoat who stepped up to the counter for the customary free coffee refill was just as likely to get the McBrush-off instead. It was all so petty and unnecessary, but I must admit that it gave me daily confirmation that Claude Lévi-Strauss got it right in *Tristes Tropiques* when he observed that a traveller's experience of any new place is inescapably coloured by his exact position in the social scale while he's there.

Even at the time, I knew my experiences as a Bluecoat would colour my memories of Portland from then on. But besides making my low status highly visible, the well-meaning folks at Columbia Sportswear had also managed to negate one of the more enjoyable aspects of my move to Portland. Before the parka came into my life, I'd been able to walk the unfamiliar streets of Old Town with the carefree certainty that my escape from New York meant I no longer had to worry about turning a corner and bumping into someone I'd let down or screwed over. Now, around every corner I turned, I ran into blue-clad versions of myself: the very person I'd let down the most, and screwed over the worst. Which was unsettling, to say the least. Though I have to admit, the whole Bluecoat fiasco provided a sobering reminder that straightening out my life would require much more than a wardrobe change.

Securing a place to live was obviously the next big change I had to shoot for, and as it turned out my quest for permanent housing gave the kindly woman at the drop-in centre a chance to atone for inadvertently turning me into a Bluecoat pariah. This was a few days after I'd collected my new parka, when I went back to the centre to ask her what I'd have to do to qualify for one of the 'leap cheques' I'd been hearing so much about on the chow line at the Blanchet House.

'It's not hard at all,' she cheerfully assured me. 'If you're enrolled in the Food Stamps programme, your income eligibility has already been established, so the only other thing I'd need from you is proof of local residence.'

Here we go again, I thought, and explained that my local residence was under a freeway overpass.

'Well, then you wouldn't be eligible, I'm afraid. LIEAP only subsidises people who need help heating their homes in wintertime. Sorry, that's a rule I have to follow.'

'I was afraid of that,' I frowned. 'So I'm out of luck then, is that what you're telling me?'

'Not necessarily,' she replied. 'We have a number of SRO hotels in the neighbourhood that participate in the LIEAP network and they'll accept a heat-subsidy cheque in lieu of rent. All you'd have to do is pay for a week's stay at one of the approved hotels, bring us your rent receipt and we'll issue a cheque for $143 directly to the hotel. Which should at least be enough to keep you indoors for the rest of the winter. If I were you, I'd consider it. Let me give you this list of the hotels we work with, and if you decide to rent a room, come back to see me and I'll be glad to help you with the paperwork.'

Thanking her for the advice, I left the drop-in centre with at least a glimmer of hope. Surely I could raise enough money selling plasma to cover a week's rent at one of the local flop-houses. If they were anything like the Bond Hotel back in Tribeca, the rates wouldn't be too steep. It was worth checking out, I figured, and as I walked back to Burnside Street I decided I'd pick a few names from the list and visit them to see how much blood money I'd have to sock away (quite literally) to cover a week's rent. But as soon as I consulted the list, I knew there was only one hotel I wanted to call home – no matter how sleazy it might turn out to be.

How could I ever pass up the opportunity to live in a place called the Joyce Hotel?

Checking the address, I realised it was right around the corner from Powell's Books, surely another sign that the Joyce was the place for me. And I wasn't disappointed when I got to Eleventh Avenue and saw the vintage-style marquee sign above the hotel's entrance, with my Irish hero's name prominently displayed.

Like most of its run-down neighbours in the Burnside District, the Joyce Hotel's four-storey brick building had seen better days. The date etched into the cornerstone read '1912' – which meant it had opened the same year that James Joyce wrote the poem 'Gas from a Burner', his famously scathing portrait of the censorious Irish printer who sabotaged publication of *Dubliners* on the grounds that Joyce's stories libelled Ireland's good name.

Something told me I wasn't likely to encounter any readers of 'Gas from a Burner' among the lodgers at the Joyce, but you could never tell. If I was any indication, maybe the hotel's august name pulled in a more literate clientele than your average flophouse. That would be a pleasant surprise.

At the moment, however, all I wanted was good news from the desk clerk, a paunchy old-timer who looked like a ringer for Weeb Ewbank, coach of the Jets in Joe Namath's glory days. Same flat-top haircut, same jowly jawline, same hard-eyed stare – which was how he sized me up as I approached the Plexiglas security barrier that topped the reception counter.

In hardship hotels like the Joyce, you speak to the desk clerk through a hole cut in the Plexiglas. Not surprisingly, the diameter of the hole is always smaller than a man's fist. Which pretty much tells you all you need to know about the company you'll be keeping if you're desperate enough to give the place your business. Then again, if you're willing to conduct business through a talk-hole, I suppose your desperation is self-evident. Mine certainly was, but I didn't care. All I cared about was a rate I could afford, and some assurance that there'd be a room available the following week, which was the soonest I figured I could raise the cash I'd need for a week's rent.

To my relief, there were several vacancies about to open up, and the weekly rate was only twenty-two dollars, so it was good news all around. Three more visits to the Stab Lab were all it would take to get me back off the streets at last! Three more visits to the Stab Lab were also all it took for me to finish reading *Down and Out in Paris and London* (which I'd carefully rationed, and only dipped into while I was bleeding for cash).

Orwell's account of his down-and-out days struck me as uncannily similar to what I'd experienced as a penniless transient since I'd hit the road. There were historical differences, to be sure. These days we have vagrancy laws. In Orwell's England, they had more restrictive 'tramping laws' – laws that forced homeless unemployed men to stay constantly on the move from poorhouse to poorhouse, or face imprisonment. But when Orwell writes about the human element of poverty – how it *feels* to be homeless, how it *feels* to go hungry, or to sleep in the cold, or to be looked down on by the public – his insights are timeless. Reading his portraits of the men he tramped with, I felt as though I could step outside onto Burnside Street and find their twins on every corner.

As it happened, I came to Orwell's closing pages (in which he offers his thoughts on improving the lot of the homeless) on the afternoon of my final rent-raising session at the Stab Lab, and as I sat in the hospital bed, squeezing my doggy ball for all I was worth – with a night's rest in a room all my own just a blood bag away – here's what Orwell had to say: 'It does not matter how small a cubicle is, the important thing is that a man should be alone when he sleeps.'

Smiling to myself, I thought, *By George, what a capital idea!* Next stop, the Joyce Hotel . . .

CHAPTER 9

*W*eeb *Ewbank's lookalike,* whose name turned out to be Vern, was once again on desk duty when I hobbled into the Joyce Hotel's lobby and pushed my blood money through the cash slot in the security barrier. In return, he shoved a registration card through the slot, and as I began filling it out it suddenly dawned on me that it was 13 March. Exactly four weeks had passed since I'd landed in Baloney Joe's on the night of my birthday. Which meant that – whether by fate or by happy coincidence – when I woke up tomorrow in a bed of my own at last, I'd be starting my *twenty-ninth* day in Portland. I'd always considered twenty-nine my lucky number, and now it had come through for me again. As soon as I'd done the math a goofy smile broke out on my face, and I made no attempt to hide it from Vern, though I noticed he was now studying me with a skeptical look. *Guy probably thinks I'm short a few marbles,* I thought. *Who else but a nut job could find anything to smile about in a flophouse like this?*

I considered explaining that the room key he was about to give me was the best belated birthday gift I could possibly have wished for but decided it was a story best saved for another day. In my experience, flophouse desk clerks are a garrulous breed. More often than not they're residents of the hotel themselves — old pensioners working off a portion of their rent by pulling shifts at the desk — and their favourite pastime while on duty is swapping long-winded stories and hotel gossip with the 'lobby rats'. So, unless you're looking to kill time, it's wise not to give them an opening. Tired as I was, I didn't care whether Vern pegged me as a head case or not. I just didn't want to get trapped at the talk-hole and have him bending my ear for the next half-hour.

'Okay, here you go, Room 222,' Vern said, sliding a tagged key and my rent receipt through the slot. 'Elevator's on the fritz, so you'll have to take the stairs up. If you stick around, we'll get to know your face pretty quick, but for the first few days make sure to stop by the desk and show your room key before you head upstairs, okay?'

'No problem,' I replied, grabbing the key and the receipt as I turned toward the stairs.

But before I could get away, Vern barked, 'Whoa, not so fast!' As a first-time guest, I was obliged to listen to a recitation of the 'house rules'. Which turned out to be the usual list of Noes.

No hotplates. No loud music. No overnight guests (unless you cleared them at the desk first and paid for their stay in advance).

'The front doors are locked at 10 p.m. every night,' Vern added. 'After ten, ring the outside buzzer, hold your room key up to the glass and the night clerk will let you in. Any questions?'

'Yeah,' I grinned. 'What time's the Continental breakfast?'

'Hey, Marvin, you hear that?' Vern called out to the other

old-timer doing bookwork behind the desk. 'We got us a comedian. Wants to know what time we serve the Continental breakfast!'

Marvin swung his swivel chair around to get a look at me and shouted back, 'That'd be right after morning yoga class, son!' Proving I wasn't the only comedian in the room.

Heading past the elevator on my way to the wide marble staircase, I noticed the curling corners of the 'Out of Order' sign taped above the call buttons and had a hunch that, in the Joyce at least, 'on the fritz' was a terminal diagnosis. Which made me thankful I hadn't gotten stuck with a room on the fourth floor. How the pensioners in the place managed without an elevator was difficult to fathom. They must have had legs like mountain goats.

Room 222 was just off the stairwell, and when I opened the door to take my first look at it there were no surprises. It was basically a clone of every other flophouse room I'd rented in recent years. Standing in the doorway, I took it all in at a glance. The sagging bed with two lumpy pillows and a threadbare bedspread. The tiny hand sink tucked into a corner, its porcelain bowl crazed with a spidery web of tiny cracks. The unframed mirror above the sink, splotched with dark patches where the silvering had flaked off over time. The indestructible, steel-framed straight-back chair, de rigueur not just in flophouses but in discriminating parole offices and psych ward rec rooms throughout the land. Then, of course, there was the room's lone window, which looked out over (you guessed it) the concrete walls of a blind airshaft – at the bottom of which lay a multicoloured glass mosaic composed of broken wine and beer bottles, an organic art installation that changed nightly as the dead soldiers came whistling down past my window and

shattered on top of their fallen brothers. And, finally, the oblig-
atory four-drawer dresser, with two missing drawer-pulls and
a cherrywood top whose edges were deckled black with cigarette burns.

All of which, I should add, sat atop a layer of crusty industrial carpet – in this case, in a mottled brown, though mottled
by what I didn't care to speculate. For twenty-two dollars a
week, that's what you get. But I wasn't disappointed in the least.
The only furnishings in the room that mattered to me were the
solid wood door and the sturdy Yale lock that secured it.
Everything else, no matter how seedy, was a bonus. Including
the thick red brick that was sitting on the windowsill – an
amenity I'd never encountered in any of my previous flops.

At first, I couldn't figure out what purpose the brick might
serve. But when I lifted up the lower half of the window to let
in some fresh air, the damned thing came crashing back down
like a guillotine blade the instant I took my hand away – and
suddenly the brick's purpose was no longer a mystery. And the
brick proved to be more versatile than I'd imagined. Depending
whether you stood it upright, or laid it down flat, or placed it
on its side, you could prop the window open at three different
heights, letting you adjust how much cold air flowed into the
room. Which was handy, since the room was hotter than a
Brooklyn tenement in August and there was no way to adjust the
flow of steam clanking through the old cast-iron radiator beside
the dresser. I know, because I tried. Only to discover that someone
had removed the handle from the radiator's regulator valve.

Shaking my head in disbelief, I thought, *Yep, Bob, you weren't
joking.* The vandals had taken the handles. And, apparently, the
window sash weights too.

Closing the door behind me, I savoured the satisfying click

of the lock. I then paused for a moment to read the notices posted on the back of the door, all of them mounted behind protective Plexiglas and securely screwed into the door's solid wood. As always, I checked the 'In Case of Emergency' map to make sure I knew which exit to head for in the event of a fire – definitely information worth knowing before you nod off in a flophouse like the Joyce, where nearly every lodger is a smoker, and the only part of the cut-rate mattresses that won't burn is their 'fire-retardant' labelling.

Beneath the emergency exit map hung a sign in bold letters that read: 'NO HOTPLATES ALLOWED! *By Order of the Portland Fire Department.*'

'Fuck the PFD!' read the comment scrawled in Magic Marker on the sign's protective plastic. That made me smile. Judging by the aromas wafting through the half-open transom window above my door, 'fuck the PFD' seemed to be the general attitude toward the no-hotplate rule. On top of the usual undertones of mildew and roach spray, I caught definite whiffs of Campbell's Chicken Noodle Soup and Dinty Moore's Beef Stew – the same two favourites that had flavoured the air in the hallways of every transient hotel I'd ever briefly called home. This was an encouraging sign. It meant the Joyce enforced the no-hotplate rule the same way the other flops did – only when the fire inspector showed up for a visit.

As soon as I could put together a little extra cash, the first thing on my 'home improvements' list would be a used hotplate. The pawnshops in the Burnside District were full of them. I could probably pick one up for five bucks or less, which was a small price to pay for the freedom it would buy me. Not just the freedom to heat up a hot meal when I felt like it, but, more importantly, the freedom to withdraw from the daily grind on the hand-out circuit. When you're forced to structure your days around the fixed schedules dictated by the Samaritan 'establishment', you forfeit all pretence of independence and just take your place among the herd. As I'd discovered, it's a routine that wearies the soul pretty quickly. I had only been on the streets of Portland for a month, but I was already tired of queuing up in the soaking rain outside the Blanchet House every afternoon, and even more tired of singing for my supper at the Rescue Mission every night. With a hotplate in my room, my time would once again be my own. I couldn't wait to get my hands on one. Come Monday, my next scheduled plasma donation day, I'd be hitting the pawn shops the minute I left the Stab Lab.

In the meantime, I'd make do with cold food. I had stopped at a bodega on my way to the Joyce and picked up a can of pork and beans, a box of doughnuts and a quart of milk, which was now chilling nicely on the wide ledge outside my brick-propped window. I was hungry after giving blood, but I put off eating for the time being. What I needed more than food was a hot shower, so I stripped down to my skivvies, tucked a frayed hotel bath towel around my waist and headed down the hall to the communal shower room, where the hotel's old boiler didn't let me down. I must have stayed in the shower for nearly half an hour, till every mirror in the room was fogged, and still the hot water never faltered. It was bliss, I tell you. Pure bliss!

Even the fact that I had nothing but the same unwashed clothes to put on once I got back to my room didn't spoil my good mood. Not after my first hot shower in nearly a month. Anyway (as John would say), a quick trip to the St Vincent de Paul thrift shop over the weekend was all it would take for me to stock my empty dresser drawers with hand-me-down clothes. And it wouldn't cost me a dime, either. Father Gary, the parish priest who ran the Sunday meal programme at St Francis of Assisi Church, had given me a voucher for the thrift shop. I'd been holding onto it for several weeks, not wanting to burden myself with extra belongings while I was still roughing it out on the streets, but now that I had a home base it was time to cash it in.

It wasn't till I'd finished dressing and sat down to eat my supper that I realised I'd forgotten to pick up a can opener at the bodega, so I had no way to open my can of pork and beans. *What now, dumbass?* I considered knocking on one of my neighbours' doors but decided it would be better to stick with the devil I knew, so I took my can of beans downstairs to the lobby and opened it with a can opener that Vern dug out of the junk drawer behind his desk. Then, as I was climbing the stairs back up to the second floor, I had an oddly unsettling encounter with one of my fellow lodgers as we passed each other on the first-floor landing.

He was a gaunt, white-haired old-timer, shuffling along on slippered feet. His checked pyjamas were covered by a blue flannel robe and atop his head sat a navy-blue ball cap with braided gold lettering that spelled out: *Pearl Harbor Survivor.* I'd never seen him before in my life, and I was pretty sure he'd never seen me either, so it was quite a surprise when he reached out a shaky hand and gripped me lightly on the shoulder as I passed. When I stopped to face him, he smiled like we were the oldest of friends and, in a solicitous tone, said, 'So, are you starting to find your way?'

What the fuck? I stood there silent for a second, dumb as the can of beans in my hand, wondering what this Ancient Mariner had seen in me that would prompt such a question. Stumped, all I could think to say was, 'Yeah, thanks, I'm starting to get the hang of it.'

'Well, good. I'm glad to hear it. I'll see you around,' he said, taking his bony hand from my shoulder to grip the bannister before resuming his trip down the stairs.

Back in my room, the Mariner's question kept ricocheting around in my brain. *So, are you starting to find your way?* The more I thought about it, the more it gave me the chills. Wasn't that exactly why I'd hit the road? To find my way?

Maybe I was reading too much into the whole encounter, but it was hard to shake the idea that an old survivor like the Mariner might have a keen eye for those who'd lost their bearings. If so, it was eerie to think that his discerning eye had unerringly picked me out on my very first night at the Joyce. What was I supposed to make of *that*? By the time I nodded off that night, I still hadn't figured it out.

On Saturday morning I slept in late for the first time in weeks and didn't awaken until I heard the sound of bagpipes faintly bleating through my open window. Which puzzled me at first, until I remembered that Portland's premature Paddy's Day parade was taking place that day. *Erin go bragh!* I muttered, rolling out of bed and reaching for my hand-me-down Oregon Ducks sweatshirt, the one piece of green clothing in my wardrobe. That would be my only nod toward the Emerald Isle this year. For the first time in twenty years (except 1985, when I was locked up on Rikers Island), I was about to celebrate St Patrick's Day as a sober man – a hopeful sign that perhaps I was, indeed, 'finding my way' at last. I chose to think so, anyway. Of course, if you're too broke to afford a drink, you can't really chalk your sobriety up to willpower, but that didn't discourage me. Breaking the cycle was all that mattered, regardless how you managed it.

I've never subscribed to the notion that the sins of the fathers (or mothers) are visited upon their children, but the truth remains that my mother's people, the McGuires, were a family much plagued by the 'Irish curse' and, sad to say, my mother was one of its unlucky victims. As a child, I got so used to seeing her with a can of Rheingold beer in her hand I never gave her drinking much thought. But as I got older and began visiting the homes of my schoolmates, I couldn't help noticing that their mothers weren't wearing their bathrobes at four in the afternoon, or doing household chores with one hand while clutching a can of beer in the other. That's when I first began to suspect that my mom had a problem. However, I didn't fully grasp the depth of her problem until the night I went rummaging through her dresser drawers.

It was the week before Christmas and I'd been left at home to babysit my brothers while my parents attended a house party down the block. I was an overly curious nine year old at the time, and I couldn't resist the urge to do a little spying while my parents were away. I was hoping for an advance peek at whatever gifts might be coming my way under the Christmas tree, but the only surprise I found waiting in my parents' bedroom was hidden in my mom's lingerie drawer: four warm cans of Rheingold, her emergency stash, tucked out of sight beneath a pile of rubbery girdles.

I couldn't look my mom in the eye for days after that. By invading her privacy, I'd uncovered a sad truth she'd surely meant to keep hidden – even from my father – and I was ashamed of myself for it. But I was ashamed of my mother too, and, to my discredit, I judged her with the naïve and self-righteous severity only a disappointed child can muster.

Though I tried not to let my feelings show, I'm sure my

mom must have noticed the sudden changes in my behaviour. On our weekend trips to the A&P, I'd still push the grocery cart through the aisles for her, just as I always had, but now when we'd get to the beer section my ears would burn red with shame as I loaded the weekly supply of Rheingold cans into the cart – the same three cases every Saturday, out of which my father never drank more than two six-packs. My mother could hardly have missed the furtive glances with which I now scanned the aisle before loading the beer into her cart. Furtive glances that telegraphed my fear of being spotted by anyone I knew from school. But though my mother must have noticed, she never questioned me about it, and for that at least I was grateful.

Happily, the passing years made me less judgemental, and by the time I dropped out of the seminary and returned home to attend public high school I had long since come down off my high horse. Now I felt perfectly at ease with my mom when she'd hand me a cold can of Rheingold at night and invite me to sit with her while she watched Johnny Carson and waited for my dad to get home from his second job. I was seventeen at the time, still a year shy of the legal drinking age, but that didn't seem to trouble my mom. She'd just give me a conspiratorial wink and caution me to keep mum about our nightly get-togethers. My brothers would be asleep by the time Johnny Carson came on, and I always retreated to my bedroom before my dad returned home from work, so we had no difficulty keeping our little secret from the rest of the family.

Our conspiracy drew us closer together than we'd been in years, and it seemed to me I was finally showing my mom the loyalty she had a right to expect from her first-born child. Which made me feel better about myself, and about my mom too. After all, what did she have to be ashamed of? Her drinking had never kept her from being a good wife to my father, or a good mother to her children, so who was anyone to judge her, least of all me? But, as I would shortly discover, she still felt judged. It just took her a while to admit it.

I turned eighteen during the winter of my senior year, and after that I began spending my nights hanging out at the local bars in Ronkonkoma with my friends instead of with my mom and Johnny Carson. At first, my mom seemed to take my defection as nothing more than a teenager's natural urge to run with the pack and she gave no sign that it bothered her. But by Eastertime I began to notice the pained look that would flicker across her face whenever my pal Kenny Brown would pull up in front of our house in his old Falcon and summon me outside with a double toot of his horn.

I saw that same hurt look in her eyes when the Falcon's horn sounded on the night of Good Friday, but I said nothing except a quick goodbye on my way out the door. I didn't return until midnight, a half-hour before my dad was due home, and when Kenny dropped me at the kerb in front of my house I was surprised to see my mother open the front door and step out onto the porch in her bathrobe, where she stood waving forlornly at Kenny's car as he pulled away.

I had a pretty good buzz on, and everything was slightly out of focus, so I didn't notice the tears streaming down my mother's cheeks until I was nearly to the doorstep. 'Mom! What's wrong?' I blurted out, alarmed and suddenly sober. I reached out to put my arms around her, but she backed away into the open doorway and just fixed me with the saddest look I'd ever seen.

'Are you really that ashamed of me, Peter? Your own mother?' she sobbed.

I was stunned.

'*Ashamed of you?* What are you saying, Mom? Of *course* I'm not ashamed of you! Why would you ever think that?'

'You never invite your friends into the house. Ever. Don't you know how that makes me feel? Like I'm not good enough, that's how. Like there's something wrong with me. Something my son's ashamed to let his friends see. Honestly, am I really that bad?'

My heart ached when I heard her say that, and then my eyes were brimming with tears just like hers. Pleading with my mom to believe me, I insisted that I'd never kept my friends away because I felt ashamed of her. But, of course, my actions had proved otherwise.

The truth was that I avoided bringing my friends into the house not because my mother drank but because she was such a voluble talker. If you gave her an opening – especially when she had a few beers in her system – she could talk your ear off for an hour before you'd ever get a word in edgewise. I'd always thought my friends would find that uncool, so I spared them the ordeal by meeting all my visitors in the street. But I had never once stopped to consider how my efforts to avoid an embarrassing situation might hurt my mother's feelings – not until that night when I was finally forced to see things through her eyes. Then the only person I was ashamed of was myself.

Though I managed to soothe her before my dad got home – and would later make a point of bringing Kenny Brown into the house whenever he stopped by to pick me up – my relationship with my mother after that Good Friday was never again as carefree as it had been on those happy nights when Johnny and Ed McMahon made us laugh so hard that I could hardly keep from choking on my 'secret beer'. A few months later I left for college, and my own career as a problem drinker got underway in earnest.

A psychologist would no doubt point to my mother's influence to explain why I took to drinking so heavily myself, but I don't buy that. Every drink I ever swallowed was raised to my lips by my own hand and I've never been tempted to blame my mother. I only wish I'd had the grace to keep my habit from hurting others – grace like my mother's. But my mom always had the family to anchor her against the idiot wind, so she was luckier than me. All I had to cling to when it began to blow was a flimsy sense of self-regard – and by now it should be clear how that worked out for me.

Still, except for the tallboy Bud I'd had on the ride into Mobile, and the two cans of Dixie beer on the ride to New Orleans, I had now gone forty-six days without a drink and, surprisingly, I felt no urge to go out and break my streak with a shot of Irish whiskey and a pint of ghastly green beer, so I counted my blessings. And there would be many more blessings to count in the coming days, as I busied myself settling into my new home.

After lunch that day I hiked out to Camp Anyway to retrieve my radio and left John a note in his stash spot, giving him my room number at the Joyce. 'Stop by and visit if you're in the neighbourhood!' I wrote, and then set off for the public library, where my rent receipt from the Joyce was the last piece of ID I needed to qualify for a library card. Wandering through the stacks for the next hour, I gathered my five-book limit: four novels (by Jack Kerouac, Knut Hamsun, Fred Exley and Saul Bellow) and a collection of essays called *The Geography of the*

Imagination by Guy Davenport. When I got to the check-out desk, the friendly librarian even threw in a shopping bag to help me tote them back to my room. Now I had everything I needed for a cozy night at the Joyce – music and books. What more could a civilised tramp ask for?

The next day I hiked across the Morrison Bridge to the southeast side of town for the Sunday afternoon meal at St Francis Church, where the charismatic Father Gary had recruited me to join the volunteer kitchen staff the previous week. When he'd approached me, I said sure, why not? I had nowhere better to be, and it seemed only fair that I pitch in after all the free lasagne I'd just eaten.

I wound up being assigned to run dishes through the kitchen's restaurant-size conveyor-belt dishwasher, a stainless-steel behemoth that certainly earned its keep. The average crowd for the Sunday meal was usually close to three hundred – not just street people but poor young families too – and the stacks of dirty dishes and trays kept me busy for nearly two hours. (Thank goodness they didn't have a manual dishwasher like the old beater at the Blanchet House, or the job would have taken a lot longer.) But even that small amount of volunteer labour left me wonderfully light-hearted when I walked out of the church for the hike back to Old Town. It had been a long time since I'd done anything so worthwhile and I was itching to work another shift in the kitchen, just to get that feeling back.

Sundays at St Francis also gave me the opportunity to stay in touch with my pal John Anyway. For whatever reason, he never chose to visit me at the Joyce, but I could always count on running into him at Sunday dinner – God bless him, that man never passed up a free meal.

On my way across the river, I remembered that the St

Vincent de Paul thrift shop was also located in the southeast part of town, and since I was early for the Sunday meal I decided to make the most of my hike by paying it a visit. The shop was located on Powell Street and 27th Avenue, painfully further from St Francis than I'd expected. My heels were throbbing by the time I got there, and as I hobbled the last few steps toward the shop I said a silent prayer that I'd finally find a pair of shoes that wouldn't torture my feet.

When I stepped inside, I was surprised to find the place mobbed by a pack of giggling college girls, scouring the racks of secondhand clothes and squealing with delight whenever they found something funky enough to qualify as 'bohemian chic'. They seemed to favour items that were so hideous they could only be worn ironically, and I confess I felt a twinge of nostalgic envy as I watched them shop. *Enjoy it while you can, girls*, I thought, remembering the days when I, too, had nothing more to worry about when I went clothes shopping than the burning question: 'Will it look "cool" on campus?'

Squeezing past the giggling girls, I made my way through the narrow aisles to the shoe section at the back of the shop but found nothing there to squeal about. There were rows and rows of cast-off shoes on the shelves, but unfortunately not one pair in my size. Which was a real letdown. But at least I had more luck in my hunt for spare clothes, and when I walked out of the shop a half-hour later I was toting my second shopping bag of the weekend. Thanks to Father Gary's voucher, I now had two fresh sets of street clothes, plus a sport coat, dress slacks and a button-down Oxford shirt that would come in handy when I started interviewing for jobs. All at a price that couldn't be beat.

I was already in a good mood after my score at the thrift

shop, so the welcoming smiles and backslaps I received from the volunteers in the St Francis kitchen made me feel even better. Most of the 'regulars' on the kitchen crew were parishioners of the church – a mix of middle-aged women and spry old retired businessmen – and I recognised many familiar faces from the week before. What surprised me was that so many of them recognised me, too, after only one stint in the kitchen. I hoped it was because I'd impressed them with my speed at the dishwasher. But it might have been just my hobbling gait that made me memorable – a few of the volunteers asked how my feet were holding up!

While we were cleaning up after the meal, Father Gary stopped in to visit the volunteers, and I thanked him again for the clothing voucher and told him I had put it to good use. Then I mentioned that I had experience working in restaurant kitchens back in New York and offered to volunteer my time as a prep cook, if the kitchen needed help on Sunday mornings. Which brought a broad smile to Father Gary's bearded face.

'Your timing is perfect, Peter,' he said. 'One of our regular morning volunteers, Mrs Quinn, just had her hip replaced. She'll be out of action for a few months, so we'll gladly take all the help you're willing to give. Can you make it next Sunday morning? The prep shift starts at nine.'

'Count on it, Father,' I said with a nod, glad to feel needed, and already looking forward to peeling and chopping onions – the newbie prep cook's inevitable first assignment, the Vale of Tears. In my book, that beat scraping dishes any day of the week.

When I said goodbye to my fellow volunteers and left St Francis that night, I was in high spirits – a man at peace with the world and happy to be homeward bound. Dusk was settling over the city and in the misty air the lights of the Morrison Bridge glowed like Chinese lanterns. It was magic hour in

Portland, and as I crossed the Willamette I paused midway and just stared down at the water for a while, content to do nothing but watch the river flow. And as I stood there in the gathering shadows, I heard a quiet voice inside me.

Right now, Pete, there is nothing more you need.

I smiled in recognition when I heard that. My inner voice was echoing the same sentiment I'd come across in *On the Road* just the night before, while skimming through my library copy before bed. Describing Dean Moriarty – newly at loose in the world after a stretch in prison – Sal Paradise says: 'He was alone in the doorway, digging the street. Bitterness, recriminations, advice, morality, sadness – everything was behind him, and ahead of him was the ragged and ecstatic joy of pure being.'

I knew I wasn't there yet, but that's where I hoped the road would take me. And for a few golden moments on the bridge that night I could almost believe I was getting close.

On Monday morning, I was up with the sun, fully rested after my second good night's sleep in a row and glad to be getting an early start to my day. It promised to be a busy one. I had the Stab Lab ahead of me, plus I'd have to swing by the drop-in centre at some point to show my rent receipt from the Joyce and take care of the paperwork for my 'leap cheque'. If I hustled, I might be able to get both chores out of the way in time to make lunch at the Blanchet House, which would be helpful, since I was just about out of Food Stamps. I had only two one-dollar stamps left in my booklet. Just enough to cover tomorrow morning's coffee at McDonald's and a fresh pouch of Bugler tobacco. Of course, neither could be purchased with Food Stamps. I'd have to convert them to cash first by doing the Food Stamp shuffle.

There were only two ways to convert Food Stamps into

cash. The first way was the easiest: you took your stamps to one of the shadier grocery stores in Old Town and sold them outright. But the scam artists who owned those places only paid you fifty cents on the dollar for your stamps, which seemed too big a rip-off to me, so I always opted for the second method: the Food Stamp shuffle. I'd walk into a grocery store, pick out a Food Stamp-approved item that cost less than a dollar, pay for it with a one-dollar stamp and leave with coins jingling in my pocket. Repeat as necessary. Keep shuffling.

Hostess Fruit Pies were my favourite purchase when I was working the shuffle. You could get them for thirty cents (or even a quarter, if there was a sale on), which yielded a healthy ratio of change. It was funny how quickly I found myself budgeting my daily expenses in units of pie. Two pies equalled one cup of McDonald's coffee, plus a pouch of Bugler. But the two stamps still in my booklet were all I had left until my regular monthly allocation came through. The DHS centre would definitely be my next stop after lunch at the Blanchet. I'd been checking in every day for the past week, but my stamps were still stuck in the pipeline. Maybe today I'd finally get lucky.

For the first time in weeks, the sky over Portland was bright blue. From the heights of downtown, you could see clear to the snow-capped peak of Mount Hood. It was milder than usual, too, with a false hint of spring, and as I hiked from McDonald's to the Stab Lab I wondered where this weather had been when I'd been freezing my nuts off at Camp Anyway! But it was a glorious morning to be out in the world, even on gimpy feet, and I was cheerier than usual when I limped into the Alpha Center. I'd arrived early enough to beat the crowd and get a bed right away.

For a change, the hours passed quickly and next thing I

knew I was standing at the cashier's window receiving the amazing news that I had just earned a twenty-dollar incentive bonus for completing my eighth donation in four weeks. I was flabbergasted. What a windfall! And I knew exactly how to spend it. And where.

The hotplate will have to wait, I told myself, as I hobbled out of the Stab Lab and set off straightaway for the local Army-Navy Surplus store. I was sick of limping around on bloody feet. It was time to do something about my ridiculous footwear situation once and for all.

I had already scouted the Army-Navy store in my travels around Old Town and for weeks I'd been coveting a pair of Vietnam-surplus 'jungle boots' on display in the window. The boots had thick rubber soles, sturdy black leather heels and toecaps, and vented nylon-canvas uppers that laced all the way to your calves. Ideal boots for a soggy town like Portland. And, even better, reasonably priced at only seventeen dollars a pair.

Having learned my lesson in New Orleans, I made sure to take my time trying on several pairs until I found a perfect fit. Then I kicked in another two dollars for a thick pair of cushiony wool socks, which I put on right there in the store. After lacing up the jungle boots, I stuffed my blood-stained socks and old boots into the new shoebox, and as soon as I was back on the street I hustled down the block to the nearest trash can and did what I'd been wanting to do for weeks. *Good fucking riddance!*

My feet were already thanking me as I hurried down Burnside Street toward the drop-in centre on Broadway to take care of my LIEAP paperwork. I was cutting along at a clip I wouldn't have thought possible when I'd rolled out of bed that morning, and I arrived in plenty of time to set up my 'leap cheque' and still make it over to Glisan Street for the final round of lunch seating at the Blanchet House. If I'd still been hobbling, I would have gone hungry – I'd never have made it in time. Though I'd barely been wearing the new boots an hour, they were already improving my life, and I sat down to lunch dazed with gratitude, still marvelling at the stroke of luck that had brought them my way.

The day had gotten off to such a good start I didn't see how it could get much better, and I was already bracing myself for bad news at the DHS centre as I hiked toward the Steel Bridge after lunch. But my run of luck wasn't over just yet. Miracle of miracles, my Food Stamp allocation had finally arrived, and all of a sudden I was sixty-eight dollars richer. What a day!

I was grinning like the Cheshire cat as I set off for downtown Portland and a shopping spree that would put plenty of miles on my new jungle boots before the afternoon was over. Fate had handed me the opportunity I'd been praying for – a chance to lay up in my room for three or four days straight and give my blistered heels a chance to finally heal – and I was determined to seize the moment. All I had to do now was hit the stores for enough supplies to see me through my convalescence.

Deciding I'd better take a moment to get organised first, I stopped off at the McDonald's on Alder Street and treated myself to a celebratory coffee while I jotted down a shopping list. Then I headed downhill to the Newberry's five-and-dime store at Fifth and Alder, a relic of the twenties that still had an antique turnstile you pushed through to enter the sales floor.

It was a sad old place, but it was the cheapest in town for toiletries and household gadgets, so it was a popular destination for the down-and-outers from the Burnside District. I wasn't surprised to spot two other Bluecoats wandering the aisles with handbaskets when I got there. I grabbed one myself and soon gathered everything on my list, plus one item I'd never thought to look for until I stumbled across it in the housewares aisle – an immersion coil heater! As soon as it caught my eye, I knew I'd have to buy it. At under two dollars it was a lot less expensive than a used hotplate and would be a hell of a lot easier to smuggle up to my room. True, you couldn't fry an egg with it, or heat up a can of beans, but it would boil water in minutes, and as long as I had boiling water there were plenty of other things I could cook, so it was a real find.

Most of the nine dollars I had left in blood money was spent by the time I walked out of Newberry's, but I now had everything I needed to set up a makeshift kitchen in my room, except groceries. The only supermarket within walking distance of skid row was the Safeway out near the art museum, twelve long blocks from the Joyce Hotel. I usually dreaded the painful hike out there, but today my new boots made it less of an ordeal, and for a change I wasn't wincing the entire way.

The best thing about the Safeway was that they had lots of cashier stations. Multiple cashiers made doing the Food Stamp shuffle a lot less embarrassing. I could buy four or five Hostess Fruit Pies, one at a time, and never have to face the same cashier twice – which eliminated all the scowling you'd have to endure if you worked the shuffle on a single cashier. It took me four pies to accumulate the change I needed for a four-day supply of Bugler, and once I had that covered I was ready to do my bulk shopping and get out of there.

My arms and shoulders were on fire by the time I lugged my two heavy grocery sacks all the way across town, and it was a relief to finally catch sight of the Fish Grotto, the restaurant that leased the southwest corner of the Joyce Hotel building. The Grotto, which had its own entrance on Stark Street, around the corner from the hotel lobby, was a curiously bipolar place. By day, it was your basic kitschy seafood joint, with cork floats and gill nets hung from the ceilings, a 'Catch of the Day' slate board propped in the window, and a desultory lunch clientele that could usually be counted on the fingers of one hand. But come five o'clock Happy Hour, the phrase 'catch of the day' took on a whole new meaning, as the Grotto morphed into a gay bar that drew a packed house nearly every night of the week.

The early crowd was already arriving when I reached the corner, and Stark Street was clogged with double-parked taxis and town cars dropping off smartly dressed men who stuck out in that neighbourhood like peacocks slumming in a flock of park pigeons. I could see them clocking me out of the corners of their eyes as I trudged through their midst with my Safeway bags. It was almost comical how deftly they stepped back and gave me room to pass. I felt like a Bluecoat Moses – parting the shiny shoes.

Inside the hotel, I saw Vern nod his flat-topped head in noncommittal greeting as I crossed the lobby, and I took that to mean I was cleared to head upstairs without showing my key at the desk any more. Progress. The Joyce was starting to feel more like home every day. And it felt even more homey when I got up to my room and began unloading groceries. I stowed my perishables – milk, mayonnaise and margarine – out on the window ledge, then pressed one of the empty dresser drawers into service as my pantry, where I stashed all the freeze-dried soup and instant oatmeal packets I'd loaded up on at the store, along with a box of tea bags, a jar of instant coffee and a supply of canned tuna fish and Cling peaches. Which pretty much filled up the drawer, so I had to store my bread and strawberry jam on top of the dresser.

Once I had my food stock organised, I opened my daypack and unloaded all the kitchen supplies I'd bought at Newberry's. In addition to the coil heater, I had picked up two wide-mouthed ceramic soup mugs (one for boiling water in, one in which to mix whatever freeze-dried convenience food the boiling water would be added to), as well as one of those little butterfly-shaped can openers, a 'Picnic Pak' of heavy-duty plastic utensils and a stubby set of throwaway cardboard salt and pepper shakers. In short, everything I needed to cook myself a hot meal, and I wasted no time putting it to good use.

Within minutes, the mug of water atop the dresser was boiling so furiously that it fogged up the mirror in the room's far corner. Of course, in an eight by ten room the 'far corner' is a relative term, but you get the idea – the gadget worked as advertised. Next thing I knew, the water was threatening to boil over the edge of the mug and I had to quickly yank the plug out of the wall socket to keep it from flooding the dresser top. This left me standing in the middle of the room nervously clutching a cord from which dangled a glowing coil that was still so hot it posed a real fire hazard. I didn't breathe easy until the infernal thing was safely hissing in the porcelain sink – the only place I could think to toss it without setting the room ablaze. Next trip to Newberry's I'd definitely have to pick up an extra ceramic mug to use as a coil-cooler.

That hairy moment didn't dull my appetite, though, and my mouth was watering by the time I finished mixing up what the Knorr packet promised would be 'a steaming cup of hearty chicken rice soup'. Since the room had no table, I improvised one by removing the last of the dresser's empty drawers and setting it upside-down on the edge of my bed. Then I pulled the chair over next to the bed. Chez Joyce was open for business.

As I sat there unwrapping a stick of margarine to spread on some bread to go with my soup ('Everything's better with Blue Bonnet on it!'), a familiar smile came over my face, as I recalled my old mentor at Dartmouth, the genial poet Richard Eberhart, who conducted his limited-enrolment poetry seminars from a big leather armchair in the fire-lit living room of his house on the edge of campus – a poet-friendly retreat over-looking the Connecticut River, haunted by the benevolent ghost of its former occupant, Robert Frost. Besides the opportunity to interact with a Pulitzer Prize-winner in an intimate setting, the six or seven students admitted to the seminar each semester were also treated to surprise visits from Eberhart's house guests – a roster that in my time included Robert Lowell, Anne Sexton, William Everson (aka Brother Antoninus) and Amiri Baraka (aka LeRoi Jones). I spent many memorable evenings talking poetry in that cozy living room, but oddly enough the night I remember best was the night Professor Eberhart offhandedly remarked that, in his opinion, the most euphonious word in the English language was (of all things!) *oleomargarine*. Ever since that night, I've never thought of the poor man's butter quite the same.

It was impossible for me to recall those happy times without also remembering the creative energy that had animated me when Richard Eberhart took me under his wing, and no doubt that's what sparked my idea to make the next four days a sort of writer's retreat. Holed up in my room, with no distractions, I'd have the perfect opportunity to get back to the one thing in my life that the idiot wind hadn't stripped away: my enduring belief in the power of words. The only belief that had sustained me after I'd dropped out of St Mary's and drifted away from the Church.

I was eager to see what could be made of the road notes I'd been gathering since I'd left New York, but first I had to collate all the scraps of paper stuffed into my original Wonder Bread bag, then transcribe them into the hardbound composition book with the old-school marbleised cover that I'd remembered to buy at Newberry's. It was a job that took me the rest of the night and a good part of the next day. Many of my notes had been sketchy and needed fleshing out as I transcribed them, which made me glad I was tackling the task while the trip was still fresh in my memory.

Whenever writer's cramp got the better of me, I'd take a break and prepare a meal, or just kick back with one of my library books, or zone out listening to the late-night jazz programming on KMHD, the student-run radio station at Mount Hood Community College. And sometimes, in the wee hours, I'd hear the clacking of typewriter keys echoing in the air shaft outside my open window. I'd smile and think, *Maybe Charles Bukowski has moved in upstairs!* Skid-row hotels were Bukowski's home turf, after all. A place like the Joyce would be right up his alley.

By the second night of my retreat, I had finished transcribing my road notes – fifty pages worth – and I began to wonder what to do with them next. I hadn't yet decided whether to use the notes as background for a novel or as the raw material for a straight-up memoir.

Might as well sleep on it, I told myself, after an hour's muddled deliberation made it clear I had no idea which path to choose. Meanwhile, Bukowski continued to hunt and peck somewhere on the upper floors, and it was hard not to take the steady clacking of his typewriter as a reproach to my own lack of productivity. But I finally said fuck it, and climbed into bed with

On the Road, which proved to be the right decision. I awoke in the morning with Kerouac's words echoing in my head and knew I had found my opening. The one line that had stuck with me was about prison being the place where a jailed man promises himself the right to live and, with that thought in mind, I belatedly realised that all the material in my road notes would have to wait. Before writing about my time on the road, my gut told me I'd have to tackle my time on Rikers Island first. As soon as I'd downed a mug of coffee, I dug out my brand-new Newberry's legal pad and began at the beginning, in an overcrowded bullpen cell, on the day I first arrived.

'Handle It!'

Upwards of thirty other inmates were already crammed into the eight by ten bullpen when I arrived at Rikers for processing, but the noise in the place was even worse than the overcrowding. It seemed like half the guys in the bullpen were shouting through the bars at once, all of them voicing complaints to the guards at the duty desk. Complaints so uniform and repetitious they took on the hypnotic quality of schoolyard singsong.

'Hey, CO! They tryin' to starve us or what? When are we getting' some chow?'

'Hey, CO! Can't you close these windows? It's *freezing* in here!'

'Hey, CO! When we gettin' beds, CO? Ain't no room in this fuckin' bullpen!'

When they deigned to answer at all, the guards' reply to this whining was always the same two words, delivered with macho disdain or weary detachment: 'Handle it!'

Handle it! Handle it! I'm sure I'll never hear another phrase that turns my stomach more than those two words did during my time behind bars. It's a phrase with a built-in sneer, a vile command that keeps your nose well-buried in the muck of your own impotence, and I wasn't in the bullpen a half-hour before I was already sick of hearing it.

In the bullpens at Rikers hours drag on into days, the guards come and go in changing shifts, but still the 'intake process' produces no 'intake'. The machinery is overstuffed and choking; it wants to break down. Too many faces to photograph. Too many fingers to be printed. Too many wallets to collect, too many receipts to issue. Too many physical exams, too few doctors.

Thirty hours after arriving in the bullpen I was frazzled with exhaustion. The noise and cramped quarters made sleep an impossible dream. Tempers in the cell were shorting out and flaring into fights more rapidly every hour, and only the frigid blasts of January air – from the windows the guards refused to close – kept the anger in the cell from boiling into a riot. Whenever a fight did break out, the guard on duty would blast his whistle and the flying squad would come running, batons and riot shields at the ready, and storm into the bullpen to drag the two oppon-ents out and hustle them away to a private cell for a 'beat-down'. These beatings were never conducted in view of the rest of us, but the groans and screams painted a picture that was clear enough to everyone – a sickening lesson in 'handling it'.

On my third day at Rikers, while I was still housed in the 'intake unit', a guard entered the cellblock and read out a list of names, among them mine, and ordered us to line up double-file on the 'count stripe' painted down the middle of the dorm's central aisle. Then the guard marched us all off to a classroom in a different wing of the prison, where a veteran corrections officer spent the next three hours lecturing us on the rules and established procedures we'd be expected to know and adhere to during our incarceration. Judging by the bored looks on the faces of most of the prisoners in the room, the CO was preaching to the choir. The only ones in the class who seemed to be paying any attention to the lecture were a handful of newbies – or, in prison parlance, 'fish' – like me.

I'll admit, getting schooled to be a proper convict was about as bizarre an example of 'continuing education' as I could possibly imagine. Still, I found it fascinating – and by the time the lecture ended my brain was crammed with all sorts of information I would never have guessed I'd need to know. For example, who knew that the guards didn't like being called *guards*? Not me, that's for sure. Apparently, our jailers preferred to be addressed as 'officer' or (the more common term) 'CO'. Nor did I know that the proper response when a riot broke out in the mess hall was to prostrate yourself on the floor, with your hands clasped behind your head, or else risk being taken for one of the rioters by the baton-wielding flying squad when they stormed in to crack heads. *Riots in the mess hall?* I remember wondering. Were riots really such a commonplace occurrence that prisoners needed to be schooled ahead of time in how to react when one broke out? If so, the months ahead were going to be more hazardous than a fish like me had envisioned.

As I would discover in the coming days, all the dos and

don'ts I had learned during that orientation session were just a fraction of what I'd need to know to survive my time behind bars. The real 'schooling' came from the jail-tattooed inmates who called the shots in the cellblocks, many of whom were serving their third or fourth sentence on the island. These repeat offenders knew more about prison life than half the guards did, and they quickly made it clear to us new fish who was really in charge – and their intimidating trash-talk left us in no doubt that the guards were the least of our problems.

Fortunately, when I was moved out of the intake unit to one of the general population cellblocks a few days later, I landed in a dormitory that housed a 'soldier' from one of the Mafia families operating in Westchester. After I had let it be known that I did business with Bobby Bats, he had one of his contacts on the outside check me out. As soon as word came back that I was telling the truth, Sal from Yonkers took me under his wing and became my 'rabbi'. Even on Rikers Island, where the black and Hispanic inmates far outnumbered the white prisoners, a connection to the Italian 'families' commanded respect, and by ducking under the umbrella that Yonkers Sal extended to me I escaped a lot of the bullshit hassles that rained down on the other fish who had to fend for themselves. Which made me glad I hadn't rolled over when the cops who'd busted me tried to get me to give up the name of my coke supplier. By keeping mum about Bobby Bats, I had proved myself a stand-up guy. As such, I was worthy of protection. So I did my time at Rikers in relative peace, shielded from the petty beefs that often sent other prisoners to the infirmary for stitches.

With Sal as my rabbi, I no longer had to put up with gang-bangers cutting ahead of me in line when I was waiting to use the cell block's one payphone at night, and nobody dared try to make me their 'biscuit' – which was the euphemism then current for inmates too weak to fight off the sexual predators who singled them out as rape targets. The only escape for these unfortunate 'biscuits' was to put in for transfer to a solo cell in the protective custody unit, which the inmates at Rikers sneeringly called 'Punk City'. Solitary confinement always seemed to me a harsh penalty to pay for being a rape victim, but, as the only remedy short of suicide, it had its share of takers.

There were no suicides in my cellblock during my time at Rikers, but an inmate in one of the adjoining blocks had hanged himself in the shower room soon after I arrived. I remember being disgusted when I heard one of the COs referring to the victim as 'another mope on a rope'. But that was early on in my sentence, before my ongoing Rikers 'education' taught me to take the callousness of the average guard for granted. The few guards who treated the inmates decently turned out to be the crooked ones who smuggled drugs into the cellblocks. Their profit motive gave them reason to consider us as potential customers, rather than just bags of meat that had to be inventoried three times a day, so in the upside-down world of prison life these black-market capitalists were actually the only guards to exhibit any human compassion. I considered it a lucky break to have been assigned to a cell block where one of these bent guards held the keys.

With our in-house smuggler on duty, the overnight hours in the dorm were a lot more mellow than they would have been if the hard-ass CO who worked the day shift had been in charge. At least at night we didn't have to worry that the smell of marijuana smoke would be reported to the shift commander and bring the flying squad rushing in to search our bunks and lockers for contraband. This was a real bonus. Our cell block was crammed with eighty inmates in a space built to house fifty, so the air in the dorm was always foul — even when the barred windows set high in the cell walls were cracked for ventilation. But the scent of burning marijuana after lights-out brought a welcome change that I came to appreciate as one of those minor blessings that made prison life slightly more toler-able. That's one lesson you can count on a place like Rikers to teach you — how to savour the little things. It was also the one lesson I promised myself I'd keep in mind once I hit the streets again . . .

It had been so long since I'd done any serious writing, it was lunchtime by the time I'd eked out those few pages, but as I reread my words over a tuna sandwich I felt as though I'd made a decent start. I'd pick up the pace once I had a few more pages behind me. In the meantime, the crucial thing was to just keep at it till I'd built up some momentum. And, as a reminder to self, my entry for that day in my composition book was a block-lettered quote from Horace (via Apelles and Pliny): NULLA DIES SINE LINEA. 'Not a day without a line.' An ironic mantra for a recovering coke addict to adopt, I'll grant you, but I'd dabbled in Latin far longer than I'd dabbled in cocaine, so I was willing to give it a shot. And — give him credit — in the weeks ahead Horace did his part in keeping me on track.

Although, I'll confess, some days my adherence to his dictum was *de minimis* – as he himself would doubtless have pointed out if he'd happened to be counting lines.

To my relief, four days proved to be all I needed for the open blisters on my heels to close up. Even the scabs were already shrinking nicely by Thursday night, so my convalescence was about complete. A few more days of bandaging my feet with gauze before I hit the streets and my gimping days would be over. Hallelujah, and God bless jungle boots!

Over the next few weeks, I would put a lot of mileage on those boots, as I chased down job openings all over the city. But despite the neatly typed résumé the volunteers at the drop-in centre had prepared for me, I never got a single call-back. If there were any employers in that city who wouldn't shy away from hiring a Bluecoat, I surely never came across one. I couldn't blame them, though. Who wants to take a chance on a job candidate who lists an SRO hotel like the Joyce as his residence? Or whose contact phone number connects to a hotel front desk?

The only business that would hire transients like me was an outfit called Oregon Advertising. Once or twice a week they'd send a passenger van down to skid row to recruit 'paper hangers' – guys willing to spend the day like mailmen, hoofing it to every house in their assigned neighbourhood – to hang advertising fliers on the doorknobs of suburban homeowners who'd just as soon set their dog on you or threaten you with a trespassing charge as read the crap you're delivering to their doorsteps. But hey, if your skin's thick enough, it's a way to pick up fifteen or twenty bucks for a day filled with healthful exercise, fresh air and the ever-cleansing rains of the Pacific Northwest. Yep, I fell for it for a few days, I'll admit it.

There was an empty warehouse a few blocks from the

Joyce and the guys who wanted a day's work would line up on the sidewalk in front of it by 7 a.m. When the Oregon Advertising van arrived, the driver would pick out eight or ten guys for his crew that day. I was younger than most of the tramps who showed up, so I got picked right away and, actually, my first two days hanging paper in the suburbs weren't too hard to take.

True, it was a pain in the ass trying to keep your bag of fliers dry when the skies opened up – and the skies *always* opened up at some point before your day was through – but with my feet all healed up I had no trouble covering the four or five miles the job required, and the extra cash came in handy. But the third time I showed up the van arrived with a different driver, a macho young Mexican guy who gave me a surly look I didn't care for. Still, when he waved me into the van I piled in like a dummy and rode off with him into the boonies – this time way out in the wilds of Beaverton. He handed me a route map for my area when we got there and I was the first crew member dropped off.

When I heard the rest of the crew laughing as the van pulled away, I had a bad feeling I'd just been played. But conscientious paper hanger that I was, I delivered all my fliers anyway – being careful not to violate company policy by cutting across any lawns – and when my route was completed I reported to the designated pick-up spot given on my route map and waited for the van to collect me. I'd arrived thirty minutes early at the rendezvous point, anxious not to miss my ride back to headquarters, and of course it was pouring rain as I waited by the roadside for the van to show up. And the rain was still bucketing down an hour and a half later, when I finally admitted to myself that the little prick had gotten one over on me.

I had a tough time getting any cars to stop for me in the

rain as I hitchhiked the ten miles back to the company office, and it was dark by the time I got back. The vans were all parked and their drivers long gone when I arrived. I cursed my luck, because I'd missed my chance to give the punk the ass-kicking he deserved. The secretary was already locking up the payroll office, but I told her what had happened and refused to let her leave until she'd written out my pay cheque. On my way home, I was sorely tempted to have a shot and a beer when I cashed the fifteen-dollar cheque at a rummy bar in Old Town, but I decided not to give the asshole that victory too. So I made do with a long, hot shower when I finally got back to the Joyce – a ritual cleansing to mark the end of my paper-hanging career.

The next day, still pissed about getting played, I decided to clear my head by taking a hike downtown to Taylor Street to treat myself to a ninety-nine-cent matinee at Portland's only discount movie theatre. I didn't care what was playing, as long as it distracted me for a couple of hours. I figured I'd just let the theatre's schedule dictate my choice. Whatever film was about to be screened next when I got to the box office, that's what I'd see. Which is how I came to purchase a ticket for *Little Shop of Horrors*, a movie I probably wouldn't have bothered with otherwise, since I'd never been a fan of Hollywood musicals.

I had no idea what I was letting myself in for, since all I knew about it was that it had made a splash as an Off-Broadway play back in the early eighties. So you can imagine my surprise when the movie kicked off with a big musical number called 'Skid Row (Downtown)'. What a hoot! As I listened to the lyrics, I couldn't help scanning the audience for any fellow Bluecoats, just to see if they were grinning as hard as I was – and sure enough, I spotted a few whose faces registered the same bewildered amusement. There we were, Burnside Street's derelict sons, ducking the rain and our troubles for a few hours in a darkened theatre, and this is what Hollywood had to offer us? Rick Moranis and Ellen Greene singing about how hard it is to escape from skid row? Pardon the pun, but it beggared belief: skid row veterans paying ninety-nine cents to be serenaded by skid row impostors? Only in Roger Corman's America!

I laughed all the way back to the Joyce, and still had a grin on my face when I cut through the lobby and nodded at Vern on my way to the stairs. But my grin faded fast when I got up to the second floor and saw the sagging pile of overstuffed trash bags outside the open door of the room across the hall from mine, and the disgusted look on the day-shift janitor's face when he stepped out of the room wearing latex gloves and a disposable breathing mask to dump another bag on the heap. I could tell right away what he was up to. I'd seen it enough to know I was witnessing an eviction – from the Latin verb *evincere*, meaning 'to overcome' or 'to defeat'. One of my neighbours, it seemed, was getting the proverbial boot.

At first, I was the only witness in the hallway, but then the Ancient Mariner emerged from his room next door – still wearing the same robe and Pearl Harbor Survivor cap he'd had on the night I first met him – and shuffled into the hall to investigate.

'Lonnie moving out?' the Mariner asked, eyeing the mound of Hefty bags.

'Yep,' the janitor replied. 'He just doesn't know it yet.'

'What, he's getting evicted?'

'Can't stay if you don't pay,' the janitor said. 'His rent was due three days ago.'

'What happened to him?' the Mariner asked. 'I haven't seen him around all week.'

'Probably still at the detox centre, drying out. Lou up in 323 says he saw the drunk wagon scoop him up on Tuesday night. Crazy bastard was passed out cold in the middle of the Burnside Bridge.'

'That's not good,' the Mariner frowned.

'Good riddance, I say. You wouldn't believe how much crap the guy had in his room,' the janitor groused, stooping to grab two cinched sacks by their throats. 'Listen to this: I found a ripped-up old pair of berry-picking pants shoved under his bed, all crusted with strawberry seeds. But nobody's picking yet, so they had to be seeds from *last* year's harvest. Unbelievable. Why in God's name would anyone hang on to such trash?'

Because, I was tempted to point out, *one man's trash is another man's proof of life*. But I just fished my room key out of my pocket and held my tongue. Something told me the janitor knew as well as I did that you don't end up living in a furnished room unless you're desperate. And once you've reached that point, you hang on to whatever you've got left, no matter how worthless, just to prove to yourself that you can still hang on to *something*.

As a former evictee myself, I was all too familiar with how the process worked. You go off on a bender, blow all your rent money, and by the time you get back to your room two or three days later some hotel minion with a pass key has hauled all your belongings off to a locked storeroom in the basement, where management will hold your stuff hostage until you pay up your back rent as ransom. Of course, for most evictees that's just one more losing proposition. If you owned anything worth ransoming, you wouldn't be staying at an SRO in the first place. So you do the only reasonable thing. You kiss it all goodbye and walk away. Now you're back out on the street again, with nothing left to lose and, take my word for it, it never feels like freedom, no matter what Janis Joplin says.

Lonnie's eviction was an unsettling reminder that I had only two weeks' worth of rent credit left on my LIEAP account. If I didn't find work soon, it wouldn't be long before I'd be out on the pavement with Mr Strawberry Fields Forever. Which wasn't something to look forward to, even though the weather was getting milder by the day. If it came to that, I figured I might just as well head south to San Francisco and take my chances with Tanner. I wasn't ready to bail just yet, though. Something could break my way any day now, if I just hung in there. Or so I kept telling myself.

I was still sweating my situation a few days later when I happened to overhear two tramps about my age swapping stories about how much money they'd both made doing seasonal work in Alaska's fish canneries when they were younger. I was standing behind them in the lunch line outside the Blanchet House at the time, engrossed in a library copy of a slim book of character sketches by Aristotle's pupil Theophrastus, but I put the book away as soon as I heard the numbers the two tramps were throwing around. *Twenty thousand bucks for a four-month gig?* How could Theophrastus compete with that? I was instantly intrigued, and immediately began pumping the two for information about fishery jobs. I couldn't really see myself working on the slime line in a canning factory, but a job as a galley cook on one of the trawlers would suit me fine.

'Hell, yeah, galley cooks make even more than the slime liners,' one of the guys claimed. 'Cooks take home a cut of the crew share, so if the catch is good, you can make bank. Sometimes double what the factory guys take home.'

This is sounding better all the time, I thought to myself, and went on pressing them for any tips they could give me about applying for work in the Alaskan fishing fleet.

'If you're serious, you'd better head on up to Seattle right quick,' the other tramp advised. 'April's when the Alaskan boats start hiring. You wait much longer you'll miss out. Most of the boats have year-round offices on the waterfront in Seattle harbour. With no connections, you'll just have to make the rounds with your résumé and hope you get lucky.'

'He's right,' his partner chimed in. 'I just hopped a freight down here from Seattle last week, and guys were already rolling into town looking for cannery work. I was you, I'd catch a train up there tomorrow.'

His mention of freight-hopping clinched the deal as far as I was concerned. My aborted attempt at catching a freight out of New Orleans hadn't satisfied my urge to give Jack Kerouac's favourite mode of travel a try. So I switched my line of questioning from boats to trains, and the freight-hopper gave me good advice on the easiest way to 'catch out' to Seattle. According to him, the Portland railyards were too heavily patrolled by yard bulls. My best bet, he said, was to catch a city bus to the Washington border, then walk across the bridge to the Vancouver train yards, where security was a lot lighter.

'Good to know,' I said. My mind was already racing, making mad plans to head for Vancouver at the earliest possible opportunity. I was so preoccupied by the time I got into the Blanchet dining room that the volunteer directing traffic had to shout at me three times before I snapped out of it and realised that the empty seat he was pointing at was meant for me. I haven't the faintest idea what they served that day. I ate in a daydream, and as soon as I left I headed downtown to the main library, where I spent a feverish half-hour huddled over a copy of the Seattle

Yellow Pages, jotting down the names and office addresses of every Alaskan fishing company I could find. It was encouraging to see how many there were. I couldn't wait to get up there and start making the rounds. But first I'd have to hit the Army-Navy store and pick up a duffel bag for my clothes and food and kitchen equipment. Easily done.

By Friday night, I had everything taken care of, and my pack and duffel were all loaded and ready for an early departure in the morning. I'd drop off my room key at the desk on my way out and then head straight to Salmon Street and Sixth Avenue to catch the metro bus that would take me to the Washington line – a budget-friendly trip that would cost me only one dollar ten cents. I barely managed three hours' sleep that night, I was so wound up and ready to go. Portland had been good to me, but after sixty-six days on skid row it was time to seek my future elsewhere.

When I awoke at dawn on Saturday and heard the rush of rainwater splashing into the airshaft outside my window, I had a feeling the weather gods were about to change my plans. I threw on some clothes and went down to the lobby to see what it looked like out in the street, and it wasn't an encouraging sight. The temperature must have taken quite a drop overnight because the rain was coming down as sleet and the sidewalks were a slushy mess.

No way you're leaving today, I muttered to myself. Hopping a freight train for the first time would be challenging enough in dry weather. I'd be crazy to try it in a freezing rainstorm. So I trudged back upstairs to my room and resigned myself to hanging out at the Joyce one more day. My room rent was paid up through to the following Wednesday anyway. And after lying awake most of the previous night I needed the extra sleep. A day's delay just meant I'd be leaving Portland on Easter Sunday, which might be a slow day for freight train traffic. But if I had to hang around Vancouver till Monday I didn't care. After a month indoors I needed to get used to roughing it again, and the banks of the Columbia River wouldn't be a bad place to start.

Easter morning dawned chilly but clear, and after a farewell coffee stop at the McDonald's on Alder, I hiked over to Salmon Street and caught the number 5 bus to Vancouver. At that early hour, the churchgoers weren't yet up and the bus was nearly empty. I had the back of the bus to myself and as we crossed the Willamette I opened my daypack and dug out the one library book I'd decided to bring along for company on the trip (confident it would find its way back to Portland with a little assistance from the librarians in Seattle). And I could hardly have chosen a better fellow traveller for a freight-hopping trip than Clyde Rice, a native Oregonian who'd ridden the rails all over the West Coast back in the thirties. By serendipitous coincidence, only days before my departure the Portland Library had featured Rice's recently published memoir, *Night Freight*, on a shelf reserved for new work by local authors. As soon as I spotted it, I knew I couldn't leave town without it.

I'd been saving *Night Freight* for my trip and hadn't cracked it open until that moment on the bus. But I knew right away that I was travelling with the right man when I read the opening lines: 'I was jungled up in some bushes alongside the tracks just outside the railroad yards in Eureka. There was a spring in the bushes and at least twenty bums around smoky fires . . .'

Save me a spot, boys, I'm on my way!

CHAPTER 10

I rode the metro bus all the way out to Jantzen Beach on the northwestern fringe of Portland and got off at the last stop on the route, a strip mall on the south bank of the Columbia River. At that hour on a Sunday morning none of the shops were open. The only sign of life was an enterprising silver-haired Mexican who was busy unloading foil-wrapped pots of Easter lilies from his cargo van and arranging them on a folding table he'd set up at the entrance to the mall's parking lot. I wished him '*Feliz Pascua*' as I trudged past his display, and he gave me a wave, but I couldn't wave back. My right hand was lugging my heavy khaki duffel, and my left was clutching a rolled-up, rope-tied sleeping bag. I'd definitely come up in the world since I'd first rolled into Portland two months earlier with nothing but a daypack on my shoulder.

The sleeping bag was a brand new Coleman that I'd scored at another LIEAP office giveaway only days after I'd picked up my blue parka. I hadn't even had a chance to christen it because

I'd moved into the Joyce the same day the bags were handed out. Unfortunately, it was insulated with synthetic Hollofil fibre instead of goose down, so it was bulkier than I'd have liked, but I was still glad to have it. I just hoped the extra gear wouldn't prove too much of a hindrance when it came time to catch a moving train 'on the fly'.

Up ahead about a quarter mile I could see the steel framework of not one but two vertical-lift bridges that looked like conjoined twins. I assumed one of the two must have been built after traffic between Portland and Seattle became too heavy for a single bridge to handle, and when I reached the bridges my hunch was confirmed. The one on my side of the road, which carried only northbound traffic, looked a lot older than its downstream twin. Though neither would have won any prizes for elegant design, their span was impressive. Bank to bank, the Columbia must have been twice as wide as any of the Willamette river crossings in downtown Portland, and I was already working up a sweat by the time I reached the far side.

Deciding there was no sense carrying extra weight while I scouted out the route to the railyards, I looked around for a spot to stash my baggage before heading into Vancouver. The tall bushes growing beside the bridge's concrete anchors looked like good cover, so I climbed down from the walkway with my gear. When I pulled back some of the branches to make room for my stuff, I uncovered a brass plaque which had been mounted to the bridge back in the make-work days of the WPA. The plaque dated the bridge's construction to 1917, which didn't surprise me – but the inspiring quote from John Ruskin inscribed on the plaque certainly did. Intrigued by this unexpected find, I immediately dug out my road journal and copied down what Ruskin had to say:

Therefore, when we build, let us think that we build forever. Let it not be for present delight, nor for present use alone, let it be such work as our descendants will thank us for. And let us think, as we lay stone upon stone, that a time will come when those stones will be held sacred because our hands have touched them, and that men will say, 'See! This our fathers did for us!'

John Ruskin was the last person I'd have expected to find skulking behind bushes beneath a bridge in Vancouver, Washington, but I was certainly glad I had found him. Whether you're a builder of bridges, laying stone upon stone, or a builder of sentences, laying word upon word, Ruskin's exhortation was advice worth heeding, and I only wished someone would get around to moving the plaque to a spot where more people could see it.

A few blocks down Vancouver's main street I came to a little park behind the public library, where a few sleepy-eyed winos were huddled at a picnic table having their first nips of the day. When I asked for directions to the Southern Pacific railyard, they told me, 'About eight blocks over, just past the Amtrak Station.'

Then the oldest of the bunch asked me, 'Where you catchin' out to?'

'Seattle,' I replied.

'Then you'll be here till tomorrow,' he informed me. 'On Sundays, ain't nothin' but passenger trains run through them yards.'

'Yeah,' I said. 'I kind of figured that might be the case. Will the cops hassle me if I bed down by the river overnight?'

'Nah, lots of guys sleep there. Long's you don't build too big a fire, the cops won't mess with you. Care for a taste?' he asked, offering up the communal mickey.

'No, thanks, I'm good,' I grinned. 'My gear's stashed back by the bridge. I'd better go collect it and start scouting out a campsite.'

Wishing them all a Happy Easter, I doubled back to my stash spot, and twenty minutes later I was eating breakfast on a stretch of shingled beach a half-mile downriver, in the shadow of an old railroad trestle bridge that looked like it had been built by a clever child with a giant Erector Set. While I sat there spreading peach jam on a few slices of Wonder Bread, a big tugboat towing a barge full of sand came down the river and sounded its horn as it got near the bridge; the horn's blast kept me from hearing the footsteps of whoever was approaching my campsite from behind – until he was practically on top of me.

Startled, I turned quickly, but relaxed when I saw it was a tramp and not a cop.

'Sorry, didn't mean to spook you,' the lanky tramp apologised, grinning through his long red beard. 'Thought I'd come over and say hi, seein's how we're neighbours. I'm campin' just down the beach. Been here two days, and you're the first company I've had. Name's Bill, by the way, but most folks just call me Red,' he said, extending his hand, which I noticed was missing its pinky finger.

'Good to meet you, Red,' I said. 'Can I offer you some breakfast?'

'Thanks, but I just had a Danish and coffee over at the Plaid Pantry. I wouldn't turn down a smoke, though, if you've got one to spare.'

'No sweat,' I said, fishing my pouch of Bugler from my coat pocket. 'Pull up a rock and make yourself comfortable.'

'Ever seen one of these old pivot bridges in action?' he asked, nodding toward the river.

'Nope,' I said. 'Is that what you call it? A pivot bridge?'

'Yep,' he grinned. 'You're in for a treat then. Watch this. Here she goes!'

As he spoke, warning lights began to flash at either end of the bridge and, moments later, the air around us was filled with the sound of massive gears turning. Then, ever so slowly, the half of the bridge closest to us began to swing away from the river-bank and, as I watched it pivot ninety degrees toward the middle of the river, the tug's horn blew one more time. The pilot leaned out of his wheelhouse to wave at the bridge operator, who was waving back from the little control house that sat atop the middle of the span.

'Pretty slick, right?' Red said, as the tug and barge eased through the gap the pivoted section of bridge had opened up.

'Never seen anything like it,' I admitted, duly impressed.

'Me neither,' Red said, firing up a smoke. 'I've hopped trains all over the country and this here's the only pivot bridge I've ever come across.'

'Glad I got to see it in action,' I said, rolling up a smoke of my own. 'What part of the South are you from, Red?' His Southern drawl was thicker than Dolly Parton's.

'Boone, North Car'lina,' he replied. 'Ever been?'

'Nope, can't say I have. But I spent a pretty strange night in Lumberton a few months back,' I said, and proceeded to describe my adventures with Sean, the Ninja Warrior for Christ. Red laughed at my story and admitted that Boone had its share of 'wing-nuts' too.

'Wing-nuts?' I repeated. That was a new one on me.

'Yeah, you know, guys with nothin' in their heads but sail-boat fuel. Don't have to be Southern to qualify either. Hell, there was a doozy right here in Vancouver last time I passed through. Some local kid who must have been certifiable. See those two big cables over there?' he asked, pointing to where a pair of thick, black underwater power lines emerged from the river, then snaked across the shingled shoreline and disappeared into the woods that bordered the riverbank. 'One of those cables is still live, but the chewed-up one was decommissioned years ago, and this wing-nut spent eight days on the beach hacking away at it with nothing but a buck knife and a railroad spike, trying to strip out the copper for scrap. That's how it got so chewed up. And you know what he collected at the scrap yard after his hands were too torn up to keep at it any more? Fifteen lousy bucks! How's that for sailboat fuel?'

'Unbelievable,' I said.

'I know, right? The local cop who told me the story said they nabbed the kid on a tip from the scrap dealer, but when they got a look at the crazy bastard's bloody hands they decided he was too psycho to even bother charging him.'

Red was two years older than me, and he'd been riding the rails ever since he'd come back to the States from Vietnam, so he had plenty of freight-hopping stories. As long as I kept plying him with tobacco, he seemed happy to share them.

Before I knew it, the sun was sinking and Red was inviting me to move my sleeping bag over by his fire pit so we could keep the gab-fest going. Red got a small fire built, and when I saw that he had a tin cookpot at his camp I broke out a can of pork and beans for our supper. While we waited for the beans to heat, he told me about the time he'd been riding the rails through Texas with a buddy of his named Willy, who was also a Vietnam vet.

They'd had to hop off in the Fort Worth railyards when the train they'd been riding stopped to take on more freight cars, and while they were waiting to re-board, a yard bull snuck up on them and started coming on all hard-ass and demanding they produce ID. But right after he cornered them, their train to El Paso began rolling again, and rather than miss it they both jumped the yard bull and knocked him out cold.

'No shit?' I said. 'You vets don't mess around.'

'Yeah, but we couldn't just leave him in the yard. Sure as shit he'd have radioed down the line as soon as he came to. So we grabbed him and heaved him up into the grain car we were riding and took him with us all the way to El Paso. Before the fat fuck woke up we had his wrists and ankles cuffed with his own zip ties, and his mouth gagged with one of Willy's old bandanas, and there was nothing he could do when he came to except give us the stink-eye and grunt like a hog in heat. When we got to El Paso, we let one of the brakemen in the caboose know the score. He thought it was so funny, he told us he'd take his time setting the yard bull free so we could di di mau before the shit hit the fan. True story.'

We were both talked out by the time we finished our supper, and when we settled into our sleeping bags on either side of the fire pit we nodded right off. But throughout the night I would wake up whenever an Amtrak train came rattling across the pivot bridge – and I was continually amazed by Red's ability to snore right through the racket undisturbed.

It must have been after midnight when the third or fourth train roused me from sleep. When I crawled out of my mummy bag to urinate, the three-quarter moon was hanging high in the night sky. I smiled a private smile as I noted its pale yellow colour – a hue distinctly more like margarine than butter. But the river was the real show. Its surface was now striped with ivory bands of reflected light from the street lamps over on the

Oregon side, and the black water between each band gave me the weird impression that I was looking at the rippling keyboard of some giant's grand piano. And as I stood there listening, momentarily transfixed, I could almost hear it playing the music of the spheres.

When we broke camp in the morning, Red stashed his gear in the riverside woods and then walked with me to the nearby Plaid Pantry, where we hung out in the parking lot drinking our morning coffee. Red rolled a few extra smokes from my pouch of Bugler, and in return for the tobacco he did me a solid by using his knot-tying skills to re-rig the rope I had tied around my sleeping bag, allowing me to attach the rolled bag to my daypack shoulder straps.

'There you go, that should do you,' he said. 'You'll need two hands free if you're catching a train on the fly,' he advised. 'Nothing I can do about your duffel bag, though. You'll just have to toss it aboard the car before you jump on.'

I took my time hiking to the railyards after Red and I parted company. He'd told me the regular Southern Pacific freight train to Seattle usually didn't come through until noon time. And I wasn't quite so worried about yard bulls because he'd told me exactly where to hide while I was waiting for the train. I stopped off at the Amtrak Station when I got to the railyard and took advantage of their restroom to wash up and refill my half-gallon water jug for the trip. Then I kept a sharp eye out for the bulls as I hiked the rest of the way to the trackside woodlot Red had described.

Ducking into the bushes, I was surprised to find a fancy cast-off Posturepedic mattress spread out beneath a big cotton-wood tree, most likely dragged there by some scavenging tramp with a taste for creature comforts. I gave it a quick check for bugs, but found none, so I made myself right at home and settled down with *Night Freight* while I waited for my train. It was a mild, sunny day and the morning passed quickly. Before I knew it, the sun was straight overhead, and I figured I'd better gather my gear and get ready to run for the train.

As I watched the yard from the cover of the bushes, I spotted two tramps heading up the tracks in my direction and wondered if they'd come to catch the Seattle train, too. They looked to be about my age, and neither was carrying a pack. The skinny one was about a head shorter than me and was sporting a wispy goatee that made him look like a Chinese herbalist. His partner was even shorter, but powerfully built, and his full black beard was wiry and thick. When they came up even with my hidey hole, I stepped out to say hello, and sure enough they were heading to Seattle after having spent the weekend in Portland celebrating a buddy's fortieth birthday. The one with the wispy goatee was named Keith; his buddy's name was Paul, but Keith just called him 'Bulldog' and it wasn't hard to see why.

Keith and Bulldog had just hiked over the bridge into Vancouver after catching the bus to Jantzen Beach, same as I'd done the day before. They were both hungover and thirsty from their hike, and when I offered them a drink from my water jug they couldn't thank me enough. They'd left all their gear back at their home base in Seattle and hadn't thought to bring a canteen along with them when they'd caught the train down to Portland. I told them I was a rookie at hopping freights and would welcome any coaching they could give me, and Keith said not to worry, they'd hop aboard first to give me a hand up when the train came through.

Thirsty as the two of them were, my water jug was emptied quickly, and Bulldog volunteered to make a run across the yard to an outdoor spigot to reload it. When he got back five minutes later, he said he'd seen a mama opossum dead on the tracks at the grade crossing, with her head crushed to a pulp by the wheels of a train, and her five orphaned babies nosing around her corpse.

'Pretty sad,' I said.

'Yeah, I felt bad for the little guys. They'll be the next ones pulped. That's the thing about trains, though. Those steel wheels'll fuck up your whole day if you let 'em.'

Not the most encouraging words I could imagine on my first day hopping trains, but I kept my worries to myself.

'Train should have been here by now,' Keith said, when twelve-thirty had come and gone. 'Must be having mechanical problems. Sure as shit hope it gets here soon or we'll never make supper at the Bride of Death.'

'The Bride of Death?' I repeated. I thought Baloney Joe's Junction was a weird name! 'Who the hell would name a mission *that*?' I asked.

'Nobody,' Bulldog laughed. 'That's just what Keith calls the Bread of Life Mission. Not too cynical, is he?'

'How long's it take to get up to Seattle anyway?' I asked.

'On a good day,' Keith said, 'about four hours. But this isn't looking like it's going to be a good day.'

At one o'clock, we saw the yellow markings of an SP locomotive rolling in from the south. Bulldog started jogging toward the tracks, with Keith and me right behind. The train braked its speed as it entered the yard and, by the time the locomotives passed us, was doing maybe ten miles per hour and still slowing down. There was an empty flatcar midway down the line of cars and Bulldog shouted, 'Jump this one, boys!' as he sprinted beside the car and got a handhold on the three-rung ladder at the tail of the car. He made it look easy as he leapt up onto the bottom rung and then scrambled aboard.

After Keith repeated the process, he shouted down to me, 'Okay, throw me your duffel!'

For the briefest of paranoid seconds, I thought twice about tossing him my bag, picturing the two of them laughing as the train rolled on without me. But I was too pumped up to stop now, so I heaved my duffel up onto the flatcar and then made a desperate lunge for the ladder. Then I felt Bulldog's vice-grip on my forearm and, before I knew it, I was hauled up the steps and standing safely on the flatcar, my heart pumping like crazy and an idiotic grin on my face. *By Christ, I did it!*

The guys were slapping me on the back as we kept rolling toward the north end of the yard, then suddenly the brakes began to squeal and the whole train jolted to a complete stop. Which immediately gave me unhappy flashbacks to my failed attempt to catch a freight train out of New Orleans. *Oh shit, not again!*

But Keith just laughed and thumped his head with his hand. 'We're morons, Bulldog! Don't you remember? The SP trains *always* stop at the end of the yard to switch radios. We didn't have to catch it on the fly. We could have just waited a minute and climbed aboard without working up a sweat!'

'How come they have to switch radios?' I asked.

''Cause Burlington Northern controls the tracks from Vancouver all the way to the Canadian border. The SP's radios are set to a different frequency. So the SP engineers always have to stop here and pick up B&N radios before they make the run north. Why the fuck didn't I remember that?'

'Too many mickeys over the weekend, probably,' Bulldog grinned.

Two minutes later, as Keith predicted, the train jerked ahead and this time we were rolling for real. As the train built up speed, we settled down against the wooden headwall at the front of the flatcar, out of the wind, and rolled up some smokes for the ride. Pretty soon we were going about thirty miles an hour, the noise too loud for conversation. Which was fine with me. I was content to just kick back and take in the scenery. Rolling north through St Helen's, I caught a glimpse of the volcano, jagged and snowcapped, many miles to the east. It had been seven years since the last big eruption, but I saw plenty of evidence of the volcano's reach. Along the railroad right of way there were several little streams whose banks were still buried under a thick layer of grey-white ash, its surface rippled by the wind like a sandy beach, and not a single stalk of vegetation had yet popped through to bring the banks back to life.

'Something's not right with this train!' Keith shouted in my ear, as our speed slacked off near the town of Kelso. *'We should be moving a lot faster than this!'*

He was right. When we got to Longview, the train braked to a stop again and we lost another twenty minutes while the brakemen uncoupled one of the train's two locomotives and swapped it out for a new one. Getting rid of the bum engine made all the difference, and when we got rolling again the engineer goosed it up to fifty or sixty, trying to make up time. Suddenly, the scenery was really flying by.

Just before Longview, we'd spotted some rainclouds blowing in from the west, so when the train stopped to switch engines we hedged our bets by moving to the shelter of an empty boxcar. Now I was sitting in front of the boxcar's wide open doorway, perched comfortably on my rolled-up sleeping bag, watching everything flash by like a video on fast-forward.

The racket from the boxcar's rattling steel doors was so loud I had to wad some tissue and stuff it in my ears to muffle the din, but that was just a minor inconvenience; it didn't spoil the show.

We roared right through a string of little towns with their lumber mills and fish hatcheries, and as they slipped past I'd hear the toy-like sound of the crossing gate's bells receding behind us, then we'd be on to the next hidden waterfall or fern-choked gorge or cow pasture dotted with black-and-white Holsteins. All the while the steady rocking of the boxcar was hypnotic. I couldn't get enough of it! Then suddenly we were into marsh country, with the salt smell of sea air, rushing along a high ridge above the edge of Puget Sound for twenty miles until we came to Tacoma, forty miles south of Seattle, just as the sun was going down.

We were stuck in Tacoma for another hour while the brakemen remade the train, dropping some cars and adding new ones. During the layover, Keith said we'd better switch back to a flatcar because we'd have to dismount on the fly in Seattle and the low ladders on either end of a flatcar made the manoeuvre much easier. To me, easier also meant safer, and I was glad to be travelling with seasoned hands.

Once the train was rolling again, Bulldog coached me on the proper technique for hopping off a train on the fly. 'Throw your pack and your duffel off first,' he said. 'Then get on the ladder and lower yourself till your feet are skimming the gravel and start running like a son-of-a-bitch to keep up with the train, without letting go of the ladder. If the train's going faster than you can run, you'll have to pull yourself back up onto the train. Never let go of the ladder unless you feel your feet keeping pace with the train. But when you feel the right pace, let go and curl *away* from the train. That's the crucial thing. Like I said, those steel wheels can fuck up your whole day.'

Keith was hoping the train would slow down enough for us to hop off near the Kingdome, in downtown Seattle, but no such luck. It kept right on chugging, and next thing we were rattling through a tunnel beneath the city that Keith called the 'Moose Hole', and when the train finally began to slow down enough for us to dismount we were two miles past the tunnel. Keith and Bulldog hopped off first, to let me see how it was done, and then I pitched my gear off the car and got down onto the ladder. I lowered my feet till they were skimming over the rough ballast stones and was glad I had my thick-soled jungle boots on.

I couldn't believe how fast I had to run to keep pace with the train. But, rookie that I was, I kept my eyes on my feet instead of looking ahead, which was dumb. I don't know why, but something (maybe the Hail Mary I'd said before the manoeuvre started) cautioned me to look up just before I was about to let go of the ladder. And it was a damned lucky thing I did because in the nick of time I spotted a steel stanchion full of track lights looming only ten feet ahead of me. If I'd let go then, I would have run right into the stanchion, with no doubt fatal results. Thank God I saw it in time and didn't let go of the ladder rung until I was safely clear of it. When I bailed out, I managed to keep my balance on the rough ballast as I curled away from the train's wheels. When I stumbled to a stop without a face-plant, I whooped triumphantly and Bulldog shouted, 'Congratulations!'

'Thanks, coach!' I shouted back, and started jogging along the tracks to retrieve my jettisoned pack and duffel.

Seattle at last! It was after eight at night, and the lights of the Space Needle were winking above the downtown skyline as we set off on the long trek back to the skid row district, near the Kingdome, to spend the night in Keith and Bulldog's camp.

We were all hungry after the long day on the train, but unfortunately we'd arrived too late to be fed at any of the local rescue missions. Bulldog managed to scavenge up some hard rolls from a dumpster behind the Spaghetti Factory restaurant near the Pike Place Market, down on the waterfront, and we gnawed on those as we continued our hike to camp. But we were still hungry when we reached skid row, so I spent my last two dollars in Food Stamps on a couple of cans of pork and beans at an all-night grocery store, where Keith and Bulldog knew all the winos loitering on the sidewalk. While I was at the counter paying for the cans of beans, Bulldog entered the store with a big smile on his face. One of the winos had lent him enough change to purchase a 'square' of Wild Irish Rose, which he and Keith wasted no time cracking open as we hiked the rest of the way to their camp.

About a mile past the Kingdome and the Salvation Army shelter, we came to the parking lot of a Jartran truck and trailer rental outlet.

'Welcome to our "trailer park",' Keith said. 'Pick any empty trailer you like. Long as we're up and out of here before the manager shows up at six to open the place, we never get hassled sleeping here.'

Bordering one side of the trailer lot was a disused railroad spur, all overgrown with weeds, and Keith and Bulldog had their bedrolls stashed in a trackside storage box the railroad had abandoned. While they were retrieving their bedrolls from the box, I opened the cans of pork and beans. After we'd polished them off, Keith set his wristwatch alarm for 5 a.m. and we all retired to separate empty trailers for the night.

I was still sleeping soundly when Keith pounded on the side of my trailer at 5.15 the next morning. I scrambled out and gathered my gear, and after I'd stored it in Keith and Bulldog's stash spot we set off in the darkness for the Union Gospel Mission, because it opened its doors the earliest.

'We'll grab some coffee and stale doughnuts at the UG, then boogie over to the Alpha Plasma Center before the crowd shows up,' Keith said, giving us our marching orders for the morning. Which sounded good to me. I'd spent the last of my cash on coffee at the Plaid Pantry back in Vancouver.

At the plasma centre, everything went smoother than I'd expected. My ID card from the Stab Lab in Portland was valid in Seattle, too, and after I passed my urine test I was pumping out a bag in no time. At the pay window, I was pleasantly surprised to find that they paid ten bucks a pint in Seattle, instead of the eight bucks you got in Old Town. The Emerald City was impressing me already!

After the Stab Lab, we headed over to the Welfare Office so I could switch my Food Stamps account to Seattle. My DHS ID from Portland made that an easy process, too, although the system in Seattle was slightly more stringent when it came to proof of local address. You couldn't get away with just marking your 'X' on a troll map in this town. If you didn't have a permanent address, they required you to spend three consecutive nights at the city-run homeless shelter on Third Avenue. Which I wasn't really keen on doing – until they told me the place's name. The Morrison Hotel! As a long-time Doors fan, I knew that the album of that name referred to a flophouse in Los Angeles, not Seattle – but still . . .

Outside the Welfare Office, Keith and Bulldog were already half in the bag from the jug they'd bought with their blood money, and when I rejoined them they blubbered it was time to hop on the free bus and take a ride to the 'Indian Center' for lunch. Like Portland, Seattle's local bus system offered a 'Fare-less Square' – a square mile of downtown in which the bus rides were free. Which was a good thing because Keith and Bulldog were rapidly getting legless.

Despite its name, the Native American Center served whites, too, and their homey dining room looked more like a grade school cafeteria than your usual soup kitchen. The food was excellent and once we'd eaten a hearty meal of baked salmon and wild rice my two wino guides were much revived.

After lunch, we hopped a free bus back to skid row, where the two of them wanted to split another jug of Rosie and hang out at Occidental Park, a tree-lined green where many of the local tramps congregated. But I didn't want to waste the afternoon, so I had them give me directions to the public library, where I figured I could find a pay-typewriter and bang out a revised résumé to use when I started making the rounds for galley cook jobs.

The résumé I'd brought with me from Portland was slanted toward editorial and clerical work. I'd have to rework it to highlight my experience in restaurant kitchens if I wanted to land a cook's job. Admittedly, my experience was rather thin. Except the four years I'd spent working in the college kitchens at Dartmouth and a few summers in the seasonal restaurant at the Dartmouth golf course, my only real culinary training had come at the hands of my friend Danny B, a Tribeca chef who'd hired me to work as a prep cook in his catering kitchen at the Washington Street Café – the last real job I'd managed to land before my coke habit made me unfit to do anything but peddle drugs in bars.

The downtown library, located in a high-rise building at

the corner of Spring Street and Fourth Avenue, would become my favourite haven from street life during my time in Seattle, especially the third-floor rooftop terrace café, where you could buy a reasonably priced cup of Seattle's famous coffee while enjoying a bird's-eye view of Elliott Bay and the islands that dot Puget Sound in the hazy distance. I doubted there was another public library in the country that could boast such a scenic perch, and I took full advantage of it on those rare days when the sun actually broke through the fog and drizzle – days that seemed to take the locals by surprise. One afternoon when I was up on the terrace I overheard two male librarians discussing the weather during their coffee break, and when the first complained it was too damned sunny, the second one asked, 'Are you afraid it will kill your mildew?' Pacific Northwest humour.

However, on that first afternoon at the library I had no time for scenic views. I was too busy burning through half my blood money at the pay-typewriter and the Xerox machine. But the revamped résumé I turned out seemed satisfactory and I was eager to start flogging it around on the waterfront the next morning. First, though, I had to survive a night at the Morrison Hotel – a place Keith and Bulldog referred to derisively as the 'Zoo'. Both of them were periodically forced to check in there themselves; they were both enrolled in a welfare programme for alcoholics and their caseworker demanded address verification from them once a month to maintain their eligibility for their monthly stipend – which of course they referred to as a 'drunk cheque'.

The programme that provided these 'drunk cheques' was called GAU, which stood for General Assistance – Unemployable, and was designed to help homeless alkies get off the streets by paying them enough each month to rent a cheap furnished room. So, Keith and Bulldog were both being paid $188 per month to be drunks and, like most of their wino brothers, they preferred to spend that windfall on fortified wine instead of housing – which goes to show that when the idiot wind is blowing, even the social engineers can't build a windbreak strong enough.

Keith and Bulldog had said they'd check into the Morrison with me that night, so I went back to Occidental Park at sunset to collect them. But before heading to the city shelter they suggested we swing by the Bread of Life (Bride of Death) Mission for some chow first. Like most Protestant missions, the BOL dished up an ear-beating before feeding us, and that night's guest preacher was an earnest young man fresh out of Bible School. The theme of his sermon was our salvation as a gift from God, it not being something we could earn on our own. According to him, no matter how much good we did in our lives, it would never outweigh our accumulated sins. To make his point, he drew an analogy to, of all things, parking tickets!

'Say you commit only three sins per day,' he said. 'Multiply those three sins times 365 days a year times seventy years of average life, and you'll be going to Judgement with seventy thousand sins on your record. Now, suppose you went before a judge with seventy thousand parking tickets. What do you think would happen?' he asked.

'Free room and board!' shouted one of the wags in the back, and the whole congregation erupted in laughter. Which left the young preacher blushing and momentarily tongue-tied. They surely hadn't prepared him for skeptics like us in Bible School. But he'd have wised up pretty quick if he'd had to spend a few nights at the Morrison Hotel, I'll guarantee it.

The Morrison, an eight-storey red-brick monstrosity, had been built in the early 1900s as the home base of the Arctic Club, a social organisation composed of survivors of the Klondike Gold Rush. Now it housed the city's largest men's shelter, and hundreds of homeless lined up every evening in the alley at the back of the building to be admitted through the transients' entrance.

'Don't worry,' Keith said, as we joined the line. 'We'll be in and out before you know it. Nobody cares if you bug out early. We just have to go upstairs to the desk, sign in for the night, then sit around on our sleeping mat in the dorm until the clipboard flunky comes around to mark us present. After that, we're free to boogie,' he grinned.

'No shit?' I said, surprised the system could be that easily manipulated. 'How do you get an address verification slip from them if you bug out early?' I asked.

'They don't hand out the AV slips till tomorrow anyway. You just swing by when you're in the neighbourhood and pick it up from whoever's working the desk. Piece of cake. Me and Bulldog are going to score a couple jugs and head back out to camp as soon as we're checked in. If I was you, I'd do the same.'

'Well, hell, if that's how it works, I'm out of here too,' I smiled. Which turned out to be a sensible decision, because when we got upstairs I could see why Keith and Bulldog called the place the 'Zoo'. Even the half-hour I spent sitting on my assigned floor mat in the dormitory – a huge, high-ceilinged room that looked as if it had once been the Arctic Club's grand ballroom – was enough to make me sure I'd be better off sleeping under the stars than putting up with the racket the Morrison crowd was making.

The variety of manias on display was something to behold.

On one of the mats in our section sat a simple soul named Billy Beck, who proudly informed me that he was hitching out to Indianapolis in the morning to pursue his dream of making his fortune as a human guinea pig at the Eli Lilly Pharmaceutical Research Center. On the mat beside him sat a short, skinny black kid in his late teens who was fervently flipping through the pages of a body-building magazine and telling all who cared to hear that he was training for the Mr America championship. He claimed he was going to pump himself up to 225 pounds before he entered the competition, which would have been quite a feat, considering he couldn't have weighed more than 125 sopping wet. Not even the steroid pills he pulled out of his backpack to show me could work a miracle like that. But you couldn't knock his enthusiasm.

'Ooowee!' he said, as he showed me the pills. 'I take these and work out at the Y, and some days my muscles start to twitchin' and I jes be watchin' 'em grow! You be scared when it happens the first time, till you get used to it.'

Yes, I was only too glad to vacate my mat as soon as the clipboard flunky marked me present. Compared to the crazy bunch at the Morrison, two alkie Vietnam vets like Keith and Bulldog seemed practically sane.

So I spent another night at the 'trailer park' and in the morning I went back to the Morrison to pick up the first of the three AV slips I needed. While I was there, I grabbed a shower and spruced up a bit for a day of job hunting, then set off downhill to the waterfront with high hopes. Only to discover, after I'd been given the same bad news at four different fishing companies, that there was no hope of me landing a galley cook's job or even a slot on a cannery slime line.

It turned out none of the Alaskan companies would hire

you unless you first came up with a security deposit to cover the cost of your airfare to Anchorage, plus the cost of any cold-weather gear you'd have to purchase to work safely in the Arctic. The numbers I was quoted ranged anywhere from five hundred to a thousand dollars. Apparently, the companies had gotten burned by too many wannabes who would fly up on the company's dime and then quit before they'd fulfilled their contract. I could see why a deposit made sense – and, as they all pointed out, you'd get the money back eventually, once your contract was up. But I knew I had no hope of raising that kind of money before all the jobs were taken, so that grand scheme had unravelled mighty quickly. It looked like my only option was to go back to scouring the daily want-ads in the *Seattle Intelligencer*. I just hoped I could stick it out on the streets of the Emerald City long enough to land a job.

Well, I thought, *at least in this town they won't hold my blue parka against me.*

I broke the bad news to Keith and Bulldog when I met up with them for lunch at the Indian Center and they both said, in that case, I'd be silly not to get over to the Welfare Office and fill out an application for the 'drunk cheque' programme.

'It's easy money, and it sounds like you could use it till you get squared away. They'll schedule you for an appointment with the house shrink, but he's a sucker for a sob story. A writer like you should have no trouble coming up with a tale of woe he'll swallow. And once he signs off, you'll get a cheque within two weeks. Go for it, man,' Bulldog urged. 'What have you got to lose?'

'Yeah, maybe I'll give it a shot,' I said, noncommittal. I wasn't really convinced it was a move I wanted to make. I'd have to sleep on it. Meanwhile, it was time to get busy checking the want-ads, so I rode the free bus back downtown to the library and went straight to the periodicals room to consult that day's *Intelligencer*. And damned if I didn't come across an intriguing ad right away – one seeking line cooks to work in Yellowstone National Park for the summer season. I'd never been to the Rockies, but in my youth I'd read so many *Field & Stream* stories about the trout fishing in Montana and Wyoming I already felt I had a sense of the place – this seemed like the perfect time in my life to go explore it.

The ad gave an 800-number you could call to request an application, which I promptly did – glad that I was already on the rolls at the Morrison Hotel because they were the only shelter in town that let you receive mail at their address. When I got through to the personnel department at TW Services, the concessionaire that ran the park's hotels and restaurants, I spoke with a friendly young woman named Carly, who gave me a quick rundown of the application process and the encouraging news that they still had available slots in the kitchen at Mammoth Hot Springs Hotel, which was due to open for the season in three weeks' time. She promised to ship an application to me in that day's mail and informed me I'd have to submit three letters of reference and a twenty-five-dollar refundable application fee when I mailed my application back. I thanked her and said I hoped I'd be meeting her in person soon. As soon as I hung up, I started dialling Information to check the phone numbers of the only three people I could think of who might give me a favourable job reference: Ace, my buddy who owned the Raccoon Lodge; Danny B, my old chef-mentor; and Father Gary, at St Francis Church in Portland, even though I'd only worked a couple of months in his kitchen. I'd have to wait until tomorrow to call them, though. I'd need to raise cash at the

Stab Lab in the morning before I could afford three long-distance calls. But I trusted all three would come through for me, and I could already picture myself in Yellowstone, cooking for tourists and fishing for cutthroat trout. After the discouraging news on the waterfront that morning, this was the break I needed, I was sure of it, and I spent the rest of the afternoon browsing through every book about Yellowstone Park that I could find in the stacks, getting more excited by the hour.

I was still all fired up when I joined the boys in camp that night, and they both said they'd keep their fingers crossed that I got the job. I even let them talk me into a gut-burning swig of Rosie to toast the occasion, but one slug was all I could take. How they drank that poisonous crap day in and day out was a mystery.

'Hell, if you land the job, you're going to need travelling money,' Bulldog said. 'You could use that drunk cheque now more than ever. If I was you, I'd get right in there to see the shrink tomorrow so you can collect a cheque before you split.'

'Yeah, it would definitely come in handy,' I agreed. 'I guess I'll have to bum a few swigs of Rosie from you after we get out of the Stab Lab tomorrow so my breath will smell convincing.'

Even with a hefty slug of Irish Rose in my system, I still had the jitters when I walked into the Welfare Office the next day. The last time I'd had any dealings with a shrink was during my intake process at Rikers, where you're forced to undergo a 'psych-eval' to see if you're suicidal before you're allowed to enter the general prison population.

The prison shrink, who spoke with a sing-song Bollywood accent, reviewed the questionnaire I'd filled out and raised his eyebrows. 'You're a Dartmouth graduate?'

'That's right,' I nodded. 'Does that surprise you?'

'Well, actually, it does,' he replied. 'We don't get many Ivy Leaguers in here.'

'I imagine not.' I shrugged. 'And yet here I am.'

The shrink then ran through a list of questions about my drug and alcohol use, which I answered truthfully, but when he got around to asking if I'd ever tried to do myself harm I laughed in his face.

'You find that question funny?' he frowned, looking perplexed.

'Come on, Doc, honestly,' I grinned. 'I'm sitting here wearing prison green. Isn't the harm I've done to myself pretty obvious?'

The Welfare Office waiting room had a separate, glassed-off smoking annexe and to calm my nerves I ducked in before my appointment with the shrink. While I was lighting up, I overheard an old wino grandma giving the business to another white-haired alkie, a guy who had the shakes so bad he could hardly get his cigarette to his mouth.

'Lookitchew!' she said. 'You better lay off for a while, or you'll never make it to your next cheque. You're shakin' like a damned dog shittin' razorblades.'

The alkie grinned at her and said, 'Yeah, this morning I thought I was usin' a 'lectric toothbrush.'

When I was finally sitting down in Dr Nelson's office, he wasn't as difficult to talk to as I'd feared. He asked me to tell him what I thought had led to my problem with alcohol, and I stammered out some bullshit about growing up with an alcoholic mom. Then I capped off my tale of woe by blaming my recent struggles with alcohol on the depression I'd been suffering since my wife Kate's death. It wasn't till I got back outside on the street that I came to the humbling realisation that most of the

317

'bullshit' I'd just fed the shrink was truer than I'd been willing to admit. But bullshit or not, my performance had earned me the doc's seal of approval, and within the next two weeks I'd be cashing my first 'drunk cheque'. My quest to amass a little getaway money was off to a promising start.

The Yellowstone application packet turned up in my mailbox at the Morrison Hotel a few days later, followed shortly thereafter by the three letters of reference I'd solicited. Everything was coming together nicely. My bighearted friend Ace at the Raccoon Lodge even tucked a twenty-dollar money order in with his letter of reference, which just about covered the application fee I had to send in with my packet, so he'd helped me out in more ways than he knew. Father Gary's reference letter was the last to arrive, and the minute I had it in hand I rushed to the post office. Now all I could do was wait and pray.

When there'd been no response through the mail for what seemed like an interminable week, my impatience got the better of me, and I crossed my fingers and called Carly at the TW Services office. My timing couldn't have been better. She cheerily informed me that she'd just put my contract in the mail the day before. I was hired! And the news got even better when she went on to tell me that she'd arranged for me to have my own private room in one of the employee dorms. I was older than the college kids who made up the bulk of the seasonal hotel staff and she figured I'd be more comfortable on my own. I told her that was fantastic, since I was trying to write a book, and the solitude would suit me fine.

The next week and a half kept me busy, as I ran around town making preparations to leave. My drunk cheque came through, and I had Keith sell half my next Food Stamp allocation for cash at the crooked grocery store where he always cashed in his monthly stamps. I was happy when he got me seventy cents on the dollar. It was better than the scam artists in Portland paid. With that money, and the cash I'd been squirrelling away from my visits to the Stab Lab, I had about $250 to spend on getting outfitted for the trip to Montana. By the time I was done buying clothes and camping gear and a serious backcountry backpack, I had spent nearly all of it, but I didn't care. I'd be earning a real pay cheque soon enough, and in the meantime I wouldn't need much money since the trip out to Montana wouldn't cost me a thing. I'd be making it by freight train.

As luck would have it, I'd met a guy from the Blackfeet reservation in Montana the previous week while I was eating lunch at the Native American Center and he'd told me I could take a city bus north to the neighbouring town of Everett and catch out from there on a train that would take me east to Spokane. He said then I'd just have switch tracks to what he called the Southern Line and I could catch a train that would take me clear through to Bozeman, Montana, only ninety miles north of Yellowstone. Depending how the trains were running, I could probably make the trip in three or four days tops, he figured, which was good to know, because now I could set the date for my departure. I had to be in Yellowstone by the start of the third week in May. If I set out from Everett a week before that, I should make it in plenty of time.

When the Sunday of my departure finally arrived, I joined Keith and Bulldog for a final breakfast at the Union Gospel Mission, and there were backslaps and fist bumps all around as I said my goodbyes. They'd been a real help to me over the past month, and good company to boot. I could only pray that one day they'd get it together and find a way off the streets the same as me. But I had a sad hunch Rosie wouldn't relinquish her grip on their lives anytime soon, so for me our parting was bittersweet.

The bus to Everett dropped me off in the downtown business section, and after getting directions from one of the locals I set off through the sleepy Sunday streets toward the railyards on the edge of town, glad not to be lugging a duffel bag for a change. My new backpack was roomy enough to stow everything I owned and, with my sleeping bag now properly stored in a waterproof stuff-sack cinched to the bottom of my pack, I'd have the use of both hands when it came time to board a train, so I was more confident than I'd been in Vancouver. I couldn't wait to get rolling.

On the way to the yards, I stopped at a park beside the tracks and read a memorial plaque commemorating the Wobblies who'd been shot up by local vigilantes in the labour riots back in 1916. I thought I could remember hearing Woody Guthrie singing about the massacre on one of his old recordings, though I couldn't recall the specific song. There were several tramps lounging on benches in the park, enjoying the mild spring weather, and I walked over to see if they knew anything about when the next eastbound freight might be passing through. They did, and it seemed I was fated to spend the night in Everett; they gave me the same bad news I'd gotten in Vancouver – no freight trains ran through on Sundays. But they showed me where to find a cut flap in the tall chain-link fence that separated the park from the tracks, and said I'd be safe making camp overnight in the bushes on the far side of the yard. *Oh well*, I thought. *Another night under the stars. No biggie.* At least with my new one-burner camp stove, I'd have coffee and hot beans for supper.

My vigil in Everett turned out to be longer than I'd hoped.

The eastbound freight I was waiting on didn't show up until almost sundown on Monday. The good thing was that it turned out to be a train full of container freight, and that usually meant a hi-ball express, so maybe I'd make up some time out on the rails. Even better, the train came to a full stop in the yards, so I didn't even have to make a run for it. I got spotted by a brakeman who was walking down the line as I scrambled aboard one of the container cars, but he just gave me a sympathetic nod and when he passed by the car he asked how far I was headed.

'Spokane first, then on to Bozeman,' I told him.

'We should make Spokane by sun-up,' he said. 'After that, we cut north to the Hi-Line, so you'll need a different train to get you to Montana.'

Though I already knew that, I thanked him anyway, but then he gave me a tip that turned out to be crucial. He warned me we'd be running through a really long tunnel on the way north through the Cascades, where the diesel smoke from the locomotives got pretty thick. 'Better tie a wet cloth around your face as soon as we enter the tunnel, or you'll be choking before we get halfway through,' he advised.

Now *there* was a wrinkle I hadn't considered. Thank goodness whatever angels looked after fools who hop freight trains had sent a kind-hearted brakeman my way. Even with a wet bandana tied over my nose and mouth, I sucked in so much eye-watering smoke on the way through that endless tunnel I was still coughing hours later when we stopped in apple country in the middle of the night to take on more cars in Wenatchee. While the train was stopped, I scouted the yard for bulls. Seeing none, I hopped down to the tracks to take a quick piss and spotted some tramps jungled up in a grove of willows at the far side of the yard. I'd have envied them their campfire if I hadn't had my sleeping bag to keep me warm. Even with the night air whipping all around me when the train was doing sixty I was comfortably snug in my bag, and when I crawled back into it as the train pulled out of Wenatchee I didn't wake up again until the morning sun was shining on my face.

We were rolling through the high desert wheat fields of eastern Washington now, and in the bright morning sun the farmers' giant irrigation wheels were spraying rainbows all around me as the train commenced a long arching sweep to the north and went barrelling over a series of high trestles that brought us to the outskirts of Spokane. I quickly stowed my sleeping bag in its stuff-sack, clipped it to my pack and got ready to toss it overboard whenever the train's speed slacked off.

The one element of a proper flying dismount that my practice session with Keith and Bulldog hadn't taught me was how to gauge when a train is travelling at a speed slow enough to safely perform the manoeuvre. That was a skill you could only get from experience, and my woeful lack of it was on display that morning as I tossed my pack overboard prematurely – and then discovered that the train was still moving way too fast for me to keep up with when I tried dangling from the ladder and running beside the container car. The instant my first foot touched the gravel I knew I was in trouble. The ground was flying by so fast beneath me it snatched my foot and threw it backwards like a shot, right toward the mauling steel wheels. *No good! Pull up!* my brain screamed, and with a panicked burst of strength I hauled myself back up onto the ladder's bottom rung and heaved a big sigh of relief.

I was two miles further down the track when the train finally slowed to a speed that seemed more manageable and this time my flying dismount went off without a hitch. However, my miscalculation had just cost me a four-mile hike back to the spot where I'd tossed my gear. As I was backtracking – and cursing myself for making such a rookie mistake – I encountered another tramp walking along the tracks and I asked him if he knew where I could catch a Montana-bound train.

'That'd be the Lo-Line you're looking for, then,' he said. 'But you're heading in the wrong direction. The Lo-Line junction's back in the main yard. You need to turn around.'

'Got to go retrieve my pack first,' I grinned. 'I threw it off the train too soon.'

'Been there, done that,' the old tramp grinned back. Then he warned me that I might have a long wait ahead of me, since not many freight trains took the Lo-Line route any more. 'You could be waiting two or three days before an eastbound train comes through,' he said.

'Shit, really?' I frowned. 'Guess I'll just have to hitchhike. I need to be in Yellowstone Park by the end of the week.'

'Well, then hitching's the way to go,' the tramp agreed. 'If you get lucky with your thumb, you might just make it by nightfall.'

By God, I hope he's right, I murmured, as I continued down the tracks to retrieve my gear. But the tramp's prediction proved to be overly optimistic. By nightfall, I'd only made it as far as Missoula, Montana, after a series of short-hop rides across the Idaho Panhandle – and a lot of time spent standing around on the outskirts of shabby little mining towns in the Bitterroot Mountains, wagging my thumb till the next Samaritan came along. Two hundred miles in eight hours of hitchhiking was pretty pathetic progress, but when my final ride of the day brought me over the crest of Lookout Pass and I got my first glimpse of Montana, the hard miles I'd put in seemed worth the effort.

I made camp that night beneath some willow trees on the bank of the Clarks Fork, the river made famous by Norman Maclean's *A River Runs Through It*. The mountain air was chilly, but the night was clear, and as I sat in the lee of my tarpaulin tent, sipping camp stove coffee beneath the million stars of Big Sky country, I was a happy man. With a little better luck tomorrow, I figured I could make it all the way to Yellowstone Park. Only three hundred miles now separated me from the fresh start I'd been chasing for the past four months, and I could hardly wait to get back on the road in the morning as soon as the sun came up.

I didn't feel quite so lucky a few hours later, though, when the sound of rain pattering on my tarpaulin tent woke me sometime after midnight and I realised that while I'd been sleeping, groundwater had seeped into my tent and soaked not only my sleeping bag but my clothing too. I had no choice but to break camp in the dark and haul my gear downriver to the nearest overpass bridge. By the time I took shelter from the rain, however, the damage had already been done, and I was soggy and miserable the rest of the night. But just before dawn, I caught a break. The rain clouds cleared off, and when the sun rose there were blue skies overhead.

As soon as there was light enough to see what I was doing, I pulled a dry change of clothes out of my backpack and stripped off all my wet things, hoping no early morning joggers would come by and catch me flashing. I could picture the report in the local papers: 'Naked Vagrant Arrested Under Clarks Fork Bridge'. So I hustled, believe me – I hadn't dressed that quickly since the night my girlfriend's merchant seaman father came home from sea two days sooner than scheduled and nearly caught us naked in his empty Bay Ridge apartment.

Once I was decent, I gathered up all my soggy clothes and my equally soggy sleeping bag and draped everything over some riverside boulders to dry in the sun. All I could do at that point was hurry up and wait. Four frustrating hours later, my stuff was finally dry enough to repack, and only then could I hike back up to the highway and get on the road at last.

By now it was eleven o'clock. I'd lost most of the morning. But I knew my luck must be turning when I caught my first ride only five minutes later and discovered that the college kid who'd picked me up was going all the way to Red Lodge. I could hardly believe it when he said he'd have me to Bozeman in three hours' time! Bozeman was only ninety miles north of Yellowstone. My odds of making it to the park before nightfall had just shot way up.

His name was Tom, and he said he was an engineering student on his way home from the University of Idaho to his family's place in Red Lodge for two weeks' vacation before he started his summer job. For a young guy, he'd done a lot of travelling, and we spent the ride swapping stories about places we'd been to. He was particularly proud of a trip he'd taken to Nepal the previous summer and had a zealot's gleam in his eyes as he described the remote Himalayan gorges he'd trekked down into with a kayak strapped on his back, all for the thrill of conquering whitewater rapids that no one had kayaked before.

Must be nice to be rich, I thought. But he was a down-to-earth kid, so it didn't come off as bragging. He seemed just as impressed by my train-hopping adventures as I was by his globe-trotting search for Class V rapids, so we hit it off just fine.

'You sure you want me to drop you in Bozeman?' Tom

asked, as we reached the city limits. 'If you're heading straight to the park, you'd be better off getting out at Livingston. You'll have to go through Livingston anyway to hook up with Highway 89. That's the only road that'll get you to the North Entrance.'

'Sure, Livingston sounds good to me,' I said. 'The closer to the park you can get me, the happier I'll be.'

East of Bozeman, we started the long climb up to the crest of Bozeman Pass. Everywhere I looked, I saw nature putting on a show that a city kid could only gawk at in goggle-eyed wonder. Alpine meadows where chestnut mares were nipping at their frisky foals. Snow-swollen creeks rushing through reedy bogs. Red-tail hawks and bald eagles carving turns in the thin blue air above the dense green slopes of the Gallatin National Forest. And the peaks of the Rockies themselves, towering all around me, so much higher than the White Mountains of New Hampshire – which had impressed me in my college days, but now seemed Lilliputian by comparison. It was a landscape that could humble a man. Even a man grown accustomed to being humbled.

There was still plenty of daylight left when Tom dropped me off in Livingston. I hiked down from the interstate and took up my station on the southbound side of Highway 89, right in front of a big green sign that said: 'North Entrance, Yellowstone Park, 52 Miles'. So close, I felt sure I'd be there before sundown.

You're on the home stretch now, Hat! I grinned to myself as I straightened my toboggan hat and stuck my thumb out in the breeze. After five thousand miles of wandering, and twenty state lines crossed, I had finally found the place I'd been looking for all along, and as each ride I caught that afternoon brought me closer to the finish line you couldn't have pried the smile off my face with a crowbar.

A mile south of Livingston, perched high in the cab of a

logger's boom truck, I got my first look at the Yellowstone River, and as we followed its course through Paradise Valley I thought of all the nights I'd sat dreaming over *Field & Stream* in study hall at St Mary's, imagining what it would be like to cast for trout from the banks of such a legendary river. Well, now I'd find out for myself – as soon as I cashed my first pay cheque and could afford to buy a rod and reel.

I was twelve miles from the park's North Entrance when the logger turned off the highway onto a gravel road that would take him up into the forest at Tom Miner Basin. I thanked him for the lift, he wished me a good summer at Mammoth, and two minutes later I was climbing into the back of a rented VW camper van driven by a young German couple on a honeymoon tour of the States. The two of them seemed as awestruck by the scenery as I was, and as we cruised through the rocky gorge of Yankee Jim Canyon and followed the river upstream to the little town of Gardiner, where a great stone arch marked the entrance to Yellowstone Park, the bride turned to me and asked, 'Do you live here?'

'I do now,' I said proudly.

'Lucky you,' she said.

'Yes,' I smiled.

Lucky me.

AFTERWORD

The rusticated stone arch at the North Entrance to Yellowstone Park is inscribed with an excerpt from the Congressional Act that established Yellowstone as the world's first national park in 1872. It reads: *For the Benefit and Enjoyment of the People.* Millions of visitors to Yellowstone have passed beneath that inscription since the Roosevelt Arch was built in 1903, but I daresay none of them ever got more benefit or enjoyment from the park than I did during the five years I worked at Mammoth Hot Springs Hotel. From the moment I climbed out of the German tourists' VW bus on that long-gone afternoon in Gardiner, my life took a turn for the better – just as I had hoped.

By happy coincidence, the executive chef in charge of all the park's kitchens, David Rees, was a fellow refugee from Brooklyn and under his tutelage I honed my kitchen skills and moved up quickly through the ranks. In two years' time, I went from line cook to head chef, and the experience I gained at

Mammoth was my springboard to a culinary career that would span the next two decades. Though it wasn't the literary career I'd envisioned for myself during my college days, it was a creatively challenging and rewarding profession nonetheless, and I never regretted the path I chose to follow once I'd put the idiot wind behind me.

Except for one scary night of backsliding when the hard-partying actor Dennis Quaid turned up at the Blue Goose Saloon in Gardiner during my first summer in Yellowstone, I'm glad to say I never snorted a line of cocaine again. And all the backcountry hiking I did on the steep mountain trails in the park soon had me feeling stronger and more fit than I'd been in years, so my health took a turn for the better in Yellowstone too. Then, to my surprise, so did my emotional life.

During my second summer at Mammoth – the summer of 1988, when more than two hundred forest fires blackened a third of the park's vast acreage – I met and fell in love with a big-hearted young Californian named Kathy Brunn, who worked in the hotel's reservations department. On the face of it, ours was an improbable romance, since Kathy was fifteen years younger than me. But she had what Buddhists would call an 'old soul' and the more time we spent together, the more I realised that fate had sent me the life companion I'd never thought would come my way after my wife Kate's untimely death.

When the forest fires forced the two of us to evacuate from Mammoth in mid-August, Kathy and I moved down to the town of Gardiner and set up house together in a rented two-room cabin up on the Jardine Hill. Then, like all the other eight hundred residents of Gardiner, we spent the next few weeks praying that the fires wouldn't sweep down into town and force us to evacuate yet again. But by the first week of September the fires reached the coffin-shaped crest of Sepulcher Mountain – the last natural barrier shielding Gardiner from the fire's advance – and it began to look as though our prayers would go unanswered.

I can still vividly recall the Saturday night when the top of Sepulcher erupted in flames. Kathy and I had gone to the Blue Goose Saloon with a crowd of other Parkies to hear a local band from Bozeman, the Hyalite Blues Band. The Blue Goose was on Park Street, on the edge of town closest to Sepulcher Mountain, and by the time the band finished its first set, the firestorm had crested the mountain. Suddenly, everyone was calling out requests for 'Fire on the Mountain', one of the Hyalite Blues Band's most popular Grateful Dead covers, and as the boys in the band obliged, most of the crowd rushed out onto the sidewalk, drinks in hand, to watch the fire show. It all bore a chilling resemblance to that scene in *Titanic* when the doomed ship's orchestra keeps right on playing, even as disaster engulfs them.

By closing time at 2 a.m. all of us left the bar convinced that we'd soon hear the three blasts of the emergency alert horn. We'd all been advised to pack getaway bags a few days earlier, so we'd be ready to evacuate to Livingston High School's gymnasium at a moment's notice. But by some miracle a freak snowstorm blew into the park early the next morning, and on Sunday, 11 September, we got the reprieve we'd been praying for, as the flames on Sepulcher died down and the wind shifted, chasing the fire back into Yellowstone and away from town.

In autumn of the following year, Kathy and I got married twice in one day – which is something I doubt many couples can claim. We held the first formal ceremony in the historic stone chapel at Mammoth, but because our marriage licence was issued in Montana and the chapel was located in Wyoming, the only way to legitimise our union was to drive back down the Mammoth hill to the state line at the 45th Parallel, where the entire wedding party reassembled on the bank of the Gardiner River to watch us repeat our vows on Montana soil.

The only thing that marred that otherwise perfect day was the absence of any members of the groom's family at the festivities. Of course, Kathy knew it would be that way. Early on in our relationship I'd told her all about my estrangement from my parents – how, when I was locked up on Rikers, I'd written a long apology letter to my parents and expressed my strong desire to make amends with them once I got out of prison. Alas, it had done me no good. My father had always left the letter-writing to my mother – during my seminary and college days, he'd never once answered any of the letters I'd dutifully written home – however, this time he broke with precedent and replied with a terse, handwritten note that left me in no doubt that he and my mother had written me off as their son and wanted nothing further to do with me.

I could hardly blame them, but the finality in my dad's tone was still a blow and I had made no other attempts to contact them in the four years before I married Kathy.

Nevertheless, when the Christmas season rolled around that year, Kathy insisted that I send my parents a card and a few pictures from our wedding in the hope that enough time had passed to soften their hearts toward me. She was always an optimist.

Though my parents never responded, I will always be grateful to Kathy for having nudged me to make the effort because, three years later, when my Aunt Mary was going through my mom's effects, she found that old Christmas card and used the return address on the envelope to contact me with the crushing news that my mother had just passed away, four years after my father's death from prostrate cancer. Which meant that my dad had died the same summer I met Kathy – and this was the first I'd heard of it.

Thank God I had Kathy to lean on, or I'd probably have crawled into a bottle and never come out. Kathy did her best to comfort me by pointing out that my mom must have still loved me because she'd saved the Christmas card instead of chucking it in the trash. And my Aunt Mary, my mother's oldest sister, said the same thing when I called her that night, so I took some small consolation from the fact that I'd followed Kathy's advice and had made one last attempt to reconcile with my parents, even though that attempt had come to naught.

In the months after I received that terrible news, I spent a lot of time fishing the Yellowstone River in the solitude of Yankee Jim Canyon, trying to distract myself from the grief and guilt I felt over my failure to be a better son. Eventually, I made peace with what I could no longer change, but I couldn't shake the feeling that for all the positive steps I'd taken in my life since moving to Yellowstone I was still a loser. That chink in my self-esteem was just wide enough to let the idiot wind come whistling through – and suddenly my life was in turmoil again. And so was Kathy's, through no fault of her own.

I had left my job at Mammoth Hotel the year before to take a higher-paying position as manager of the Blue Goose Saloon, which, like most bars in Montana, derived a good portion of its monthly income from the rolls of quarters its gambling patrons pumped into the gaudy row of slot machines that were strategically placed just inside the front door. I'd never been tempted to waste my time or money playing the slot machines – whatever quarters I was willing to part with went into the coin-op pool table. But in the year after I got word that my parents were gone I began obsessively squandering my tip money playing the Keno machines, chasing the high that every gambler seeks – the adrenaline rush of hitting a big jackpot, which momentarily makes you forget that you're still just a loser in the grip of a destructive habit. Before long, I was as addicted to Keno as I'd been to cocaine, and unbeknownst to Kathy I'd racked up so much debt on credit card advances that we were thousands of dollars in the hole by the time my guilty conscience finally forced me to confess what a selfish fool I'd been.

To make matters worse, I'd also been fiddling the books at the Blue Goose and pocketing the bar's money to support my habit, so I would have been facing jail time if the Goose's owner hadn't mercifully given me the opportunity to avoid criminal charges by repaying my debt to him in instalments over the next twenty-four months.

For me, it was a welcome relief to finally confess the secret I'd been hiding for many guilty months, but for Kathy there was no relief. My revelations blindsided her, and she was devastated – not just by my betrayal, but also by the damage I had done to her clean credit rating. I feared she'd wash her hands of me right then and demand a divorce. And I wouldn't have blamed her if she had. I had turned her world upside-down. But divorcing me wouldn't have freed her from the debts I'd run up on our joint accounts, so in the end she stuck with me and reluctantly agreed to go along with the only plan I could think of that might quickly restore us to solvency – a move to Las Vegas. It might seem like an outlandish proposal for a compulsive gambler to make, but logistically and financially it made perfect sense. My good friend Greg Hahn – the former pastry chef at Mammoth, and best man at our wedding – had recently relocated to Vegas with his wife Mary and the two of them had been urging us to do the same. Greg had landed a well-paid position in the bakery at the Stardust Hotel and Casino and, according to him, chefs in Las Vegas were earning salaries more than double what I was bringing home in Montana, so a move to the desert seemed like the best solution to my problem.

With Greg and Mary's generous help, we settled in Las Vegas at the start of 1996. The town was going through a boom at the time and there were plenty of jobs available for trained chefs and professional reservationists. Kathy landed a position in the Luxor's ersatz pyramid on the downtown Strip and I was hired as head chef of the Stockyard, the high-end steak and seafood restaurant in the just-opened Texas Station Casino, the Fertitta family's latest venture out on the north end of town. It was a high-pressure job that kept me in the kitchen sixty hours a week, but the salary was good and the quarterly bonuses I earned helped us pay off our debts at a steady pace. And thankfully, despite the fact that we spent two and a half years in the gambling capital of America, the hard lesson I'd learned from my folly in the Blue Goose kept me from squandering any more money at the slot machines. I escaped from 'Lost Wages' unscathed – and once again solvent – when we finally moved back to Montana in the spring of 1998.

For a couple of years, it had been nice to escape the snow and sub-zero temperatures of Montana's six-month winters, but by the time my Blue Goose debt was paid I was longing to get back to the Rockies. When another of our old Yellowstone Park friends, Paul Mineau, turned up in Vegas for a visit and offered me a position as catering chef at Montana State University in

Bozeman, I used all the persuasion I could muster to convince Kathy to move back north.

She wasn't easily convinced. Why would she be? I'd already dragged her away from a job that she loved in Yellowstone, and now I was asking her to quit a good job at the Luxor and pull up stakes all over again to move back to a low-wage state like Montana, where, unlike me, she had no new position awaiting her. But in the end, loyal to a fault, Kathy agreed to give it a try for my sake. I was pushing fifty at that point, and she knew that the retirement benefits that came with the MSU job were something I desperately needed, so she let me accept Paul's offer. (Now, every pension cheque I cash reminds me to be grateful for her sacrifice.)

Back in Bozeman, we bought ourselves a single-wide mobile home in a trailer park on the Gallatin River, just two lots downstream from the trailer where Richard Brautigan had lived two decades earlier, back when he was fighting – and tragically, losing – his own long struggle with the idiot wind. Luckily, my sojourn on the Gallatin was more therapeutic, and I never again engaged in any self-destructive behaviour – even when, four years later, Kathy announced that she was leaving me to resume her life in Yellowstone Park as a single woman.

Naturally, after fourteen years together, I was sorry to see her go, but I could understand her urge to explore a new life without me. She was thirty-eight at the time, the same age I'd been when I hit the road to find a fresh future elsewhere, and I knew what it was like to feel the need to move on. So I helped her U-Haul her things down to Gardiner and wished her a tearful farewell, but I never felt betrayed by her decision, and to this day we remain good friends.

One of the perks of working at MSU was access to the

university's email system, and after I was on my own again I began a regular correspondence with an old Bay Ridge buddy of mine who I'd worked with at Harcourt Brace Jovanovich during my early years in the publishing business. Gerry was my oldest friend, and over the years he'd built up a solid reputation as a book editor, earning the respect of an illustrious list of writers, including Don DeLillo and David Foster Wallace. Gerry and I had been out of touch since I'd left New York, but after some internet sleuthing he'd managed to track me down in Las Vegas shortly before I moved back to Montana. I was delighted when I received his unexpected letter asking me for news of what I'd been up to, and I spent the next week writing a twenty-page reply that sketched out the highlights of my four-month journey to Yellowstone.

After reading my reply, Gerry began a years-long campaign to convince me that I should expand that letter into a book-length memoir. I resisted taking his advice for a long time. I still wanted to believe that I had a novel in me, and it seemed to me I'd be abandoning my youthful dreams by writing a memoir before I'd published any fiction (although I suspect that the main reason I kept dragging my feet was because of my reluctance to re-engage with the man I was when the idiot wind chased me out of New York). However, after Kathy moved back to Yellowstone, I began to spend the quiet nights in my trailer working on the memoir Gerry had been urging me to write, and over the next few years I kept sporadically emailing chapters to New York for Gerry to review.

Though Gerry's enthusiasm for the project was unflagging, halfway through that early incarnation of this memoir I became disheartened by my seeming inability to find a suitable voice for the story I was trying to tell, and my dissatisfaction eventually led me to the conclusion that Gerry's faith in me had been misplaced. So I shelved the hundred pages of that draft memoir with all the other half-finished manuscripts I'd given up on over the years and there it would languish for the better part of a decade.

After my divorce from Kathy, I had begun to visit my two younger brothers on Long Island every summer, and each visit had left me feeling more and more troubled by their steadily declining health. My youngest brother, Kevin, who'd inherited my parents' house, had been confined to a wheelchair ever since the early seventies, a result of spinal damage he'd suffered in a car wreck when he was still in his teens. My brother Steve, the second-born son in our family, had taken over as Kevin's sole caregiver after my parents died. He had his own ailments to deal with, and the stress of caring for Kevin all by himself was getting to be more than he could handle. So, as soon as I was eligible to collect my pension and Social Security benefits, I took early retirement, sold my trailer and moved back to my parents' old home in Lindenhurst to give my brothers the help they needed.

My assistance came in handy almost right away. Only two weeks after I arrived from Montana, Hurricane Sandy struck Long Island and turned my brothers' front yard into a jumbled maze of wind-toppled maple trees – which kept Steve and me busy with chainsaws for the rest of that autumn. 'Jesus, Steve,' I remember joking, 'if I'd wanted to be a lumberjack, I could have stayed in Montana!'

The three of us shared many laughs and good times during the next three years after my return to the family homestead, all of them blessings I would have missed out on had I stayed in Montana, but my reunion with my brothers was far too brief.

By the summer of 2015, they had both been diagnosed with terminal cancers – Steve in his lungs, and Kevin in his liver – and I spent most of June and July keeping vigil at their bedsides in Good Samaritan Hospital, until the heartbreaking week when they both passed away, only four days apart. In a way, I suppose that was a blessing too. After all the years they'd spent living together, it seemed only right that their brotherly bond should remain unbroken – even by death.

In the first few months after I lost my brothers, I consoled myself with the thought that I'd done everything for them that I could do. And I took comfort, too, from the thought that Kevin and Steve would let my parents know that I'd stepped up when it counted and had shown my family loyalty in the end. Still, I missed my brothers terribly. Awakened by noises in the night, I'd momentarily mistake the old house's creaking for the sound of them going about their business – and then I'd break out crying when I remembered that was something I would never hear again.

The next few months were a dark time for me, as I struggled to come to terms with being a sole survivor. Thankfully, Gerry and his wife Susanne were able to lift my spirits when I paid them a visit in mid-September and unburdened my sorrows during a long afternoon on their patio. They were the only people I had left in the world to tell my story to, and after they'd heard me out I felt more relieved and hopeful than I'd have thought possible. So hopeful, in fact, that I didn't even cringe when Gerry later popped the inevitable question: 'So, Peter, what's happening with your memoir?'

'You know what, Gerry?' I smiled. 'I think maybe now I'm ready to make it happen.'

That very evening when I got home I dug out my old road journals and began to reimagine the shape the memoir should take. I decided not to try to salvage any of my earlier drafts but to start over from scratch so I could find a style that rang truer in my inner ear. By Thanksgiving, I was ready to sit down at the keyboard to give the project one last-ditch try and, to my continuing amazement, the chapters began to flow at an encouraging pace. *Idiot Wind* was growing longer by the day.

Before I knew it, ten months had passed, and I was whooping for joy as I typed out the book's final page. On that happy afternoon – which came almost exactly one year to the day after Gerry's 'patio pep talk' – the story I'd been carrying around in my head for twenty-nine years was finally out in the world, and as I sat giving thanks in my parents' old house, the Prodigal Son come home at last, I found myself recalling my favourite lines from T.S. Eliot's 'Little Gidding':

> *And the end of all our exploring*
> *Will be to arrive where we started*
> *And to know the place for the first time.*

Or, as Neal Cassady would say, 'Keep rollin' and you'll always eventually cross your line again.'

ACKNOWLEDGEMENTS

Without the encouragement and unflagging support I received from Gerry Howard and Susanne Williams, this book would never have been written, and for that reason (and many others) I dedicate *Idiot Wind* to them.

Thanks also to my literary agent, David McCormick, who wasn't afraid to put his faith in a late-blooming first-time author. David's editorial input was invaluable right from the start and I have no doubt that the revisions he suggested played a key role in the book's eventual acceptance for publication.

Many people gave generously of their time to read early drafts of *Idiot Wind*, and I owe a debt of gratitude to all of them. I'd especially like to thank Don DeLillo, Walter Kirn, Donald Ray Pollock, Jay McInerney, Joel Rose, Paul Slovak, Emmanuelle Heurtebize and Sander VanVlerk for their feedback.

Thanks also to Kathy Maravetz, John and Kathy Nappi, Jakob and Maria Hoyland, Andreas Nowara, Susan Dumois,

Rebecca Cole, Greg and Mary Hahn, Paul Mineau, Brenda Biddy-Hoffman, Sandi Tansey, Richard Young, Greg Daskalogrigorakis, Patricia Davis, Kenneth Brown, Geoffrey Gerow, William Sharkey, Jeff Dahlman, Edward Kozelka, John Clemente, Bill Procaccini and, last but not least, my 'fishing family' in Montauk, NY, the Quaresimos: Capt. Jamie, Capt. Anthony, Capt. Tyler and 'Admiral' Sharon.

Finally, I'd like to acknowledge the outstanding work done by the amazing Jamie Byng and his colleagues at Canongate Books: my editor, Hannah Knowles; Jon Gray, who designed the cover; Leila Cruickshank, Vicki Rutherford and Debs Warner, who handled copy-editing and permissions; and Andrea Joyce and Jessica Neale, my angels in the foreign rights department. Thanks to one and all!